— A HANDBOOK ON —
COMMERCIAL
COURT PRACTICE

PANKAJ PRASAD

INDIA • SINGAPORE • MALAYSIA

Notion Press Media Pvt Ltd

No. 50, Chettiyar Agaram Main Road,
Vanagaram, Chennai, Tamil Nadu – 600 095

First Published by Notion Press 2021
Copyright © Pankaj Prasad 2021
All Rights Reserved.

ISBN 978-1-63850-844-1

This book has been published with all efforts taken to make the material error-free after the consent of the author. However, the author and the publisher do not assume and hereby disclaim any liability to any party for any loss, damage, or disruption caused by errors or omissions, whether such errors or omissions result from negligence, accident, or any other cause.

While every effort has been made to avoid any mistake or omission, this publication is being sold on the condition and understanding that neither the author nor the publishers or printers would be liable in any manner to any person by reason of any mistake or omission in this publication or for any action taken or omitted to be taken or advice rendered or accepted on the basis of this work. For any defect in printing or binding the publishers will be liable only to replace the defective copy by another copy of this work then available.

CONTENTS

Preface		*5*
1	The Commercial Courts Act, 2015: An Overview	13
2	The Pre-Litigation Mediation & Settlement	29
3	Institution of Suit	38
4	Statement of Defence	63
5	Disclosure, Discovery & Inspection of Documents	73
6	Case Management Hearing	91
7	Leading Evidence and Argument	99
8	Judgment and Decree	107
9	Interest and Cost	117
10	Summary Procedure	127
11	Arbitration Matter	134
12	Appeal, Revision & Civil Writ	155
13	Execution of Decree and Award	168
14	Enforcement and Breach of Contract	187
15	Interpretation of Contracts	196
16	Frustration of Contract	211

17	Warranties, Conditions and Terms	220
18	Time, Exemption and Force Majure Clauses	226
19	Penalties and Damages	240
20	Privity of Contract and Sub Contractor	262

Bibliography *277*

PREFACE

In our society where the economy is having a predominating effect on every other facet of life, the role of law is to serve three main tasks: standardizing and enforcing contracts, defining property rights, and punishing fraud. While standardizing contracts is being done by way of prescribing 'model forms,' enforcing contracts has been a time-consuming process in Courts of law, legislative resorts to take some species of contractual disputes to Multi-Member Tribunals have also not met the great expectations it generated. There is further indication that courts have shown an increasing interest in advancing this model of legal regulation by enhancing protection for private property and contractual obligation by approving the use of criminal remedies concomitantly with civil liability. But at the same time, the propagation of the mediative process apart from improving adjudicative efficacy is the true need of hour to improve upon administration of justice in the country. The plethora of cases in courts and their long pendency has elevated the procedural law from its classical position of 'handmaid of justice' to that of 'headmaster of justice'. While reducing the pendency of cases has been a buzzword, improving the adjudicative process has been somewhat not given due attention.

The classical theory of breach of contract, as a purely civil breach, has been scrutinized with more penetrative eyes to cull out whether there was any *mens rea* at the inception of the deal. 'Fraud' as defined under section 17 of the Contract Act has been further stretched to see whether the word "Fraudulently" and "Dishonestly" encapsulates the defendant's act of breach. With property rights no more a fundamental right in India, the right to enforce contracts becomes more important to protect business interest and investment in property, but even this judicial acknowledgment of criminality in contractual dispute has not produced desired results.

The establishment of Commercial Courts, enactment of Insolvency Code, and amendment in Arbitration & Conciliation Act show legislature's will to provide an efficient, if not better, legal framework for addressing civil remedies in the matter of contractual disputes. The civil remedies by way of invoking the principles of the sanctity of contract and bringing actions for damages for breach of contracts are going to be the hallmark of the new legal framework.

The enactment of the Commercial Courts Act, 2015 has led to the establishment of newly designated Commercial Courts to conduct the trial of civil disputes which are 'commercial disputes' as defined under the Act. As amended in 2018, this Act contains substantial provisions relating to the establishment, jurisdiction, and infrastructure of commercial courts and commercial appellate courts with the central idea to lessen the time consumed in civil trials in the country. The present book is an attempt to present the summary of the provisions which are to be followed while pursuing or defending a suit arising out of commercial disputes. The chapters of the book are arranged in a manner that a lawyer or a litigant may find easy and handy. Familiarity with the existing Code of Civil Procedure is a prerequisite for conducting a civil trial in Commercial Court. This book presents only those changes/amendments that have been brought by the Act to the Code of Civil Procedure apart from a brief analysis of existing provisions that are to be read and followed along with the amended provisions.

The present legislation should be seen in congruence with the ongoing attempt at the international arena to bring a sort of uniformity in the field of commercial law. The two main bodies are UNIDROIT and UNICITRAL. The International Institute for the Unification of Private Law (UNIDROIT) is an independent intergovernmental Organisation with its seat in the Villa Aldobrandini in Rome. Its purpose is to study needs and methods for modernizing, harmonizing, and coordinating private and in particular commercial law as between States and groups of States and to formulate uniform law instruments, principles and rules to achieve those objective UNIDROIT has worked extensively in the area of contract law and adopted a variety of instruments intended to offer harmonized and effective rules to respond to the evolving needs of modern transactions. The UNIDROIT Principles of International Commercial Contracts (UPICC) constitute a non-binding codification or "restatement" of the general part of international contract law, adapted to the special requirements of modern international commercial practice. Similarly, the United Nations Commission on International Trade Law is the core legal body of the United Nations system in the field of international trade law. A legal body with universal membership specializing in commercial law reform worldwide for over 50 years, UNCITRAL's business is the modernization and harmonization of rules on international business. The UNICITRAL code on arbitration has been largely adopted in the current arbitration law regime in India. Accordingly, superior courts in the country have not shied away from referring to the formulated principles of these two bodies, even though they do not have a binding effect. The model law suggested by these two bodies is also going to have some persuasive impact on the domestic commercial dispute redressal process.

Part- I of this book aims to have a limited purpose to discuss the procedural law applicable to a trial involving certain specifically classified civil disputes. The thirteen chapters are the milestones of a civil suit culminating in a decree followed by an appeal. As such, this part of the book is to supplement the existing material on procedural law in respect of commercial dispute as a readable summary suitable for a broad reference on the subject with necessary citations of the Supreme Court and High Courts for the better elucidation of the subject.

Part- II of the book relates to some complex yet frequently encountered aspects of the law of contracts. It aims to present the finer points of the law of contracts keeping in mind the need for lawyers to equip themselves with it. Contract law in all its manifestations is a vast subject having a great historical and analytical perspective that is beyond the ambit of the present handbook but an attempt has been made to highlight the broad principles on some contentious issues emerging in courtroom trials.

Attempts have been made to keep the error at a minimal level. However, to err is human and as such if any error is found, endeavour shall be made to correct the same. I hope, this book will be fruitful for all who have an interest in the subject.

26.05.2021

Author

pankaj026@gmail.com

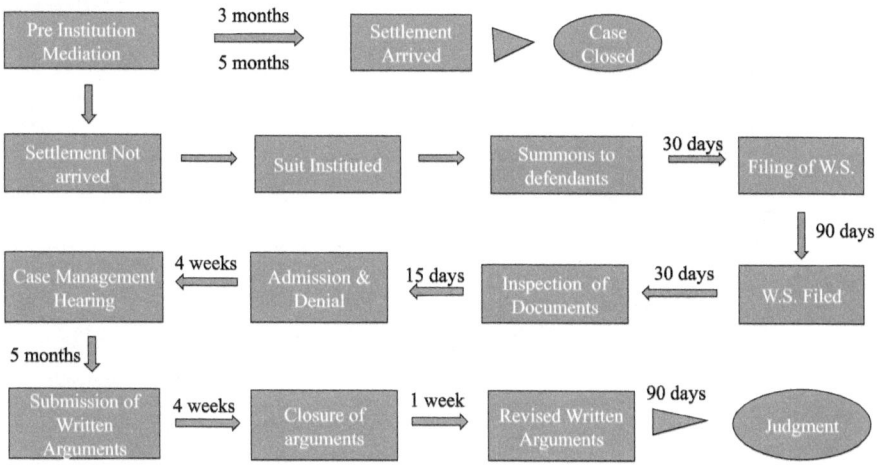

PART - 1

1

THE COMMERCIAL COURTS ACT, 2015: AN OVERVIEW

"The essence of law lies in the spirit, not in its letter, for the letter is significant only as being the external manifestation of the intention that underlies it"

– Salmond

BACKGROUND

The Commercial Courts Act, 2015[1] is a new law legislated with a view to make the courts in India more efficacious while dealing with commercial disputes which are primarily disputes falling within ambit of 'contract' as defined under section sec. 2 (h) of Indian Contract Act. From classical point of view, the Commercial Courts Act comes within realm of procedural law but it has created some substantial rights for the parties to get expeditious adjudication of certain disputes and from that point of view, the legislative expectation from courts is to assist India gaining better rankings in the eyes of global business community. Broadly speaking four types of accounts are possible of any area of the law- (1) historical, (2) prescriptive (3) descriptive and (4) interpretative. Historical accounts seek to explain how and why

---

1 [NO. 4 OF 2016 [31ˢᵗ December, 2015.]

the law has developed the way it has; they reveal the law's causal history. For example, an explanation of modern contract law as the product of changing forces of production in the 18th and 19th century is a historical as is an explanation of modern contract law as the product of medieval scholars' concerns for Aristotelian notions of virtue. Prescriptive accounts of the law are accounts of what the law should be of the ideal law. An argument that contract law should promote economic efficiency is a prescriptive account, as is an argument that the consideration rule in contract law should be eliminated. Descriptive accounts, as the name suggests, aim to describe the law as it is now or as it was at a certain time. When lawyers explain contract law to their clients, they are typically engaged in a descriptive exercise, and most textbooks on contract law are, in large part, descriptive accounts. The fourth type of account, an interpretative account, aims to enhance understanding of the law by highlighting its significance or meaning.[2] In practice, nearly all interpretative theories include historical, prescriptive, and descriptive elements.[3] It would be, therefore, of significance if the current law of commercial dispute is examined in view of the aforesaid theory/ies.

Historically, Commercial Courts have been under conception since new economic policy was announced in 1992. In the year 2003, the Law Commission *suo motu* took up the issue of proposing the constitution of Commercial Divisions in High Courts, in view of the vast changes in the economic policies of the country post-1991; the perception that the Indian judicial system had "collapsed" due to inordinate delays; and the need to ensure the fast disposal of high value commercial disputes to provide assurance to domestic and foreign investors[4]. In its 188th Report titled "Proposals for Constitution of Hi-tech Fast-Track Commercial Divisions in High Courts", the Commission examined the international practice

---

2   Contract Theory by Stephen A Smith, Oxford University Press at pp.4-5
3   Ibid
4   Para 1.2 of Law Commission 253rd Report

of setting up Commercial Courts to deal with high value or complex commercial cases, and the need for such Commercial Courts in India. Its aim was to give a clear assurance to investors that high value commercial suits would directly go before the Commercial Division to be constituted in all High Courts, which would follow fast track procedures similar to those recommended in the 176th Report on "Arbitration and Conciliation (Amendment) Bill, 2002". These Commercial Divisions would also be equipped with high-tech video conferencing facilities along the lines used in Commercial Courts abroad[5] (Needless to say, the present Covid 19 pandemic saw video conferencing a reality in Indian courts and tribunals) The Law Commission carried out an in-depth study of the Commercial Courts in the United Kingdom (hereinafter "UK"); the United States of America, specifically the States of New York and Maryland; Singapore; Ireland; France; Kenya and nine other countries to examine the procedures followed and the kinds of cases handled by the Commercial Courts in such countries[6].

Law Commission in its 253rd Report said in Para 4.1, "While the need for Commercial Courts is obvious in India, the institution of such courts should be seen as a stepping-stone to reforming the civil justice system in India. At the same time, the reforms should be tailored to keep in mind the existing institutions and should focus on improving them within the existing legal framework." It further said in Para 4.2, "The Commercial Courts, the Commercial Divisions and the Commercial Appellate Divisions of High Courts that have been recommended are intended to serve as a pilot project in the larger goal of reforming the civil justice system in India. The goal is to ensure that cases are disposed of expeditiously, fairly and at reasonable cost to the litigant. Not only does this benefit the litigant, other potential litigants (especially those engaged in trade and commerce) are also advantaged by the reduction in backlog caused by the quick

---

5   Para 1.3 of Law Commission 253rd Report
6   Para 1.4 Law Commission 253rd Report

resolution of commercial disputes. In turn, this will further economic growth, increase foreign investment, and make India an attractive place to do business. Further, it also benefits the economy as a whole given that a robust dispute resolution mechanism is a *sine qua non* for the all-round development of an economy."

The legislative attempt to overhaul the civil procedure *vis-à-vis* amendment in 1999 and 2002 seemed to have not attained the purpose of making courts act fast. The Supreme Court in **Salem Bar Association v. Union of India**[7] further watered down some of the most effective measures on the basis of twin principles of directory-mandatory provisions. The present Act shows strong legislative will to make procedure expeditious and making litigants, lawyers and courts to adhere to timelines.

Doing Business report is a report under auspices of World Bank which presents quantitative indicators on business regulations and the protection of property rights that can be compared across 190 countries of world. It covers 12 areas of business regulation. Ten of these areas—starting a business, dealing with construction permits, getting electricity, registering property, getting credit, protecting minority investors, paying taxes, trading across borders, enforcing contracts, and resolving insolvency—are included in the ease of doing business score and ease of doing business ranking. The two parameters-enforcing contracts and resolving insolvency are two areas in which the Central Govt. brought reforms by way of amending and codification of law. The Indian Bankruptcy Code, Commercial Courts Act and Amendment of Arbitration Act are three such measures to improve overall ranking in the abovesaid *Doing Business*. It appears that early resolution of commercial disputes creates positive image amongst investors about the strong and responsive Indian legal system.

---

7   (2005) 6 SCC 344

The Commercial Courts Act envisages swift conduct of commercial disputes brought before the Court for which suitable provisions have been made in the Act. The Act has brought necessary amendments in Code of Civil Procedure vide section 16 which clearly provides that the trial of a suit in the Commercial Court shall follow the amended provision with further provision that the provision under this Act shall have effect notwithstanding anything inconsistent therewith contained in any other law for the time being in force or in any instrument.

STATEMENT OF OBJECT & REASONS OF THE ACT

Purpose clause is an express statement of legislative intention. Such a clause is optional. When present, it is included in the body of the Act. It may apply to the whole or a part of the Act. Instead of a preamble, an Act may contain one or more purpose clauses in the body of it. The term 'purpose' or some equivalent terms such as 'objective' may be used.[8] The book- Benion on Statutory Interpretation further says, "The purpose clause may be taken as a guide to legislative intention; indeed that is its function. However, it is unlikely to be taken to override the clear words of an operative provisions of the Act."

The Supreme Court in **K.P. Varghese v. Income Tax Officer, Ernakulam**[9] held that interpretation of statute being an exercise in the ascertainment of meaning, everything which is logically relevant should be admissible. A Rule is a uniform or established course of things. There are three rules of interpretation of statutes- Literal, Golden and Mischief. An Aid, on the other hand is a device that helps or assists. For the purpose of construction or interpretation, the Court has to take recourse to various internal and external aids. One of such internal aids is the Statement of object and reasons appended to the Bill while presented to the parliament.

The Commercial Courts Act, 2015 enshrines object and reasons for bringing this legislation which necessarily means for providing a robust

---

8   Benion on Statutory Interpretation, Fifth Edition at p.734
9   AIR 1981 SC 1922 ; (1981) 4 SCC 173

mechanism for redressal of commercial disputes within the existing judicial structure without creating any new tribunal or *quasi* judicial authority, yet with improved efficacy of the Courts. It was the need of time in today's economic world. A definite time limit for successive stages in a *lis*, that includes suit, application and execution has been provided for. The Act provides a time span of nearly one and half year for disposal of a suit from date of inception to date of the judgment. This includes the proceedings conducted by an arbitral tribunal, in which the Commercial Courts or Commercial Divisions of a High Court as the case may be, shall play pivotal role as contemplated in the Arbitration and Conciliation Act, 1996, as amended till date.

The statement of object and reasons of the Act provides that it is an "An Act to provide for the constitution of Commercial Courts, Commercial Appellate Courts, Commercial Division and Commercial Appellate Division in the High Courts for adjudicating commercial disputes of specified value and matters connected therewith or incidental thereto." BE it enacted by Parliament in the Sixty-sixth Year of the Republic of India as follows:—

The proposal to provide for the speedy disposal of High value commercial disputes has been under consideration of the government for quite some time. The high value commercial disputes involve complex facts and question of law. Therefore, there is need to provide for an independent mechanism for their early resolution. Early resolution of commercial dispute shall create a positive image to the investor world about the independent and responsive Indian legal system.

The Act No-4 of 2016 has been further amended in the year 2018 to bring suit of lower denomination within reach of designated 'Commercial Court' and a flexible mechanism within the jurisdiction of State Govt. to establish Commercial Courts and Commercial Appellate Courts.

The Commercial Courts, Commercial Division and Commercial Appellate Division of High Courts Act, 2015 (Now Commercial Courts Act) has been enacted for the constitution of Commercial Courts, Commercial Division and Commercial Appellate Division in the High Courts for adjudicating commercial disputes of specified value and for matters connected therewith or incidental thereto. 2. The global economic environment has since become increasingly competitive and to attract business at international level, India needs to further improve its ranking in the World Bank 'Doing Business Report' which, *inter alia*, considers the dispute resolution environment in the country as one of the parameters for doing business. Further, the tremendous economic development has ushered in enormous commercial activities in the country including foreign direct investments, public private partnership, etc., which has prompted initiating legislative measures for speedy settlement of commercial disputes, widen the scope of the Courts to deal with commercial disputes and facilitate ease of doing business. Needless to say, an early resolution of commercial disputes of even lesser value creates a positive image amongst the investors about the strong and responsive Indian legal system. It is, therefore, proposed to amend the Commercial Courts, Commercial Division and Commercial Appellate Division of High Courts Act, 2015. 3. As Parliament was not in session and immediate action was required to be taken to make necessary amendments in the Commercial Courts, Commercial Division and Commercial Appellate Division of High Courts Act, 2015, to further improve India's ranking in the 'Doing Business Report', the President promulgated the Commercial Courts, Commercial Division and Commercial Appellate Division of High Courts (Amendment) Ordinance, 2018 on 3rd May, 2018. 4. It is proposed to introduce the Commercial Courts, Commercial Division and Commercial Appellate Division of High Courts (Amendment) Bill, 2018 to replace the Commercial Courts, Commercial Division and Commercial Appellate Division of High Courts (Amendment) Ordinance, 2018, which inter alia, provides for the following namely:—

i. to reduce the specified value of commercial disputes from the existing one crore rupees to three lakh rupees, and to enable the parties to approach the lowest level of subordinate Courts for speedy resolution of commercial disputes;

ii. to enable the State Governments, with respect to the High Courts having ordinary original civil jurisdiction, to constitute Commercial Courts at District Judge level and to specify such pecuniary value of commercial disputes which shall not be less than three lakh rupees and not more than the pecuniary jurisdiction of the district Courts;

iii. to enable the State Governments, except the territories over which the High Courts have ordinary original civil jurisdiction, to designate such number of Commercial Appellate Courts at district judge level to exercise the appellate jurisdiction over the Commercial Courts below the district judge level;

iv. to enable the State Governments to specify such pecuniary value of a commercial dispute which shall not be less than three lakh rupees or such higher value, for the whole or part of the State; and

v. to provide for compulsory mediation before institution of a suit, where no urgent interim relief is contemplated and for this purpose, to introduce the Pre-Institution Mediation and Settlement Mechanism and to enable the 7 8 Central Government to authorise the authorities constituted under the Legal Services Authorities Act, 1987 for this purpose. 5. The Bill seeks to achieve the above objectives

The Commercial Courts Act, 2015, as amended, provides for constitution of Commercial Courts at District level and Commercial Division at High Court with original jurisdiction. Similarly, the Act provides for constitution of Commercial Appellate Courts in District Courts as well as in High Courts. The constitution of Courts as dealt with in Chapter II of the Act can be looked into from two angles-

i. **Where High Courts do not have ordinary original civil jurisdiction:** The State Govt. may after consultation with the concerned High Court, by notification, constitute such number of

Commercial Courts at District level as it may deem necessary[10]; and specify such pecuniary value which shall not be less than three lakh rupees or such high value as it may deem necessary[11]. The State Govt. shall, after consultation with the concerned High Court specify the local limits of the area to which jurisdiction of Commercial Court shall extend[12]. The judge or judges of a Commercial Court either at level of District Judge or a Court below the level of District Judge[13].

Similarly, section 3-A of Commercial Courts Act, 2015 provides that the State Govt. may after consultation with the concerned High Court, by notification designate such number of Commercial Appellate Courts at District Judge level as it may deem necessary. Section 5 of the Commercial Courts Act, 2015 provides that the Chief Justice of the concerned High Court shall, by order, constitute Commercial Appellate Division having one or more Division Benches for the purpose of exercising the jurisdiction and powers conferred on it by the Act.

ii. **Where High Courts have ordinary original civil jurisdiction:** With respect to the High Courts having ordinary original civil jurisdiction, the State Govt. may, after consultation with the concerned High Court, by notification, constitute Commercial Courts at the District Judge level[14]. Sec 4 of the Act, however, provides that Chief Justice of the Concerned High Court may by order constitute Commercial Division having one or more Benches consisting of a Single Judge for exercising the jurisdiction and powers conferred on it under the Act. Appeal from the decisions of Commercial Division shall lie to the Commercial Appellate Division, as constituted, under sec. 5 of the Act.

---

10 Sec 3 (1) of Commercial Courts Act, 2015
11 Sec 3 (1A) of Commercial Courts Act, 2015
12 Sec 3 (2) of Commercial Court Act, 2015
13 Sec 3 (3) of Commercial Court Act, 2015
14 Sec 3 (1) Proviso, Commercial Courts Act, 2015

These Commercial Courts and Commercial Divisions in High Courts (having ordinary original civil jurisdiction) have been constituted to exercise jurisdiction and power under the Act to adjudicate commercial disputes only as defined and described under sec. 2(c) of the Act, which gives an exhaustive list of such disputes in clause (i) to (xxii). Meaning of 'arising out of' according to Collins Dictionary is "If something arising from particular situation, or arises out of it, it is created or caused by the situation." The Black's Law Dictionary defines it as "To originate, to stem; to result (litigation routinely arises from such accidents)". Any dispute caused by the aforesaid matters fall within ambit of the commercial dispute. However, commercial dispute of certain specified value only can be brought for adjudication before a Commercial Court. Sec 6 of the Act provides as follows:

Section 6. Jurisdiction of Commercial Court—The Commercial Court shall have jurisdiction to try all suits and applications relating to a commercial dispute of a Specified Value arising out of the entire territory of the State over which it has been vested territorial jurisdiction.

***Explanation.*—For the purposes of this section, a commercial dispute shall be considered to arise out of the entire territory of the State over which a Commercial Court has been vested jurisdiction, if the suit or application relating to such commercial dispute has been instituted as per the provisions of sections 16 to 20 of the Code of Civil Procedure, 1908 (5 of 1908).**

The word 'specified value' has been defined in sec. 2(i) of the Act as, "Specified Value", in relation to a commercial dispute, shall mean the value of the subject-matter in respect of a suit as determined in accordance with section 12 [which shall not be less than three lakh rupees] or such higher value, as may be notified by the Central Government. It is significant to note here that the clause 'which shall not be less than three lakh rupees' has been brought in the Act vide Amendment Act, no 28 of 2018.

This amending provision needs to be notified by the concerned State Govt. after consultation with the respective High Court. In all such states where this notification has not been made, the jurisdiction of commercial Court remains as per original Act i.e. Act of 2015.

The Jharkhnad State vide notification dated 08.02.2021 has notified the constitution of commercial courts superseding the earlier notification as follows:

1. One Court of the Civil Judge (Senior Division) in each district of the State of Jharkhand, as Commercial Court to exercise original jurisdiction in respect of commercial disputes where the value of the suit or dispute is not less than Rs. three lakhs and upto Rs. One Crore.

2. One court of District Judge in each district of the State of Jharkhand as Commercial Court to exercise original jurisdiction in respect of commercial disputes where the value of the suit or dispute exceeds Rs. One Crore.

3. The Court of District Judge in each District as Commercial Appellate Court to exercise appellate jurisdiction and dispose of the appeals arising out of the judgments and orders passed by a Commercial Court below the level of the District Judge.

4. The deputed officers shall execute above assignment in addition to their allotted work.

The combined effect of the aforesaid notification is that there shall be two tier of Courts for original jurisdiction based on the value of the suit- Civil Judge (Senior Division) from Rs. 3 Lakhs to 1 Crore; and that of District Judge from above 1 crore. Further, the appellate jurisdiction in respect of the commercial cases has also been made two tier- at District Judge level up to Rs. 1 Crore and Commercial Appellate Division above Rs. 1 Crore. The value of the suit and the dispute shall be done on the basis of definition and calculation of specified value which has been dealt with under the next chapter.

To attain its object and reasons the Commercial Courts Act has introduced certain watershed amendments in some of the provisions of the Code of Civil Procedure. Section 16 provides-

1. **Amendments to the Code of Civil Procedure, 1908 in its application to commercial disputes.—(1) The provisions of the Code of Civil Procedure, 1908 (5 of 1908) shall, in their application to any suit in respect of a commercial dispute of a Specified Value, stand amended in the manner as specified in the Schedule.**

2. **The Commercial Division and Commercial Court shall follow the provisions of the Code of Civil Procedure, 1908 (5 of 1908), as amended by this Act, in the trial of a suit in respect of a commercial dispute of a Specified Value.**

3. **Where any provision of any Rule of the jurisdictional High Court or any amendment to the Code of Civil Procedure, 1908 (5 of 1908), by the State Government is in conflict with the provisions of the Code of Civil Procedure, 1908, as amended by this Act, the provisions of the Code of Civil Procedure as amended by this Act shall prevail.**

All the amending provision as aforesaid have been incorporated in 'Schedule', which amends only a selected part of the Code like sec. 26, 35 and 35A. In the First Schedule of the Code of Civil Procedure following Orders have been amended with certain inserting provisions. These can be shown in tabular form as below:

Section		Details
26		*Proviso* inserted
35		Substituted
35A		Sub section(2) omitted

Section		Details
Order	Rule	Details
V	1(1)	Substituted, Second proviso
VI	3-A	Inserted, pleading forms to be prescribed by High Court
	15A	Inserted, Verification of pleadings
VII	2-A	Inserted, statement in respect of interest sought; Rule14 not to apply
VIII	1	Substituted, *Proviso*; Rule 1A not to apply
	3-A	Inserted, manner of denial in written statement
	5	Inserted, *Proviso* after first proviso in sub rule(1)
	10	Inserted, *Proviso* Omitted, *Proviso*
XI		Substituted, Disclosure, discovery & inspection of documents
XIII-A		Inserted, Summary judgment
XV		Omitted
XV-A		Inserted, Case management Hearing
XVIII	2	Substituted, Sub rule 3A to 3F
	Rule 4	Inserted, Sub rule 1, 1A to 1C
XIX	4, 5, 6	Inserted, after Rule 3, Control, rejection & form of affidavits of evidence
XX	1	Substituted, Rule 1

In addition to the aforesaid amendments of orders and rules, an Appendix I has also been inserted after Appendix H. By virtue of newly inserted Order XI Rule 7, it is hereby clarified that Order XIII Rule 1, Order VII Rule 14 and Order VIII Rule 1A of the Code of Civil Procedure, 1908 (5 of 1908) shall not apply to suits or applications before the Commercial Divisions of High Court or Commercial Courts."

This has to be further read with section 21 of the Commercial Courts Act, 2015 which provides that **save as otherwise provided, the provisions of this Act shall have effect, notwithstanding anything inconsistent therewith contained in any other law for the time being in force or in any instrument having effect by virtue of any law for the time being in force other than this Act.**

This Act has set strict timelines for different stages of a trial right from the appearance of parties to conclusion of trial. Timelines for pre-institution mediation has also been provided in the Act which can be summarised in tabular form as below:

Stage of the Case	Reckoning of Time	Time provided for
Pre-institution Mediation	Date of application by plaintiff	3 months, can be extended for 2 further months
Appearance of defendant	Date of service of summons	30 days
Written Statement	30 days, can be further extended to 120 days	Date of service of summons
Application for summary judgment	Prior to issue framing	
Reply to such application	Date of receipt of notice of application or hearing	30 days

Stage of the Case	Reckoning of Time	Time provided for
Additional docs. by respondent	Before date of hearing	15 days'
Additional documents by applicants	Before date of hearing	5 days
Hearing of application for summary judgments		After 30 days notice
Case Management Hearing	From the date of filing of affidavits	Not later than 4 weeks
Fixing of dates and time limits		After hearing parties and framing issues
Cross-Examination		day to day
Closure of arguments by both parties	From date of framing of issues	6 months
Filing of additional documents	From date of institution of suit	30 days
Inspection of documents	From date of filing of WS	30 days
Admission & denial of documents	From date of inspection of docs	15 days
Written arguments	Before commencing oral arguments	4 weeks
Revised written argument	After conclusion of oral arguments	1 week
Judgment	After conclusion of arguments	within 90 days

This Act itself contains provision for constant monitoring of the commercial cases data. The statistical data regarding the number of suits, applications, appeals or writ petitions filed before the Commercial Courts, Commercial Appellate Courts, Commercial Division, or Commercial Appellate Division, as the case may be, the pendency of such cases, the status of each case, and the number of cases disposed of, shall be maintained and updated every month by each Commercial Courts, Commercial Appellate Courts, Commercial Division, Commercial Appellate Division and shall be published on the website of the relevant High Court.[15] The Commercial Courts (Statistical Data) Rules, 2018 seeks 'average no. of days taken to decide the case.' Rule 3 prescribes following format.

S.No	Name of the Court	No. of cases pending (on the 1st day of month of ___)	No. of new cases instituted (during the month as per column 3)	Total cases pending in the court (on the last day of the month as per column 3)	No. of cases disposed (during the month as per column 3)	Average no. of days taken to decide the case
(1)	(2)	(3)	(4)	(5)	(6)	(7)

---

15 Sec.17 Commercial Courts Act, 2015

2

THE PRE-LITIGATION MEDIATION & SETTLEMENT

"The entire legal profession... has become so mesmerized with the stimulation of the courtroom contest, that we tend to forget that we ought to be healers of conflict... trial by adversarial contest must in time go the way of the ancient trial by battle and blood... our system has become too costly, too painful, too destructive, too inefficient for truly civilized people."

– Chief Justice Warren Burger, excerpt from the 1984 "The State of Justice" speech

Mediation is one of the most time saving and cost-effective mechanisms of alternate dispute redressal methods. It may be classified into three variants- Pre-litigation mediation, Court-mandated mediation and Post-filing mediation. While Pre-Litigation mediation begins before the dispute reaches to the Courts, the other two begins only on intervention of the Courts. Court-mediation means that the case has already been filed in Court. Then, the Court enters an order that requires the opposing parties to attend mediation. Generally, the Court order selects the given mediator. For example, the Family Courts Act, 1984 provides for making of such endeavour at the first instance and it keeps the room open for later stage also. Section 9 of Family Courts Act, 1984 reads as

"(1) In every suit or proceeding, endeavour shall be made by the Family Court in the first instance, where it is possible to do so consistent with the nature and circumstances of the case, to assist and persuade the parties in arriving at a settlement in respect of the subject-matter of the suit or proceeding and for this purpose a Family Court may, subject to any rules made by the High Court, follow such procedure as it may deem fit.

(2) If, in any suit or proceeding, at any stage, it appears to the Family Court that there is a reasonable possibility of a settlement between the parties, the Family Court may adjourn the proceedings for such period as it thinks fit to enable attempts to be made to effect such a settlement.

(3) The power conferred by sub-section *(2)* shall be in addition to, and not in derogation of, any other power of the Family Court to adjourn the proceedings."

The Code of Civil Procedure (Amendment) Act, 1999 inserted section 89 provides for this settlement of disputes outside the code. It was suggested by Law Commission of India that the court may require attendance of any party to the suit or proceedings to appear in person with a view to arriving at an amicable settlement of disputes between the parties and make an attempt to settle the dispute between the parties amicably. Section 89 provides that where it appears to the Court that there exist elements of a settlement which may be acceptable to the parties, the court shall formulate the terms of settlement and give them to the parties for their observations and after receiving the observations of the parties, the court may reformulate the terms of a possible settlement and refer this same for arbitration, conciliation, judicial settlement including settlement through *lok adalat*, or the mediation. Order X Rule 1A, 1B and 1C provide the necessary procedure for any mode of alternative dispute resolution. This procedure is to be adopted only after ascertainment of admission and denial of the contents of the plaint and the written statements viz. pleadings, as contemplated in Rule 1 of Order X of the Code of Civil Procedure.

In recent years, mediation has been given further impetus by the inclusion of a provision in the Companies Act, 2013, which makes it mandatory for the central government to maintain a mediation and conciliation panel, comprising experts for mediating commercial disputes between the parties.[1] Further, tribunals under the Companies Act or the central government may also refer a dispute to mediation where it deems it appropriate. The maximum time to conclude a mediation is three months. Similarly, the Consumer Protection Act, 2019 provides for mediating disputes at the first instance of admission of a complaint before any consumer disputes redressal agency.[2] Chapter V of the Consumer Protection Act, 2019 envisages the establishment of consumer mediation cells at the national, state, and district levels, to whom the consumer disputes redressal agencies shall refer their cases. The Real Estate (Regulation and Development) (RERA) Act, 2016 also encourages amicable conciliation of disputes between promoters and allottees through dispute settlement forums established by consumer or promoter forums.[3]

However, the pre-litigation mediation is characterized by marked difference, as stated above. A dispute heard in pre-litigation mediation has not been filed with the Courts, thus information about the dispute is not public. If the potential exists for all phases of a trial and evidence presented to be available to the public, privacy is a great advantage for the contesting parties to enter the mediation process before the dispute reaches to the Court. Confidentiality is one of the greatest benefits of pre-mediation. The knowledge that an informal, honest, and confidential discussion can take place with the mediator adds to the speed and success of mediation. It is also cost effective for both parties. The Commercial Courts Act calls it as

---

[1] Section 442(1) of Companies Act, 2013
[2] Section 37 of Consumer Protection Act, 2019
[3] Section 32(g)

Pre- Institution Mediation, instead of pre-litigation mediation, and keeps the time consumed therein out of limitation period.

The Commercial Courts Act 2015 provides mandatory mediation between the parties before institution of the suit itself save and except where urgent relief is required. The amendment act inserted a new chapter III A and a new section 12A as follows

12A. Pre-Institution Mediation and Settlement—

1. **A suit, which does not contemplate any urgent interim relief under this Act, shall not be instituted unless the plaintiff exhausts the remedy of pre-institution mediation in accordance with such manner and procedure as may be prescribed by rules made by the Central Government.**

2. **The Central Government may, by notification, authorise the Authorities constituted under the Legal Services Authorities Act, 1987 (39 of 1987), for the purposes of pre-institution mediation.**

3. **Notwithstanding anything contained in the Legal Services Authorities Act, 1987 (39 of 1987), the Authority authorised by the Central Government under sub-section (2) shall complete the process of mediation within a period of three months from the date of application made by the plaintiff under sub-section (1):**

   Provided that the period of mediation may be extended for a further period of two months with the consent of the parties:

   Provided further that, the period during which the parties remained occupied with the pre-institution mediation, such period shall not be computed for the purpose of limitation under the Limitation Act, 1963 (36 of 1963).

4. **If the parties to the commercial dispute arrive at a settlement, the same shall be reduced into writing and shall be signed by the parties to the dispute and the mediator.**

5. **The settlement arrived at under this section shall have the same status and effect as if it is an arbitral award on agreed terms under sub-section (4) of section 30 of the Arbitration and Conciliation Act, 1996 (26 of 1996).]**

The Central Govt. exercising powers under section 21 of the Commercial Courts Act 2015 has framed Rules titled as The Commercial Courts (Pre-Institution Mediation and Settlement) Rules, 2018 provides for procedures for initiation of mediation process, venue for such mediation, role of mediator, mediation fee etc. Rule 3 provides that a party to a commercial dispute may make an application to the Authority (as notified by the Central Govt.) in the prescribed form online or by Post or by hand for initiation of mediation process under the Act along with fee of one thousand rupees payable to the Authority either by way of demand daft or through online. The Authority shall issue notice to the opposite party to appear. If both parties appear before the Authority and give consent to participate in the mediation process, the Authority shall assign the commercial dispute to a Mediator. The Authority shall ensure that the mediation process is completed within three months which can be further extended for a period of two months by consent of both parties viz. applicant and the opposite party. Rule 7 provides the procedure of mediation in detail and Rule 12 provides the set of ethics to be followed by the mediator. So, the adherence to the timeline has been made a responsibility of the Authority, which shall get the same through the mediator. Rule 11 provides that before the commencement of the meditation, the parties to the commercial dispute shall pay to the Authority a one-time mediation fee to be shared equally as per the quantum of claim.

One of the characteristic features of these Rules is the emphasis on confidentiality of mediation. Rule 9 provides that the Mediator, parties or their authorized representatives or Counsel shall maintain confidentiality about the mediation and the Mediator shall not allow stenographic or audio or video recording of the mediation sittings. Rule 12(ix) provides that mediator shall not meet the parties, their representatives, or their counsels or communicate with them, privately except during the mediation sittings in the premises of the Authority. Rule 12(x) further provides that mediator shall not interact with the media or make public the details of commercial dispute case, being mediated by him or any other allied activity carried out by him as a Mediator, which may prejudice the interests of the parties to the commercial dispute.

In case, the mediation succeeds, the terms of settlement shall be reduced to writing to be signed by the parties and the mediator which shall have an effect of an 'award' and shall be enforceable accordingly.

However, if the suit is instituted without complying with the provision of 12A, the plaint shall be returned forthwith under provision of Order VII Rule 10 of Code of Civil Procedure Code, provided however that there is no urgent relief prayed for in the plaint. One such case came before the Telengana High Court in **M/s M. K. Food Products v M/s S. H. Food Products**[4] where the suit instituted by the petitioner was for a permanent injunction restraining the respondent from infringing the copyright that the petitioner has in the design of the packing in which their product is sold. The suit was returned by the office pointing out certain defects. After complying with the returns, which are relevant and after pointing out that two returns, which related to registration, were irrelevant, the petitioner represented the papers. Yet the office insisted upon the irrelevant returns, which related to the registration under the Copyright Act and the Patent Act. The petitioner sought hearing in the open Court. After hearing the petitioner, the Commercial Court returned the plaint in terms of Section 12(A)(1) of the Commercial Courts Act, 2015 on the ground that the petitioner should first exhaust the remedy of pre-institution mediation. Therefore, the petitioner preferred a civil revision before the High Court. After hearing the parties, the Court held, "8. In addition, the learned Judge has directed to return the plaint on the

---

[4] CRP 3690/2018

ground that the petitioner should first exhaust the remedy of pre-institution mediation under Section 12(A)(1) of the Act. ...."

9. It can be seen from what is extracted above that it is only in cases where the suit does not contemplate any urgent interim relief that there is a bar for institution of the suit without the plaintiff exhausting the remedy of pre-institution mediation. The expression used in Section 12(A)(1) of the Act is "A suit which does not contemplate any urgent relief".

10. Unfortunately, the learned Judge has read the above expression to mean as if only in cases where the plaintiff is entitled to urgent interim relief, the provision will not apply. The entitlement of a party to an urgent relief is a matter that would come up for consideration if the suit is numbered and several aspects taken into account. What is required to satisfy Section 12(A)(1) of the Act is the contemplation of an urgent relief."

The Madhya Pradesh High Court (Indore Bench) in **GSD Constructions Pvt. Ltd v Balaji Febtech Engineering Pvt. Ltd.**[5] adjudged a similar matter where the appellants filed a civil suit for declaration, recovery of money and for grant of injunction and they also moved applications under Order 7 Rule 1 of the Code of Civil Procedure, 1908 and under Order 39 Rule 1 and 2 read with Section 151 of the Code of Civil Procedure, 1908. THE High Court held, "looking to the urgency of interim relief prayed by the appellants in the present matter, the trial Court is directed to hear the applications filed by the appellants and proceed ahead in the matter without forcing the appellants to avail the pre-institution remedies as observed by the learned Judge."

The application for such mediation has to be filed in the prescribed form as provided in the Rules as below:

---

5   MA 4081 / 2019

Schedule-I

Form-1: Mediation Application Form

[*See* Rule 3(1)]

Name of the Authority and address

Details of Parties:

1. Name of applicant :
2. Address and contact details of applicant:

   Address:-

   Telephone. No._____ Mobile._____ E-mail ID:_____
3. Name of opposite party:
4. Address and contact details of opposite party:

   Address:-

   Telephone. No._____ Mobile._____ E-mail ID:_____

Details of Dispute:

1. Nature of dispute as per section 2 (1)(c) of the Commercial Courts Act 2015 (4 of 2016):
2. Quantum of claim:
3. Territorial jurisdiction of the competent court:
4. Brief synopsis of commercial dispute (not to exceed 5000 words):
5. Additional points of relevance:

Details of Fee Paid:

Fee paid by DD No. _____ dated _____

Name of Bank and branch _____

Online transaction No. _____ dated _____

Date:

Signature of Authority

Note: Form shall be submitted to the Authority with a fee of one thousand rupees.

For Office Use:

Form received on :

File No. allotted:

Mode of sending notice to the opposite party:

Notice to opposite party sent on:

Whether Notice acknowledged by opposite party or not:

Date of Non-starter report/ Assignment of commercial dispute to Mediator:

3
INSTITUTION OF SUIT

The importance of the art of pleading is insufficiently realized in this country. It is at least as important as any other part of the duties of an advocate. Moreover, it demands a high degree of skill, and the final form of any pleading should be settled only by advocates who have the necessary skill and experience.

– Ramprasad Chimanlal v. Hazarimal Lalchand,
AIR 1931 Cal 458

Once a dispute referred to mediation under section 12A of the Commercial Courts Act, 2015 is not resolved by settlement, the same becomes amenable for adjudication by the Courts specifically constituted under the Act known as 'Commercial Courts' or 'Commercial Division' of a High Court as the case may be. Section 26 of the Code of Civil Procedure, as amended, provides that every suit shall be instituted by presentation of a plaint or in such manner as may be prescribed. In every plaint, facts shall be proved by affidavit, provided that such affidavit shall be in the form and manner as prescribed under order VI Rule 15 A.

There are, broadly speaking four essential elements of a suit-

a. **Parties**: There must be two parties to every suit, i.e. a plaintiff and a defendant. There may be, however, more than one plaintiff and more than one defendant in a suit. The Code provides for a necessary party and a proper party and also contains provisions relating to joinder, non-joinder and mis-joinder parties in a suit. Order I deals with the provisions relating to parties, consequences of non- impleading a necessary and/or proper party. The main object before the court is to bring all interested parties before it so that the underlying dispute may be fully and completely adjudicated. The court has the power and jurisdiction to add, strike out or substitute any party in a suit which is discretionary but subject to statutory provisions. Like any other suit, a commercial suit shall follow the law relating to party.

b. **Cause of action:** There is no definition of cause of action in the Code. However, the term has been interpreted by the Supreme Court and High Courts to mean a bundle of facts which it is necessary for the plaintiff to prove to entitle him to a decree in the suit. Every plaint must disclose a cause of action (Order VII Rule 1(e), otherwise the plaint may be rejected under order VII Rule 11(a). While reaching to a conclusion the plaint must be read into whole and it is not essential, though desirable, to dedicate a separate paragraph in the plaint to cause of action and the time when it arose. In a suit for damages for breach of contract two facts shall be required to be proved- *firstly*, the making of contract and *secondly*, the breach of contract which has to be separately proved apart from other relevant facts ancillary to it. Since commercial disputes relate to contracts which are very specific, classified into various category with every possibility of further sub classification it is essential to have deep understanding of substantive law applicable in that branch. For example, in a case involving insurance contract, apart from Indian Contract Act, 1872, the Insurance Act, 1938 and Rules framed therein and Regulations framed by the nodal agency- Insurance Development & Regulatory Authority are pre-requisites.

c. **Subject matter**: Generally speaking, the subject matter of a suit is the property claimed in the suit. The property may be movable or immovable. The Commercial Courts Act, however, provides an exhaustive list of such commercial disputes in section 2 (c) under clause (i) to (xxii).

 i. **ordinary transactions of merchants, bankers, financiers and traders such as those relating to mercantile documents, including enforcement and interpretation of such documents;**
 ii. **export or import of merchandise or services;**
 iii. **issues relating to admiralty and maritime law;**
 iv. **transactions relating to aircraft, aircraft engines, aircraft equipment and helicopters, including sales, leasing and financing of the same;**
 v. **carriage of goods;**
 vi. **construction and infrastructure contracts, including tenders;**
 vii. **agreements relating to immovable property used exclusively in trade or commerce;**
 viii. **franchising agreements;**
 ix. **distribution and licensing agreements;**
 x. **management and consultancy agreements;**
 xi. **joint venture agreements;**
 xii. **shareholders agreements;**
 xiii. **subscription and investment agreements pertaining to the services industry including outsourcing services and financial services;**

xiv. mercantile agency and mercantile usage;

xv. partnership agreements;

xvi. technology development agreements;

xvii. intellectual property rights relating to registered and unregistered trademarks, copyright, patent, design, domain names, geographical indications and semiconductor integrated circuits;

xviii. agreements for sale of goods or provision of services;

xix. exploitation of oil and gas reserves or other natural resources including electromagnetic spectrum;

xx. insurance and re-insurance;

xxi. contracts of agency relating to any of the above; and

xxii. such other commercial disputes as may be notified by the Central Government.

Explanation.—A commercial dispute shall not cease to be a commercial dispute merely because—

a. it also involves action for recovery of immovable property or for realisation of monies out of immovable property given as security or involves any other relief pertaining to immovable property;

b. one of the contracting parties is the State or any of its agencies or instrumentalities, or a private body carrying out public functions;

It is of utmost importance to satisfy that the disputes leading to institution must satisfy any one or more of the aforesaid class of disputes as it would be subject to judicial scrutiny at the time of admission and afterwards it may come under challenge of the defendants. This may also be challenged in view of section 15 of the Commercial Courts Act, 2015 which provides-

15. Transfer of pending cases.—

1. All suits and applications, including applications under the Arbitration and Conciliation Act, 1996 (26 of 1996), relating to a commercial dispute of a Specified Value pending in a High Court where a Commercial Division has been constituted, shall be transferred to the Commercial Division.

2. All suits and applications, including applications under the Arbitration and Conciliation Act, 1996 (26 of 1996), relating to a commercial dispute of a Specified Value pending in any civil court in any district or area in respect of which a Commercial Court has been constituted, shall be transferred to such Commercial Court:

   Provided that no suit or application where the final judgment has been reserved by the Court prior to the constitution of the Commercial Division or the Commercial Court shall be transferred either under sub-section (1) or sub-section (2).

3. Where any suit or application, including an application under the Arbitration and Conciliation Act, 1996 (26 of 1996), relating to a commercial dispute of Specified Value shall stand transferred to the Commercial Division or Commercial Court under sub-section (1) or sub-section (2), the provisions of this Act shall apply to those procedures that were not complete at the time of transfer.

4. The Commercial Division or Commercial Court, as the case may be, may hold case management hearings in respect of such transferred suit or application in order to prescribe new timelines or issue such further directions as may be necessary for a speedy and efficacious disposal of such suit or application in accordance 3[with Order XV-A] of the Code of Civil Procedure, 1908 (5 of 1908):

   Provided that the proviso to sub-rule (1) of Rule 1 of Order V of the Code of Civil Procedure, 1908 (5 of 1908) shall not apply to such transferred suit or application and the court may, in its discretion, prescribe a new time period within which the written statement shall be filed.

5. In the event that such suit or application is not transferred in the manner specified in sub-section (1), sub-section (2) or sub-section (3), the Commercial Appellate Division of the High Court may, on the application of any of the parties to the suit, withdraw such suit or application from the court before which it is pending and transfer the same for trial or disposal to the Commercial Division or Commercial Court, as the case may be, having territorial jurisdiction over such suit, and such order of transfer shall be final and binding.

In **Anant Gopal Sheoray v. State of Bombay AIR 1958 SC 915** it was held that no person has a vested right in any course of procedure. He has only the right of the prosecution or defence in the manner prescribed for the time being by or for the court in which the case is pending and if by an Act of Parliament, the mode of procedure is altered he has no other right than to proceed according to altered mode.

The definition of commercial dispute is exhaustive but not restricted to the exact terms used in the Act. In a case Madhuram Properties v. Tata Consultancy 2017 SCC Online Guj 725 the plaintiff and defendant entered into one indenture of sub-lease in respect of 216 flats of residential blocks. Plaintiff agreed to grant sub lease of such lease for a period three years. The dispute arose between the parties and renewal of lease did not materialize and lease came to an end. The suit was brought for recovery of possession and mesne profits. The Commercial Court returned the plaint for placing it before the appropriate court. The plaintiff aggrieved from the order filed an appeal before the High Court. It was held, "As the agreement/indenture for which dispute has arisen is with respect to immovable property and used exclusively for residential purposes and cannot be said to be immovable property used exclusively in trade or commerce, the learned Commercial Court has rightly held that dispute between the parties cannot be said to 'commercial dispute' within definition of section 2(c) of the Commercial Courts Act."

In another case Manyata Dealcom Pvt. Ltd. v Dinkar Mishra & Ors, 2020 SCC Online Jhar 1109 the matter was that the plaintiff-company had taken plots on lease at Deoghar for erecting building thereon and to let them out on rent/lease on the property described in the schedule of the plaint. The plaintiff started constructing buildings on registered lease-hold land and property and started making various types of constructions for the purposes of business transactions and setting on long term leases as per the terms of the original leases executed and registered by the defendants in favour of the plaintiff company with respect of the lands fully described in Schedules 1 to 4 of the plaint which was the subject-matter of the suit and were referred to as suit properties. The plaintiff after doing the needful started construction work and constructed basement, lower ground floor and few shops on the upper ground floor on the lease out premises and out of the constructed portion, the plaintiff settled a few of them to various persons. Dispute arose between the parties and the suit was filed for declaration of right, title, interest and possession of the properties and also for recovery of loss and damages. The defendant appeared in the suit and prayed for rejection of the plaint on the ground that the commercial dispute does not include dispute arising out of lease and that the plaint on its reading would reveal that the relief claimed by the plaintiff and the grounds set in the plaint are purely arising out of lesser- lessee relationship.

Relying on Supreme Court judgment in **Ambalal Sarabhai Enterprises Ltd. v. K.S. Infraspace LLP and Another 2019 SCC Online SC 1311**, the Jharkhand High Court held, "17. Upon perusal of the plaint (Annexure-1), this Court finds that the dispute arises out of agreements of lease which was entered into between the parties for commercial exploitation of the immoveable property and as per the plaint, the construction had already started and upon advertisement, arrangements were already entered into with third parties. In view of the aforesaid this court is of the considered view that as per the plaint, the present suit arises out of agreements relating to immovable property used exclusively in trade or commerce and such dispute would squarely fall within the term "commercial dispute" as defined in Section 2 (1) (c) (vii) of the Act when read in the light of the aforesaid judgment passed by the Hon'ble Supreme court which has been heavily relied upon by the Plaintiff/Appellant." It was further held by the High Court, "The law is well settled that when a term is defined in a statute the same is to be given full effect unless the context otherwise requires and in the present case there is no occasion to give and different meaning to the term "commercial dispute" other than its definition in the Act".

Ambalal Sarabhai Enterprises Ltd. v. K.S. Infra Space LLP and Another, *supra,* the facts which led to dispute was that the plaintiff-appellant executed an agreement to sell in favour of the respondent No. 2 who assigned and transferred all his rights under the said agreement to sell in favour of respondent No.1 by executing an assignment deed who was to purchase the lands which were the subject matter of the agreement from the appellant herein. Accordingly, the sale was made under a Deed of Conveyance but other aspects were to be completed regarding the change relating to the nature of the use of the land for conclusion of the transaction, the right of the appellant in respect of the land was to be protected. In that view a Memorandum of Understanding entered into between the appellant and the respondents herein. As per the same, a Mortgage Deed was required to be executed by respondent No. 1 herein in favour of the appellant. Accordingly, a Mortgage Deed dated was executed but the same had not been registered. It is in that light the appellant herein filed the Commercial Civil Suit so as to enforce the execution of a Mortgage Deed. Consequently, the relief of permanent injunction and other related reliefs were sought. It is in the said suit, summon was issued to respondents herein who are the defendants in the suit, wherein on filing the written statement the application under Order VII Rule 10 of CPC was filed. The Commercial Court while rejecting the application had referred to the Memorandum and Articles of Association of the appellant company and in that light taking note of the business that they were entitled to undertake has arrived at the conclusion that the plaintiff seems to be carrying on the business as an estate agent and in that circumstance has further arrived at its conclusion that it is a commercial dispute. The High Court on the other hand had found fault with the manner in which the Commercial Court had rested its consideration on the Memorandum and Articles of Association and had examined the matter in detail to come to a conclusion that the immovable property in the instant case was not being used for trade or commerce. In that regard, the legal position enunciated by the various decisions was referred to and had accordingly directed the return of the plaint to be presented in an appropriate Court which is assailed herein. The Supreme Court after detailed examination of plaint, observed, "……In the entire plaint there is no reference to the nature of the land or the type of use to which it was being put as on the date of the Agreement to Sell/Sale Deed/Memorandum of Understanding or as on the date of the suit." It was further observed, "Even though in the paragraph describing jurisdiction the plaintiff has stated with regard to the territorial jurisdiction since the office and land being at Vadodara, there is no reference indicating the reason for which the plaintiff pleads that the Court which is the Commercial Court exclusively constituted to try the commercial disputes has jurisdiction to try the instant suit." The Court then held, "Even if the immovable property under the Mortgage Deed was the subject matter it was necessary to plead and indicate that the same was being used in trade or commerce due to which the jurisdiction of Commercial Court is invoked. Without such basic pleadings in the plaint, any explanations sought to be put forth subsequently would only lead to a situation that if an objection is raised, in every suit a consideration would be required based on extraneous material even to ascertain as to whether the intended transaction between the parties was of such nature that it is to be construed as a commercial dispute." Ultimately, the Supreme Court upheld the decision of the High Court to return the plaint in following words, "Therefore, if all these aspects are kept in view, we are of the opinion that in the present facts the High Court was justified in its conclusion arrived through the order dated 01.03.2019 impugned herein. The Commercial Court shall therefore return the plaint indicating a date for its presentation before the Court having jurisdiction."

The aforesaid judgment clearly mandates that the plaint for a commercial dispute must contain specific pleadings on point of jurisdiction vis-à-vis the definition of commercial dispute as provided in section 2(c) of the Commercial Courts Act.

    d. **Reliefs Claimed**: Every suit shall be instituted by presenting a plaint before the competent commercial court having pecuniary and territorial jurisdiction. Every plaint shall comply with provisions of Order VI and VII. In suits on contracts, aggrieved party can claim three kinds of reliefs- (i) specific performance; (ii) damages and (iii) injunction. While, claiming specific performance of contract shall be subject to conditions laid down in Specific Relief Act, the explanation to sec. 2(c) of the Commercial Courts Act does not take away all rights to claim specific performance of contract involving immovable property. It provides that a commercial dispute shall not cease to be a commercial dispute merely because it also involves action for recovery of immovable property or for realisation of monies out of immovable property given as security or involves any other relief pertaining to immovable property. This is in line with general accepted principle that where there is breach of contract to transfer immovable property, the plaintiff is entitled to specific performance of contract but where the breach is of a contract to transfer movable property the plaintiff is not entitled to specific performance but to damages only. Injunction is one of the major reliefs applicable in commercial contract. In some of the suits like dispute involving intellectual property rights, injunction is a rule than exception.

There are two particular methods of giving relief in respect of contracts – one is specific performance of contract and the other is relief of damages or compensation for non- execution of the contract. The specific performance of contract is its actual execution according to its stipulations and terms which is enforceable under Specific Relief Act, 1963 and largely governed by principles of equity. On the other hand, relief for damages or compensation is based on breach of contract where specific performance is not possible or ruled out by specific provisions of Specific Relief Act. However, the relief of damages or compensation is so encompassing that even in a suit for specific performance the claim of damages or compensation can be claimed in alternative or conjunctive.

According to Fry on Specific Performance, Universal Publishing Co. From every contract there immediately and directly results an obligation on each of the contracting parties towards the other of them to perform such of the terms of the contract as he has undertaken to perform. And if the person on whom this obligation rests fail to discharge it, there results in morality to the other party a right at his election either to insist on the actual performance of the contract or to obtain satisfaction for the non-performance of it.

It is certain that the Roman Law gave a title to damages as the sole right resulting from default in performance, and did not enforce specific performance directly or in any other manner than by giving such right to damages. It held to the maxim "*Nemo potest pratcise cogi ad factum.* In like manner the Common Law of England made no attempt actually to enforce the performance to contracts, but gave to the injured party only the right to satisfaction for non-performance (Ibid).

It would be worth reproducing an interesting example cited by Fry in his Treatise on Specific Performance of Contract "If a contract were entered into between A and B for the delivery by B of a certain chattel on payment of a certain sum by A, and A made the payment, but B refused to deliver the chattel, an action for its detention would lie in a Court of Common Law at the suit of A, and at his election execution might issue for the return of the chattel. This looks very like a specific performance of the contract, but was not such in fact. The complaint of A, in the case supposed, was not that the contract had been broken, but that the chattel had been detained. He did not aver that the contract ought to be performed and that the chattel ought to be made his; but he alleged that the contract had been performed, and that therefore the chattel was his, and the defendant's detention wrongful. In short, the contract came into controversy, if at all, only as the title of the plaintiff." Even in early times in England a court of equity assumed jurisdiction to compel a party to a contract for breach of which damages were not an adequate remedy, to perform part of his contract. The remedy by way of damages for breach of contract gives pecuniary compensation for failure to carry out the terms of the contract. Specific performance of contract cannot be claimed as a matter of right and the grant of relief is the discretion of the court. The claim of damages or compensation for breach of contract is the rule of law since ancient time and it is still the most common remedy in actions for breach of contract.

Breach connotes infringement or violation of a promise or obligation, as per Wharton's Law Lexicon, and breach of contract means violation of a contractual obligation, either by failing to perform one's own premise or by interfering with another party's performance. To appreciate an action based on breach, both as plaintiff and defendant it is essential to comprehend the law relating to performance of contract, person who is liable to perform, time and place to perform, impossibility to perform, acquiescence, waiver and estoppel of the party by conduct or otherwise etc. as most often than not even the party at fault is likely to defend its case with counter allegation of breach on its adversary. The damages are the consequences of breach to be paid by the party at fault to the party who suffers. Then there is question of quantum of damages which pose herculean task before the party as no straight jacket formula could be adopted to decide it. Several theories have evolved and relied upon by the Courts while pronouncing its judgment on quantum of damages. Incidental to this question, there is aspect of interest and sometimes currency (in case of contract involving parties of different countries). Over and above, question of jurisdiction and mode of resolution of dispute also crop up.

Contract law facilitates the movement of private property to those who value it most highly by executing transfer agreements legally enforceable in a court. In general, contract law favours enforcement of agreements without judicial review of either the overall fairness or individual terms of the exchange. Indeed, under the prevailing "objective" theory of contract, parties who do not consciously consent to be subject to contractual duties, nevertheless, are bound so long as their conduct reasonably manifests assent. The reasons for this heavy presumption in favour of contract enforcement are not difficult to fathom. Where courts to engage in detailed, substantive review of the terms of each transaction presented to them, individual contracting parties would suffer a significant loss of freedom over their own economic lives, transaction costs would soar, courts would be overwhelmed by the task of judicial review. Despite the general need to enforce contracts as written, the law recognizes a number of occasions when judicial review of agreements is warranted. Defences based on public policy are among the most ancient of these exceptions. In its narrowest application, the public policy doctrine bars enforcement of "illegal" bargains--contracts enforcement of which would involve the court in sanctioning conduct outlawed by well-established criminal or civil law.

Chapter IV of Indian Contract Act, 1872 contains provisions relating to performance of contract. While sections-37 to 39 deal with contracts which *must* be performed, sections- 40 to 45 deal with **by whom** the contracts *must* be performed. The word, "must" in the abovesaid provisions lead us to simple inference that the law considers sanctity of contract as sacrosanct provided, however, that the 'contract-in-question' must meet the requirements of provisions of Chapter II thereof and the same must not be vitiated on the grounds of being void or voidable invoked by the party who defends case of valid contract.

Most contracts, in general, consist of reciprocal promises performance of which is called for by both parties. Sections-51 to 58 deal with such matters. Whereas section 37 provides that the parties to a contract must either perform or offer to perform their respective promises which are binding on their legal representatives after their death, unless excused by the act or any other law; section 51 provides that when a contract consists of reciprocal promises to be simultaneously performed no promisor need perform his promise unless the promisee is ready and willing to perform his reciprocal promise. A modern example is "cash on delivery" mode of sale of goods in online market. It can be seen that the provisions of sections 51 to 58 cover in their fold all such transactions, howsoever, complex they may be. After conclusion of a contract, situation may arise where it becomes impossible to perform due to emerging facts or law which leads to frustration of contracts. It is always adopted as measure of defence to escape from liability under a contract on this ground; but dexterity of the adversary flourishes in his attempt to weed out the non-applicable pleas to fathom the correct facts with help of credible evidence.

PLEADINGS IN COMMERCIAL SUIT

Order VI of the Code deals with pleadings in general. The word pleading has been defined in Rule 1 itself as "plaint" or "written statement". In proceedings before the Civil Court, it may include a petition whereby proceedings are initiated under any law for the time being in force and reply thereto by the respondent whether in form of an affidavit or otherwise.

Pleadings fulfil several functions and their principal objects, as described by Bullen & Leake & Jacob are as follows:

"1. First, the objects of pleadings are to define with clarity and precision the issues or questions which are in dispute between the parties and fall to be decided by the court."

"2. Secondly, the object of pleadings is to require each party to give fair and proper notice to his opponent of the case he has to meet to enable him to frame and prepare his own case for trial"

"3. Thirdly, the object of pleadings is to inform the coat what are the precise matters in issue between the parties which alone the court may determine, since they set the limits of the action which may not be extended without due amendment properly made".

"4. Fourthly, the object of pleadings is not only to provide a brief summary of the case of each party, which is readily available for reference, and form which the nature of the claim and defence may be easily apprehended, but also to constitute a permanent record of the issues and questions raised in the action and decided therein so as to prevent future litigation upon matters already adjudicated upon between the litigants or those privy to them."

Order VI provides that every pleading shall contain statement in concise form of material facts on which the party pleading relies for his claim. This rule involves and requires four separate things:

i. Every pleading must state facts and not law.

ii. It must state material facts and material facts only.

iii. It must state facts and not evidence by which they are to be proved.

iv. It must state such facts concisely in a summary form.

The Commercial Courts Act provides for forms of pleading to be prescribed by concerned High Court. Order VI Rule 3A provides,

"3A. Forms of pleading in Commercial Courts.—In a commercial dispute, where forms of pleadings have been prescribed under the High Court Rules or Practice Directions made for the purposes of such commercial disputes, pleadings shall be in such forms."

Rule 4 mandates that the party relying on any misrepresentation, fraud, breach of trust, wilful default or undue influence or any other manner with respect to which particulars may be necessary to give full particulars, with dates and items, if necessary, in his pleadings. Wherever the contents of any document are material it shall be sufficient in any pleading to state the effect thereof as briefly as possible without setting out the whole or any part thereof unless the precise words of document or any part thereof are material. Every pleading shall be signed by the party and his pleader provided where a party pleading is by reason of absence or for other good cause unable to sign the pleading it may be signed by any person duly authorised by him to sign the same or to sue or defend on his behalf. Every pleading shall be verified at the foot by the party or by one of the parties pleading or by some other person proved to the satisfaction of the Court to be acquainted with the facts of the case. The person verifying shall specify, by reference to the numbered paragraphs of the pleading, what he verifies of his own knowledge and what he verifies upon information received and believed to be true. The verification shall be signed by the person making it and shall state the date on which and the place at which it was signed. 1 The person verifying the pleading shall also furnish an affidavit in support of his pleadings. The Commercial Courts Act has inserted a new Order 15A to provide further specific manner in which the pleadings in commercial suit are to be verified.

15A. Verification of pleadings in a commercial dispute—

1. **Notwithstanding anything contained in Rule 15, every pleading in a commercial dispute shall be verified by an affidavit in the manner and form prescribed in the Appendix to this Schedule.**

2. **An affidavit under sub-rule (1) above shall be signed by the party or by one of the parties to the proceedings, or by any other person on behalf of such party or parties who is proved to the satisfaction of the Court to be acquainted with the facts of the case and who is duly authorised by such party or parties.**

3. **Where a pleading is amended, the amendments must be verified in the form and manner referred to in sub-rule (1) unless the Court orders otherwise.**

4. **Where a pleading is not verified in the manner provided under sub-rule (1), the party shall not be permitted to rely on such pleading as evidence or any of the matters set out therein.**

5. **The Court may strike out a pleading which is not verified by a Statement of Truth, namely, the affidavit set out in the Appendix to this Schedule.]**

"APPENDIX-I

STATEMENT OF TRUTH

(Under First Schedule, Order VI- Rule 15A and Order XI- Rule 3)

I ----------- the deponent do hereby solemnly affirm and declare as under:

1. I am the party in the above suit and competent to swear this affidavit.
2. I am sufficiently conversant with the facts of the case and have also examined all relevant documents and records in relation thereto.
3. I say that the statements made in ---------paragraphs are true to my knowledge and statements made in ----------paragraphs are based on information received which I believe to be correct and statements made in ---paragraphs are base d on legal advice.
4. I say that there is no false statement or concealment of any material fact, document or record and I have included information that is according to me, relevant for the present suit.
5. I say that all documents in my power, possession, control or custody, pertaining to the facts and circumstances of the proceedings initiated by me have been disclosed and copies thereof annexed with the plaint, and that I do not have any other documents in my power, possession, control or custody.
6. I say that the above-mentioned pleading comprises of a total of ---- pages, each of which has been duly signed by me.
7. I state that the Annexures hereto are true copies of the documents referred to and relied upon by me.
8. I say that I am aware that for any false statement or concealment, I shall be liable for action taken against me under the law for the time being in force.

Place:

Date:

DEPONENT

VERIFICATION

I, ... do hereby declare that the statements made above are true to my knowledge.

Verified at [place] on this [date]

DEPONENT."

What would be the consequences of non-compliance with the Or.VI Rule 15A is yet to see much judicial scrutiny. However, it is well settled that the provision of Or. VI Rule 15 is directory and not mandatory. In *Salem Bar Association*, it was held, "The affidavit required to be filed under amended Sec. 26(2) and Or. 6 R. 15(4) of the Code has the effect of fixing additional responsibility on the deponent as to the truth of the facts stated in the pleadings. It is, however, made clear that such an affidavit would not be evidence for the purpose of the trial. Further, on amendment of the pleadings, a fresh affidavit shall have to be filed in consonance thereof."[1] The position has been further reaffirmed by the Supreme Court, "The intention of the legislature in bringing about the various amendments in the Code with effect from 1.07.2002 were aimed at eliminating the procedural delays in the disposal of civil matters. The amendments effected to Sec. 26, Or. 4 and Or. 6 R. 15, are also geared to achieve such object, but being procedural in nature, they are directory in nature and non-compliance thereof would not automatically render

---

[1] 2005 (6) SCC 344, AIR 2005 SC 3353

the plaint non-est, as has been held by the Division Bench of the Calcutta High Court."

"In our view, such a stand would be too pedantic and would be contrary to the accepted principles involving interpretation of statutes. Except for the objection taken that the plaint had not been accompanied by an affidavit in support of the pleadings, it is nobody's case that the plaint had not been otherwise verified in keeping with the unamended provisions of the Code and Rule 1 of Ch. 7 of the Original Side Rules. In fact, as has been submitted at the Bar, the plaint was accepted, after due scrutiny and duly registered and only during the hearing of the appeal such an objection was raised."

"Considering the aforesaid contention, even though the amended provisions of Or. 6 are attracted in the matter of filing of plaints in the Original Side of the Calcutta High Court on account of the reference made to Or. 6 and R. 1 of Ch. 7 of the Original Side Rules, non-compliance thereof at the initial stage did not render the suit non-est. On account of such finding of the Division Bench of the Calcutta High Court, not only have the proceedings before the learned Single Judge been wiped out, but such a decision has the effect of rendering the proceedings taken in the appeal also *non-est*.[2] Sub rule (4) and (5) of Rule 15A envisage the consequences of non-compliance of sub rule (1) and (2) the party shall not be permitted to rely on such pleading as evidence or any of the matters set out therein and the Court may strike out a pleading which is not verified by a Statement of Truth, the affidavit set out in the Appendix to this Schedule. The Andhra Pradesh High Court in **Unitech-NCC JV v. I. S. N. Infrastructures (P) Ltd.**[3] held that it is settled and well established provision of law that procedural laws are intended and meant obviously for advancement of justice and the same cannot be used for cuttling the valuable and substantial rights of the parties. In the considered view of this Court, the non filing of truth

---

2   AIR 2013 SC 1549
3   2020 SCC Online AP 1997

statement is a curable defect and it cannot be construed as fatal to the defendant.

CONTENTS OF PLAINT

The plaint shall contain the following particulars:—

a. the name of the Court in which the suit is brought;
b. the name, description and place of residence of the plaintiff;
c. the name, description and place of residence of the defendant, so far as they can be ascertained;
d. where the plaintiff or the defendant is a minor or a person of unsound mind, a statement to that effect;
e. the facts constituting the cause of action and when it arose;
f. the facts showing that the Court has jurisdiction;
g. the relief which the plaintiff claims;
h. where the plaintiff has allowed a set-off or relinquished a portion of his claim, the amount so allowed or relinquished; and
i. a statement of the value of the subject-matter of the suit for the purposes of jurisdiction and of Court-fees, so far as the case admits[4].

Where the plaintiff seeks the recovery of money, the plaint shall state the precise amount claimed but where the plaintiff sues for mesne profits, or for an amount which will be found due to him on taking unsettled accounts between him and the defendant, or for movables in the possession of the defendant, or for debts of which the value he cannot, after the exercise of reasonable diligence, estimate, the plaint shall state approximately the amount or value sued for[5]. The newly inserted Rule 2A deals with interest specifically as below-

---

4   Or. VII R.1
5   Or. VII R 2

2A. Where interest is sought in the suit, —

1. Where the plaintiff seeks interest, the plaint shall contain a statement to that effect along with the details set out under sub-rules (2) and (3).

2. Where the plaintiff seeks interest, the plaint shall state whether the plaintiff is seeking interest in relation to a commercial transaction within the meaning of section 34 of the Code of Civil Procedure, 1908 (5 of 1908) and, furthermore, if the plaintiff is doing so under the terms of a contract or under an Act, in which case the Act is to be specified in the plaint; or on some other basis and shall state the basis of that.

3. Pleadings shall also state—
   a. the rate at which interest is claimed;
   b. the date from which it is claimed;
   c. the date to which it is calculated;
   d. the total amount of interest claimed to the date of calculation; and
   e. the daily rate at which interest accrues after that date.

The plaint shall show that the defendant is or claims to be interested in the subject-matter, and that he is liable to be called upon to answer the plaintiff's demand[6]. Where the suit is instituted after the expiration of the period prescribed by the law of limitation, the plaint shall show the ground upon which exemption from such law is claimed, provided that the Court may permit the plaintiff to claim exemption from the law of limitation on any ground not set out in the plaint, if such ground is not inconsistent with the grounds set out in the plaint. Every plaint shall state specifically the relief which the plaintiff claims either simply or in the alternative, and it shall not be necessary to ask for general or other relief which may always be

---

[6] Or VII R5

given as the Court may think just to the same extent as if it had been asked for. And the same rule shall apply to any relief claimed by the defendant in his written statement[7]. Where the plaintiff seeks relief in respect of several distinct claims or causes of action founded upon separate and distinct grounds, they shall be stated as far as may be separately and distinctly.[8]

Where suits instituted and contested by parties are juridical persons like Company, partnership firms etc., the compliance of Or. XXIX of the Code is mandatory according to which any pleading may be signed and verified on behalf of the corporation by the secretary or by any director or other principal officer of the corporation who is able to depose to the facts of the case.

Sections 2(c)(xi) and 2(c)(xv) of the Commercial Courts Act, 2015 consist of joint venture and partnership agreements, the provision of Order XXX shall also be complied with. (1) Any two or more persons claiming or being liable as partners and carrying on business in, India may sue or be sued in the name of the firm (if any) of which such persons were partners at the time of the accruing of the cause of action, and any party to a suit may in such case apply to the Court for a statement of the names and addresses of the persons who were, at the time of the accruing of the cause of action, partners in such firm, to be furnished and verified in such manner as the Court may direct. Where persons sue or are sued partners in the name of their firm under sub-rule (1), it shall, in the case of any pleading or other document required by or under this Code to be signed, verified or certified by the plaintiff or the defendant, suffice if such pleading or other document is signed, verified or certified by any one of such persons.

Order XI Rule 1 Sub Rule (3) of the Code of Civil Procedure as amended by the Commercial Courts Act casts a further duty on the plaintiff regarding contents of the plaint which is follows:

---

[7] Or VII R7
[8] Or. VII R8

(3) The plaint shall contain a declaration on oath from the plaintiff that all documents in the power, possession, control or custody of the plaintiff, pertaining to the facts and circumstances of the proceedings initiated by him have been disclosed and copies thereof annexed with the plaint, and that the plaintiff does not have any other documents in its power, possession, control or custody.

Explanation.—**A declaration on oath under this sub-rule shall be contained in the Statement of Truth as set out in the Appendix.**

Order VII Rule 1 Sub rule (i) of the Code of Civil Procedure necessitates a statement to be incorporated in the plaint about value of the subject-matter of the suit for the purposes of jurisdiction and of Court fees so far as the case admits. Sec.2(1)(i) of the Commercial Courts Act describes specified value as in relation to a commercial dispute, shall mean the value of the subject-matter in respect of a suit as determined in accordance with section 12 which shall not be less than three lakh rupees or such higher value, as may be notified by the Central Government. Clearly, the valuation of the subject matter in a plaint shall be determined in accordance with section 12 of the Commercial Courts Act as below:

12. Determination of Specified Value—(1) The Specified Value of the subject-matter of the commercial dispute in a suit, appeal or application shall be determined in the following manner:—

   a. **where the relief sought in a suit or application is for recovery of money, the money sought to be recovered in the suit or application inclusive of interest, if any, computed up to the date of filing of the suit or application, as the case may be, shall be taken into account for determining such Specified Value;**

   b. **where the relief sought in a suit, appeal or application relates to movable property or to a right therein, the market value of the movable property as on the date of filing of the suit, appeal or** application, as the case may be, shall be taken into account for determining such Specified Value;

c. where the relief sought in a suit, appeal or application relates to immovable property or to a right therein, the market value of the immovable property, as on the date of filing of the suit, appeal or application, as the case may be, shall be taken into account for determining Specified Value; 1[and]

d. where the relief sought in a suit, appeal or application relates to any other intangible right, the market value of the said rights as estimated by the plaintiff shall be taken into account for determining Specified Value;

2. The aggregate value of the claim and counterclaim, if any as set out in the statement of claim and the counterclaim, if any, in an arbitration of a commercial dispute shall be the basis for determining whether such arbitration is subject to the jurisdiction of a Commercial Division, Commercial Appellate Division or Commercial Court, as the case may be.

WORDS AND STYLE

There is something to be said for the view that a legal document should be special- if someone is summoned to court he or she should feel it is something more than an ordinary letter. But on the other hand, it should be possible to understand the document sent, whether it is pleading of the court or some other document drafted by a lawyer. Good drafting is not necessarily long words and lots of sub-clauses, but the essential facts of a case set out in clear and concise way, and using the right words in good English.[9]

Brevity, clarity and simplicity are hallmarks of the skilled pleader.[10] It is important to remember always that the basic purpose of pleading is to

---

9 A Practical Approach to Legal Advice and Drafting by Susan Blake at p. 99
10 In re Brickman's Settlement [1982] 1 All ER 336

summarise a case and define issues in it. This is to help the parties in the preparation of their case, and to help the judge to see immediately what the case is about.[11] But the pleading should not be argumentative. It shall not contain evidence either. There is no magic in drafting with long words, antiquated phrases or bad grammar though the inexperienced lawyer will sometimes get this impression from some of the drafting examples available. There is sometimes good justification for complicated constructions and special words, but they should be used where there is good cause.[12]

---

11 A Practical Approach to Legal Advice & Drafting by Susan Blake at p.104
12 Ibid at p.116

4

STATEMENT OF DEFENCE

Ignorance of law excuses no man; not that all men know the law, but because 'tis an excuse every man will plead, and no man can tell how to confute him.

— Jhon Sheldon: Table Talk (1689) 'Law'

The word written statement has not been defined in the Code of Civil Procedure. It may be called statement of defense. It is the assertions by a defendant esp. in England; the defendant's answer to the plaintiff's statement of claim.[1] It is pleading of the defendant in a suit and the rule of general pleading as provided in Order VI shall apply both to the plaint and written statement. It is the law of limitation, which governs time limit for filing of plaint which leads to institution of suit. A suit is instituted when the plaint is presented to the proper officer. However, the Code of Civil Procedure prescribes the limitation of period under which written statement is allowed to be filed. Prior to amendment in the year 2002, there was no fixed time for filing the written statement. However, limiting the period of filing of written statement has been the focal point of legislative reforms towards expeditious disposal of a suit.

---

1   Black's Law Dictionary

One of the hallmarks of Commercial Courts Act is the law amended in respect of drafting and filing of written statement, and the strict adherence to the provision has been envisaged by bringing amendments to all such provisions in the Code of Civil Procedure that has been interpreted to give leeway to the defendants. These enabling provisions have been made to give effect to the object and reasons of the Act. A comparative study of Order VIII Rule 1 of the Code of Civil Procedure, as existing in respect of suits other than commercial suits, with the present law applicable to commercial suits would show the legislative intent to rule out any waiver in respect of the tile limits. The Order VIII Rule 1 of the Code of Civil Procedure as applicable to other suits provides that "The defendant shall, within thirty days from the date of service of summons on him, present a written statement of his defence:

Provided that where the defendant fails to file the written statement within the said period of thirty days, he shall be allowed to file the same on such other day, as may be specified by the Court, for reasons to be recorded in writing, but which shall not be later than ninety days from the date of service of summons.

This amendment was brought in the Code by Code of Civil Procedure (Amendment) Act, 2002, prior to which the provision read as below:

"The defendant shall at or before the first hearing or within such time as the Court may permit, present a written statement of his defence." So, a maximum limit of ninety days was put by way of Amendment Act of 2002, which was challenged in the Supreme Court in the landmark case **Salem Bar Association v. Union of India**[2], which held "Clearly, therefore, the provision of Order VIII Rule 1 providing for upper limit of 90 days to file written statement is directory. Having said so, we wish to make it clear that the order extending time to file written statement cannot be made in routine. The time can be extended only in exceptionally hard cases. While

---

2 (2005) 6 SCC 344

extending time, it has to be borne in mind that the legislature has fixed the upper time limit of 90 days. The discretion of the Court to extend the time shall not be so frequently and routinely exercised so as to nullify the period fixed by Order VIII Rule 1."

In arriving to this conclusion the Supreme Court observed, "In construing this provision, support can also be had from Order VIII Rule 10 which provides that where any party from whom a written statement is required under Rule 1 or Rule 9, fails to present the same within the time permitted or fixed by the Court, the Court shall pronounce judgment against him, or make such other order in relation to the suit as it thinks fit. On failure to file written statement under this provision, the Court has been given the discretion either to pronounce judgment against the defendant or make such other order in relation to suit as it thinks fit. In the context of the provision, despite use of the word 'shall', the Court has been given the discretion to pronounce or not to pronounce the judgment against the defendant even if written statement is not filed and instead pass such order as it may think fit in relation to the suit. In construing the provision of Order VIII Rule 1 and Rule 10, the doctrine of harmonious construction is required to be applied. The effect would be that under Rule 10 of Order VIII, the Court in its discretion would have power to allow the defendant to file written statement even after expiry of period of 90 days provided in Order VIII Rule 1. There is no restriction in Order VIII Rule 10 that after expiry of ninety days, further time cannot be granted. The Court has wide power to 'make such order in relation to the suit as it thinks fit".

This judgment was invariably relied upon by the Courts and party as defendant took liberty to file their written statement at their convenience. To address this issue and to set the Supreme Court decisions at naught in this respect, the legislature plugged in all the loopholes from where laxity could be claimed in respect of commercial dispute. To begin with Order V Rule 1 was amended as follows:

In the Order V, in Rule 1, in sub-rule (1), for the second proviso, the following proviso shall be substituted, namely:—

"Provided further that where the defendant fails to file the written statement within the said period of thirty days, he shall be allowed to file the written statement on such other day, as may be specified by the Court, for reasons to be recorded in writing and on payment of such costs as the Court deems fit, but which shall not be later than one hundred twenty days from the date of service of summons and on expiry of one hundred twenty days from the date of service of summons, the defendant shall forfeit the right to file the written statement and the Court shall not allow the written statement to be taken on record."; in Order VIII,—

i. in Rule 1, for the proviso, the following proviso shall be substituted, namely:—

"Provided that where the defendant fails to file the written statement within the said period of thirty days, he shall be allowed to file the written statement on such other day, as may be specified by the Court, for reasons to be recorded in writing and on payment of such costs as the Court deems fit, but which shall not be later than one hundred twenty days from the date of service of summons and on expiry of one hundred twenty days from the date of service of summons, the defendant shall forfeit the right to file the written statement and the Court shall not allow the written statement to be taken on record.";

(iv) in Rule 10, the following proviso shall be inserted, namely:—

"Provided that] no Court shall make an order to extend the time provided under Rule 1of this Order for filing of the written statement."

A combined effect of aforesaid provisions can be rendered as below:

a. Defendant is required to file written statement within thirty days from date of service of summons on him;

b. Defendant shall be allowed to file written statement not later than one hundred twenty days from date of service of summons by the Court;

c. The Court while allowing written statement later than thirty days shall record its reasons in writing;

d. The Court shall allow for such delayed written statement on payment of cost at its discretion;

e. On expiry of one hundred twenty days from the date of service of summons, the defendant shall forfeit his right to file written statement;

f. On expiry of one hundred twenty days from the date of service of summons, the Court shall not allow the written statement to be taken on record;

g. No Court shall make an order to extend the time provided under Rule 1of this Order for filing of the written statement where party fails to present written statement called for by the Court.

Can a petition filed by defendant under Order VII Rule 11 of the Code of Civil Procedure could extend the aforesaid time of 120 days in filing the written statement Court in view of judgment in **R.K. Roja v. U.S. Rayudu and Another**[3] came for decision in **M/S SCG Contracts India Pvt. Ltd. v Ks Chamankar Infrastructure Pvt**[4] before the Supreme Court which held that ordinarily a written statement is to be filed within a period of 30 days. However, grace period of a further 90 days is granted which the Court may employ for reasons to be recorded in writing and payment of such costs as it deems fit to allow such written statement to come on record. What is of great importance is the fact that beyond 120 days from the date of service of summons, the defendant shall forfeit the right to file the written statement and the Court shall not allow the written statement to be taken

---

3   (2016) 14 SCC 275
4   (2019) 12 SCC 210

on record. This is further buttressed by the proviso in Order VIII Rule 10 also adding that the Court has no further power to extend the time beyond this period of 120 days.

The Supreme Court settled the matter fully in **Desh Raj V. Balkishan(D) Thr. Proposed LR Ms. Rohini** [5] in Para 12: "Hence, it is clear that post coming into force of the aforesaid Act, there are two regimes of civil procedure. Whereas commercial disputes [as defined under section 2(c) of the Commercial Courts Act, 2015] are governed by the CPC as amended by section 16 of the said Act; all other non-commercial disputes fall within the ambit of the unamended (or original) provisions of CPC." In Para 14, it has been held, "As regard the timeline for filing of written statement in a non-commercial dispute, the observations of this Court in a catena of decisions, most recently in **Atcom Technologies Ltd. v. Y. A. Chunawala and Co.**[6] holds the field. Unamended Order VIII Rule1, CPC continues to be directory and does not do away with the inherent discretion of Courts to condone certain delays."

Contents of written statement are guided by the special provisions made in Order VIII of the Code of Civil Procedure. The rules of pleading, verification and affidavit as laid down in Order VI of the Code are applicable to written statement as well. Order VIII of the Code, so far as drafting of written statement to plaint in a commercial dispute is concerned, the provisions are as below:

The defendant must raise by his pleading all matters which show the suit not be maintainable, or that the transaction is either void or voidable in point of law, and all such grounds of defence as, if not raised, would be likely to take the opposite party by surprise, or would raise issues of fact not arising out of the plaint, as, for instance, fraud, limitation, release, payment, performance, or facts showing illegality[7]. It shall not be sufficient for a

---

5   2020 SCC Online SC 49; AIR 2020 SC 621
6   2018 Scc Online SC 499
7   Or VIII R2 of Code of Civil Procedure

defendant in his written statement to deny generally the grounds alleged by the plaintiff, but the defendant must deal specifically with each allegation of fact of which he does not admit the truth, except damages.[8] The Commercial Courts Act inserts a new Rule 3A in Order VIII which is as follows:

3A. Denial by the defendant in suits before the Commercial Division of the High Court or the Commercial Court.—

1. **Denial shall be in the manner provided in sub-rules (2), (3), (4) and (5) of this Rule.**

2. **The defendant in his written statement shall state which of the allegations in the particulars of plaint he denies, which allegations he is unable to admit or deny, but which he requires the plaintiff to prove, and which allegations he admits.**

3. **Where the defendant denies an allegation of fact in a plaint, he must state his reasons for doing so and if he intends to put forward a different version of events from that given by the plaintiff, he must state his own version.**

4. **If the defendant disputes the jurisdiction of the Court he must state the reasons for doing so, and if he is able, give his own statement as to which Court ought to have jurisdiction.**

5. **If the defendant disputes the plaintiff's valuation of the suit, he must state his reasons for doing so, and if he is able, give his own statement of the value of the suit.**

Where a defendant denies an allegation of fact in the plaint, he must not do so evasively, but answer the point of substance. Thus, if it is alleged that he received a certain sum of money, it shall not be sufficient to deny that he received that particular amount, but he must deny that he received that sum or any part thereof, or else set out how much he received. And if an allegation is made with diverse circumstances, it shall not be sufficient

---

8 Or VIII R3 of Code of Civil Procedure

to deny it along with those circumstances.[9] Rule 5 of Order VIII deals with Specific denial, in which a second proviso has been inserted to sub rule (1)- Every allegation of fact in the plaint, if not denied specifically or by necessary implication, or stated to be not admitted in the pleading of the defendant, shall be taken to be admitted except as against a person under disability:

Provided that the Court may in its discretion require any fact so admitted to be proved otherwise than by such admission:

Provided further that every allegation of fact in the plaint, if not denied in the manner provided under Rule 3A of this Order, shall be taken to be admitted except as against a person under disability.

Before analysis of the contents of written statement, a question arises whether it would be possible to take benefit of Rule 9 of Order VIII, which has remained unamended, by a defendant who fails to file complete written statement within the stipulated time and chose to file a preliminary or brief written statement to avoid the rigour of forfeiture of his right; and thereafter file detailed additional written statement may be filed by taking leave of the Court. It is not uncommon to include a paragraph/clause in written statement to the effect of 'reserving rights of filing additional written statement' and/or 'seeking leave of the Court to file additional written subsequently'. It is submitted that any such attempt shall stand scrutiny by the Court in light of the 'object and reasons' of the Act which does not propound any such construction and interpretation of law. The additional written statement, if at all, can be put forward only to meet the requirements arising out of discovery of new facts only. Secondly, the provision of Rule 15A of Rule 6 shall not allow the defendant to resort to such tactics as it provides a comprehensive declaration in matters of documents in possession, knowledge and custody of the documents. Thirdly, Rule 10 of Order VIII shall come in the way of such delaying attempts.

---

9   Or VIII R4 of Code of Civil Procedure

Rule 3A of the Code casts a duty on the defendant to put forth his denial in the ways and manner exclusively provided under sub rules- (2), (3), (4) and (5) thereof. Sub rule(2) provides four Heads under which the written statement shall be based-

- Allegations that defendant denies: Sub rule (3) provides where defendant denies an allegation, he must state his reasons for doing so and if he intends to put forward a different version of events from that given by the plaintiff, he must state his own version.
- Allegations that defendant is unable to admit or deny but wants plaintiff to prove
- Allegations that defendant admits
- Sub rule (4) provides that if the defendant disputes the jurisdiction of the Court, he must state the reasons for doing so, and if he is able, give a statement as to which Court ought to have jurisdiction. The word jurisdiction denotes pecuniary and territorial ones. It would also be examined in view of specified value of the subject matter, nature of dispute whether it is within ambit of sec. 2(c) of Commercial Courts Act.
- Sub rule (5) provides that if the defendant disputes the plaintiff's valuation of the suit, and if he is able, give his own statement of the value of the suit. The question of valuation of value shall be determined under purview of sec. 2(i) and sec. 12 and also rule 2A of Order VII.

Second proviso to the Rule 5 of Order VIII presents the consequences of not adhering to the aforesaid provisions of Rule 3A whereby it has been provided that every allegation of fact in plaint, if not denied in the manner provided under Rule 3A of this Order, shall be taken to be admitted except as against a person under disability.

Although there is no word like replication used in the Code of Civil Procedure, in practice it may be filed in certain circumstances. Replication and Additional written Statement fall within ambit of Order VIII Rule 9 of the Code of Civil Procedure which deals with the subsequent pleadings. It provides that no pleading subsequent to the written statement of a defendant other than by way of defence to set off or counter claim shall be presented except by the leave of the Court and upon such terms as the Court thinks fit; but the court may at any time require a written statement or additional written statement from any of the parties and fix a time of not more than thirty days for presenting the same. Under this rule, either party may, with the leave of the Court, file a supplementary statement. In an old case, Kerela High Court considered the question whether replication can be filed by the plaintiff under Order VIII Rule 9[10]. It was observed in that case that the word "replication" is the plaintiff's answer to the defendant's plea and "rejoinder" is the defendant's answer to the plaintiff's replication. It is lawful to the plaintiff to file a replication to add his pleas already made in the plaint and the only condition thereon is the leave of the Court. Even in cases that require leave, it is open to the Court to grant leave with or without conditions. The Court may permit filing of an additional written statement from any of the parties but the Court must fix the outer limit of not more than 30 days for presenting the same. Where additional written statement is concerned, Order VIII Rule 9 gives ample power to the court to grant leave to file additional written statement and it does not prescribe by restricting what defence has to be taken.

---

10 Kochukesavan Nair v. Gouri Amma 1967 KLT 257

5

DISCLOSURE, DISCOVERY & INSPECTION OF DOCUMENTS

Disclosure is one of the big costs drivers of commercial litigation. It is not only the process of identifying and handing over appropriate documents which is expensive. The resultant bundle, whether electronic or in hard copy, then has to be considered by the other side. Finally counsel, solicitors, experts and others all set to work on the documents and may devote many expensive hours to the process. Therefore, getting a grip on disclosure is one of the keys to controlling litigation costs.

– Lord Justice Jackson At The Law Society's Commercial Litigation Conference On 10 October 2016.

The Commercial Courts Act, 2015vide section 16 amends Order XI of the Code of Civil Procedure stands substituted by a the following

"ORDER XI

DISCLOSURE, DISCOVERY AND INSPECTION OF DOCUMENTS IN SUITS BEFORE THE COMMERCIAL DIVISION OF A HIGH COURT OR A COMMERCIAL COURT

1. **Disclosure and discovery of documents.—**
   1. Plaintiff shall file a list of all documents and photocopies of all documents, in its power, possession, control or custody, pertaining to the suit, along with the plaint, including:—
      a. documents referred to and relied on by the plaintiff in the plaint;
      b. documents relating to any matter in question in the proceedings, in the power, possession, control or custody of the plaintiff, as on the date of filing the plaint, irrespective of whether the same is in support of or adverse to the plaintiff's case;
      c. nothing in this Rule shall apply to documents produced by plaintiffs and relevant only—
         i. for the cross-examination of the defendant's witnesses, or
         ii. in answer to any case set up by the defendant subsequent to the filing of the plaint, or
         iii. handed over to a witness merely to refresh his memory.
   2. The list of documents filed with the plaint shall specify whether the documents in the power, possession, control or custody of the plaintiff are originals, office copies or photocopies and the list shall also set out in brief, details of parties to each document, mode of execution, issuance or receipt and line of custody of each document.
   3. The plaint shall contain a declaration on oath from the plaintiff that all documents in the power, possession, control or custody of the plaintiff, pertaining to the facts and circumstances of the proceedings initiated by him have been disclosed and copies thereof annexed with the plaint, and that the plaintiff does not

have any other documents in its power, possession, control or custody.

Explanation.—A declaration on oath under this sub-rule shall be contained in the Statement of Truth as set out in the Appendix.

4. In case of urgent filings, the plaintiff may seek leave to rely on additional documents, as part of the above declaration on oath and subject to grant of such leave by Court, the plaintiff shall file such additional documents in Court, within thirty days of filing the suit, along with a declaration on oath that the plaintiff has produced all documents in its power, possession, control or custody, pertaining to the facts and circumstances of the proceedings initiated by the plaintiff and that the plaintiff does not have any other documents, in its power, possession, control or custody.

5. The plaintiff shall not be allowed to rely on documents, which were in the plaintiff's power, possession, control or custody and not disclosed along with plaint or within the extended period set out above, save and except by leave of Court and such leave shall be granted only upon the plaintiff establishing reasonable cause for non–disclosure along with the plaint.

6. The plaint shall set out details of documents, which the plaintiff believes to be in the power, possession, control or custody of the defendant and which the plaintiff wishes to rely upon and seek leave for production thereof by the said defendant.

7. The defendant shall file a list of all documents and photocopies of all documents, in its power, possession, control or custody, pertaining to the suit, along with the written statement or with its counterclaim if any, including—

    a. the documents referred to and relied on by the defendant in the written statement;

b. the documents relating to any matter in question in the proceeding in the power, possession, control or custody of the defendant, irrespective of whether the same is in support of or adverse to the defendant's defence;

c. nothing in this Rule shall apply to documents produced by the defendants and relevant only—

> (*i*) for the cross-examination of the plaintiff's witnesses,
>
> (*ii*) in answer to any case set up by the plaintiff subsequent to the filing of the plaint, or
>
> (*iii*) handed over to a witness merely to refresh his memory.

8. The list of documents filed with the written statement or counterclaim shall specify whether the documents, in the power, possession, control or custody of the defendant, are originals, office copies or photocopies and the list shall also set out in brief, details of parties to each document being produced by the defendant, mode of execution, issuance or receipt and line of custody of each document.

9. The written statement or counterclaim shall contain a declaration on oath made by the deponent that all documents in the power, possession, control or custody of the defendant, save and except for those set out in sub-rule (*7*) (*c*) (*iii*) pertaining to the facts and circumstances of the proceedings initiated by the plaintiff or in the counterclaim, have been disclosed and copies thereof annexed with the written statement or counterclaim and that the defendant does not have in its power, possession, control or custody, any other documents.

10. Save and except for sub-rule (7) (c) (iii), defendant shall not be allowed to rely on documents, which were in the defendant's power, possession, control or custody and not disclosed along with the written statement or counterclaim, save and except by leave of Court and such leave shall be granted only upon the defendant establishing reasonable cause for non-disclosure along with the written statement or counterclaim.

11. The written statement or counterclaim shall set out details of documents in the power, possession, control or custody of the plaintiff, which the defendant wishes to rely upon and which have not been disclosed with the plaint, and call upon the plaintiff to produce the same.

(12) Duty to disclose documents, which have come to the notice of a party, shall continue till disposal of the suit.

2. Discovery by interrogatories.—

1. In any suit the plaintiff or defendant by leave of the court may deliver interrogatories in writing for the examination of the opposite parties or any one or more of such parties, and such interrogatories when delivered shall have a note at the foot thereof stating which of such interrogatories each of such persons is required to answer:

Provided that no party shall deliver more than one set of interrogatories to the same party without an order for that purpose:

Provided further that interrogatories which do not relate to any matters in question in the suit shall be deemed irrelevant, notwithstanding that they might be admissible on the oral cross-examination of a witness.

2. On an application for leave to deliver interrogatories, the particular interrogatories proposed to be delivered shall be submitted to the court, and that court shall decide within seven days from the day of filing of the said application, in deciding upon such application, the court shall take into account any offer, which may be made by the party sought to be interrogated to deliver particulars, or to make admissions, or to produce documents relating to the matters in question, or any of them, and leave shall be given as to such only of the interrogatories submitted as the court shall consider necessary either for disposing fairly of the suit or for saving costs.

3. In adjusting the costs of the suit inquiry shall at the instance of any party be made into the propriety of exhibiting such interrogatories, and if it is the opinion of the taxing officer or of the court, either with or without an application for inquiry, that such interrogatories have been exhibited unreasonably, vexatiously, or at improper length, the costs occasioned by the said interrogatories and the answers thereto shall be paid in any event by the party in fault.

4. Interrogatories shall be in the form provided in Form No. 2 in Appendix C to the Code of Civil Procedure, 1908 (5 of 1908), with such variations as circumstances may require.

5. Where any party to a suit is a corporation or a body of persons, whether incorporated or not, empowered by law to sue or be sued, whether in its own name or in the name of any officer of other person, any opposite party may apply for an order allowing him to deliver interrogatories to any member or officer of such corporation or body, and an order may be made accordingly.

6. Any objection to answering any interrogatory on the ground that it is scandalous or irrelevant or not exhibited *bona fide* for the purpose of the suit, or that the matters inquired into are not

sufficiently material at that stage, or on the ground of privilege or any other ground may be taken in the affidavit in answer.

7. Any interrogatories may be set aside on the ground that they have been exhibited unreasonably or vexatiously, or struck out on the ground that they are prolix, oppressive, unnecessary or scandalous and any application for this purpose may be made within seven days after service of the interrogatories.

8. Interrogatories shall be answered by affidavit to be filed within ten days, or within such other time as the court may allow.

9. An affidavit in answer to interrogatories shall be in the form provided in Form No. 3 in Appendix C to the Code of Civil Procedure, 1908 (5 of 1908), with such variations as circumstances may require.

10. No exceptions shall be taken to any affidavit in answer, but the sufficiency or otherwise of any such affidavit objected to as insufficient shall be determined by the court.

11. Where any person interrogated omits to answer, or answers insufficiently, the party interrogating may apply to the court for an order requiring him to answer, or to answer further, as the case may be, and an order may be made requiring him to answer, or to answer further, either affidavit or by *viva voce* examination, as the court may direct.

3. Inspection

   1. All parties shall complete inspection of all documents disclosed within thirty days of the date of filing of the written statement or written statement to the counterclaim, whichever is later. The Court may extend this time limit upon application at its discretion, but not beyond thirty days in any event.

   2. Any party to the proceedings may seek directions from the Court, at any stage of the proceedings, for inspection or production of

documents by the other party, of which inspection has been refused by such party or documents have not been produced despite issuance of a notice to produce.

3. Order in such application shall be disposed of within thirty days of filing such application, including filing replies and rejoinders (if permitted by Court) and hearing.

4. If the above application is allowed, inspection and copies thereof shall be furnished to the party seeking it, within five days of such order.

5. No party shall be permitted to rely on a document, which it had failed to disclose or of which inspection has not been given, save and except with leave of Court.

6. The Court may impose exemplary costs against a defaulting party, who wilfully or negligently failed to disclose all documents pertaining to a suit or essential for a decision therein and which are in their power, possession, control or custody or where a Court holds that inspection or copies of any documents had been wrongfully or unreasonably withheld or refused.

4. Admission and denial of documents.—

1. Each party shall submit a statement of admissions or denials of all documents disclosed and of which inspection has been completed, within fifteen days of the completion of inspection or any later date as fixed by the Court.

2. The statement of admissions and denials shall set out explicitly, whether such party was admitting or denying:—

   a. correctness of contents of a document;
   b. existence of a document;
   c. execution of a document;

d. issuance or receipt of a document;

   e. custody of a document.

   Explanation.—A statement of admission or denial of the existence of a document made in accordance with sub-rule (2) (*b*) shall include the admission or denial of the contents of a document.

   3. Each party shall set out reasons for denying a document under any of the above grounds and bare and unsupported denials shall not be deemed to be denials of a document and proof of such documents may then be dispensed with at the discretion of the Court.

   4. Any party may however submit bare denials for third party documents of which the party denying does not have any personal knowledge of, and to which the party denying is not a party to in any manner whatsoever.

   5. An Affidavit in support of the statement of admissions and denials shall be filed confirming the correctness of the contents of the statement.

   6. In the event that the Court holds that any party has unduly refused to admit a document under any of the above criteria,- costs (including exemplary costs) for deciding on admissibility of a document may be imposed by the Court on such party.

   7. The Court may pass orders with respect to admitted documents including for waiver of further proof thereon or rejection of any documents.

5. Production of documents.—

   1. Any party to a proceeding may seek or the Court may order, at any time during the pendency of any suit, production by any party or person, of such documents in the possession or power of such party or person, relating to any matter in question in such suit.

2. Notice to produce such document shall be issued in the Form provided in Form No. 7 in Appendix C to the Code of Civil Procedure, 1908 (5 of 1908).

3. Any party or person to whom such notice to produce is issued shall be given not less than seven days and not more than fifteen days to produce such document or to answer to their inability to produce such document.

4. The Court may draw an adverse inference against a party refusing to produce such document after issuance of a notice to produce and where sufficient reasons for such non-production are not given and order costs.

6. Electronic records.—

1. In case of disclosures and inspection of Electronic Records (as defined in the Information Technology Act, 2000 (21 of 2000)), furnishing of printouts shall be sufficient compliance of the above provisions.

2. At the discretion of the parties or where required (when parties wish to rely on audio or video content), copies of electronic records may be furnished in electronic form either in addition to or in lieu of printouts.

3. Where Electronic Records form part of documents disclosed, the declaration on oath to be filed by a party shall specify—

   a. the parties to such Electronic Record;

   b. the manner in which such electronic record was produced and by whom;

   c. the dates and time of preparation or storage or issuance or receipt of each such electronic record;

   d. the source of such electronic record and date and time when the electronic record was printed;

e. in case of email ids, details of ownership, custody and access to such email ids;

f. in case of documents stored on a computer or computer resource (including on external servers or cloud), details of ownership, custody and access to such data on the computer or computer resource;

g. deponent's knowledge of contents and correctness of contents;

h. whether the computer or computer resource used for preparing or receiving or storing such document or data was functioning properly or in case of malfunction that such malfunction did not affect the contents of the document stored;

i. that the printout or copy furnished was taken from the original computer or computer resource.

4. The parties relying on printouts or copy in electronic form, of any electronic records, shall not be required to give inspection of electronic records, provided a declaration is made by such party that each such copy, which has been produced, has been made from the original electronic record.

5. The Court may give directions for admissibility of Electronic Records at any stage of the proceedings.

6. Any party may seek directions from the Court and the Court may of its motion issue directions for submission of further proof of any electronic record including metadata or logs before admission of such electronic record.

7. Certain provisions of the Code of Civil Procedure, 1908 not to apply.—For avoidance of doubt, it is hereby clarified that Order XIII Rule 1, Order VII Rule 14 and Order VIII Rule 1A of the Code of Civil Procedure, 1908 (5 of 1908) shall not apply to suits or

applications before the Commercial Divisions of High Court or Commercial Courts.".

The unamended Order XI of the Code is titled as " Discovery and Inspection" which contains twenty three rules in it.

Order VII Rule 14 of the unamended Code mandates production of documents at the time of presenting plaint

14. Production of document on which plaintiff sues or relies.—

1. Where a plaintiff sues upon a document or relies upon document in his possession or power in support of his claim, he shall enter such documents in a list, and shall produce it in Court when the plaint is presented by him and shall, at the same time deliver the document and a copy thereof, to be filed with the plaint.

2. Where any such document is not in the possession or power of the plaintiff, he shall, wherever possible, state in whose possession or power it is.

3. A document which ought to be produced in Court by the plaintiff when the plaint is presented, or to be entered in the list to be added or annexed to the plaint but is not produced or entered accordingly, shall not, without the leave of the Court, be received in evidence on his behalf at the hearing of the suit.]

4. Nothing in this rule shall apply to document produced for the cross-examination of the plaintiffs witnesses, or handed over to a witness merely to refresh his memory.

Order VIII Rule 1A of the unamended Code provided production of documents along with the written statement

1A. Duty of defendant to produce documents upon which relief is claimed or relied upon by him.—

1. Where the defendant bases his defence upon a document or relies upon any document in his possession or power, in support of his

defence or claim for set-off or counter-claim, he shall enter such document in a list, and shall produce it in Court when the written statement is presented by him and shall, at the same time, deliver the document and a copy thereof, to be filed with the written statement.

2. Where any such document is not in the possession or power of the defendant, he shall, wherever possible, state in whose possession or power it is.

3. A document which ought to be produced in Court by the defendant under this rule, but, is not so produced shall not, without the leave of the Court, be received in evidence on his behalf at the hearing of the suit.]

4. Nothing in this rule shall apply to documents—
   a. produced for the cross-examination of the plaintiff's witnesses, or
   b. handed over to a witness merely to refresh his memory.

Order XIII Rule 1 of the Code provides that the documents enclosed with the plaint and the written Statement are to be original.

1. **Original documents to be produced at or before the settlement of issues.—**
   1. The parties or their pleader shall produce on or before the settlement of issues, all the documentary evidence in original where the copies thereof have been filed along with plaint or written statement.
   2. The Court shall receive the documents so produced:
      Provided that they are accompanied by an accurate list thereof prepared in such form as the High Court directs.
   3. Nothing in sub-rule (1) shall apply to documents—

a. produced for the cross-examination of the witnesses of the other party; or

b. handed over to a witness merely to refresh his memory.

Order XI Rule 7 of Code seeks to non-applicable to commercial dispute

7. **Certain provisions of the Code of Civil Procedure, 1908 not to apply.—** For avoidance of doubt, it is hereby clarified that Order XIII Rule 1, Order VII Rule 14 and Order VIII Rule 1A of the Code of Civil Procedure, 1908 (5 of 1908) shall not apply to suits or applications before the Commercial Divisions of High Court or Commercial Courts.".

The cumulative effect of the above provisions is that at the time of filing of the suit, the plaintiff shall file a list of all documents and photocopies of all documents as relied upon or referred to in the plaint. Similarly, defendant is required to file photocopy of all documents referred to and relied upon in the written statement. The mandatory provision of filing 'original' documents has been done away with. However, the plaint shall contain a declaration on oath from the plaintiff that all documents in the power, possession, control or custody of the plaintiff, pertaining to the facts and circumstances of the proceedings initiated by him have been disclosed and copies thereof annexed with plaint. Also, the Written Statement shall contain a declaration on oath from the defendant that all documents in the power, possession, control or custody of the defendant, pertaining to the facts and circumstances of the proceedings initiated by him have been disclosed and copies thereof annexed with written statement.

Both plaintiff and defendant shall not be allowed to rely on documents which were in their possession, control or custody and not disclosed in the plaint and the written statement as the case may be, without seeking leave of the Court but such leave shall be granted only upon showing reasonable cause establishing non-disclosure of the documents.

Section 30 of the Code of Civil Procedure deals with discovery and production of documents and provides that subject to such conditions and limitations as may be prescribed, the Court may, at any time, either of its own motion or on the application of any party(*a*) make such orders as may be necessary or reasonable in all matters relating to the delivery and answering of interrogatories, the admission of documents and facts, and the discovery, inspection, production, impounding and return of documents or other material objects producible as evidence; (*b*) issue summonses to persons whose attendance is required either to give evidence or to produce documents or such other objects as aforesaid; (*c*) order any fact to be proved by affidavit. In **Maria Margadia Sequeria v. Erasmo Jack De Sequeria (D)**[1] a three judges bench of the Supreme Court held that in civil cases, adherence to Section 30 CPC would also help in ascertaining the truth. It seems that this provision which ought to be frequently used is rarely pressed in service by our judicial officers and judges.

This shall be read with Order XI Rule (5) of the Code (As amended) which provides that (*1*) Any party to a proceeding may seek or the Court may order, at any time during the pendency of any suit, production by any party or person, of such documents in the possession or power of such party or person, relating to any matter in question in such suit; (*2*) Notice to produce such document shall be issued in the Form provided in Form No. 7 in Appendix C to the Code of Civil Procedure, 1908 (5 of 1908); (*3*) Any party or person to whom such notice to produce is issued shall be given not less than seven days and not more than fifteen days to produce such document or to answer to their inability to produce such document; (*4*) The Court may draw an adverse inference against a party refusing to produce such document after issuance of a notice to produce and where sufficient reasons for such non-production are not given and order costs.

The Code (As amended) mandates filing of list of all documents for both-plaintiff and defendants along with plaint and written statement

---

1 (2012) 5 SCC 370

respectively in their power, possession, control or custody but there is no mandate of giving copy of the documents to the opposite parties. Rule (3) of Order XI provides that (1) All parties shall complete inspection of all documents disclosed within thirty days of the date of filing of the written statement or written statement to the counterclaim, whichever is later. The Court may extend this time limit upon application at its discretion, but not beyond thirty days in any event. (*2*) Any party to the proceedings may seek directions from the Court, at any stage of the proceedings, for inspection or production of documents by the other party, of which inspection has been refused by such party or documents have not been produced despite issuance of a notice to produce. (*3*) Order in such application shall be disposed of within thirty days of filing such application, including filing replies and rejoinders (if permitted by Court) and hearing. (*4*) If the above application is allowed, inspection and copies thereof shall be furnished to the party seeking it, within five days of such order. (*5*) No party shall be permitted to rely on a document, which it had failed to disclose or of which inspection has not been given, save and except with leave of Court. (*6*) The Court may impose exemplary costs against a defaulting party, who wilfully or negligently failed to disclose all documents pertaining to a suit or essential for a decision therein and which are in their power, possession, control or custody or where a Court holds that inspection or copies of any documents had been wrongfully or unreasonably withheld or refused.

Once inspection is complete by each party of the other party's document, the Code calls for submission of a statement of admission or denial of all documents disclosed and of which inspection has been completed within 15 days of completion of inspection or any later date as fixed by the Court. Such admission and denial shall be about five aspects of the documents-

a. correctness of contents of a document;
b. existence of a document;

c. execution of a document;

d. issuance or receipt of a document;

e. custody of a document.

Many a time, a huge number of documents are filed in commercial suits running into hundred or thousand of pages and each of such documents needs to be specifically dealt with on four aforesaid parameters. In case of denial, reason is to be given. A simple workable approach could be presenting the statement in tabular form as below:

Description of docs.	Correctness of contents	Existence of docs.	Execution of docs.	Issuance or Rect. of docs	Custody of docs	Reasons for denial, if any

The 'admission and denial' as contemplated under this Order XI Rule 4 is in respect of documents only. Order XI Rule 4 further provides that in the event that the Court holds that any party has unduly refused to admit a document under any of the above criteria- cost (including exemplary cost) for deciding on admissibility of a document may be imposed by the Court on such party.

A distinction has to be made with statement and denial of the contents of the pleading as contemplated in Order X Rule 1 of the Code which provides that at the first hearing of the suit the Court shall ascertain from each party or his pleader whether he admits or denies such allegations of fact as are made in the plaint or written statement (if any) of the opposite party, and as are not expressly or by necessary implication admitted or denied by the party against whom they are made. Since, this provision has not been subjected to any amendment, this stage in any commercial suit is of tremendous importance. The provision of Order XI Rule 4 has to be complied with within 15 days of inspection of documents, there seems to be incongruence between the provision of Order X Rule 1which contemplates admission/denial at first hearing and the instant provision which provides filing of statements of admission/denial in respect of documents within 15 days of inspection.

Admission of facts or documents are different yet both are significant. admitted by the parties to a suit need not be proved. The Supreme Court held in **Nagindas Ramdas v Dalpatram Iccharam**[2] that admission in pleadings or judicial admissions made by parties, at or before the hearing of the case, stand on a higher footing than evidentiary admissions and are binding on the party making them and constitutes waiver of proof. Order XII Rule 6 of the Code provides that where admissions of fact have been made either in the pleading or otherwise; whether orally or in writing, the Court may at any stage of the suit, either on the application of any party or of its own motion and without waiting for the determination of any other question-between the parties, make such order or give such judgment as it may think fit, having regard to such admissions. According to the Supreme Court "the object behind the rule is laudable. The court should be able to make an order at least where there are no disputes between the parties. It need not wait till other disputed matters are resolved or adjudicated. However, judgment on admissions cannot be claimed as a matter of right and depends on the discretion of the court, which must be satisfied that the admission relied upon is clear, definite and unequivocal."

---

2   AIR 1974 SC 471

6

CASE MANAGEMENT HEARING

The great thing in the world is not so much where we stand, as in what direction we are moving.

– Oliver Wendell Holmes

One may conceive of many reasons for the cost, delay and complexity of civil litigation. The intricacy of substantive laws, the conduct of the legal profession and the conduct of the courts are three distinct possible reasons. Yet Lord Woolf nominated the lack of judicial case management as the overriding concern. "Without effective judicial control", he wrote, the adversarial process is likely to encourage an adversarial culture and to degenerate into an environment in which the litigation process is too often seen as a battlefield where no rules apply. In this environment, questions of expense, delay, compromise and fairness may have only low priority. The consequence is that expense is often excessive, disproportionate and unpredictable; and delay is frequently unreasonable[1]. "......the call for a more active judiciary had been made in England as far back as 1953, when a committee chaired by Sir Raymond Evershed MR recommended that judges "should pursue a more active and dominant course in the interests of the litigant". As long ago as 1906 Roscoe Pound identified one cause of

---

1   Report on Access to Justice, 2006

dissatisfaction with the administration of justice as the "sporting theory of justice" and its behavioural manifestations. The result of such diagnoses is case management.[2] It emerged under the label of 'case flow management' in the United States in the early 1970s. An early proponent was Maureen Solomon, whose recommendations led to the Australian Federal Court's adoption of the docket system. She described 'case flow management' as follows: [A]s now generally accepted in the courts community, case flow management connotes supervision or management of the time and events involved in the movement of a case through the court system from the point of initiation to disposition, regardless of the type of disposition.[3]

In India, the Supreme Court in the case of **Salem Advocate Bar Association v. Union of India**[4] discussed the concept of case flow management – a concept that lies at the core of effectively managing the workload of a court. Based on the recommendations of the committee headed by Justice M. Jagannadha Rao, the Court in this case urged the High Courts to adopt the Model Case Flow Management Rules for High Courts and subordinate courts, with or without modifications, so as to ensure fair, speedy, and inexpensive justice. The crux of the report is fixation of time at every point of a case.

Recently, the Supreme Court in ***In re*: to issue certain guidelines regarding inadequacies And deficiencies in criminal trials V. The State of Andhra Pradesh & ors.**[5] held, "This court is of the opinion that the courts in all criminal trials should, at the beginning of the trial, i.e. after summoning of the accused, and framing of charges, hold a preliminary case management hearing. This hearing may take place immediately after the framing of the charge. In this hearing, the court should consider the total number of witnesses, and classify them as eyewitness, material witness, formal witness (who would be asked to produce documents, etc)

---

2   Ibid
3   Ibid
4   2005(6) SCC 344; AIR 2005 SC 3353
5   Suo moto writ (crl) no.(s) 1/2017

and experts. At that stage, the court should consider whether the parties are in a position to admit any document (including report of experts, or any document that may be produced by the accused, or relied on by her or him). If so, the exercise of admission/denial may be carried out under Section 294, Cr. PC, for which a specific date may be fixed. The schedule of recording of witnesses should then be fixed, by giving consecutive dates. Each date so fixed, should be scheduled for a specific number of witnesses. However, the concerned witnesses may be bound down to appear for 2-3 consecutive dates, in case their depositions are not concluded. Also, in case any witness does not appear, or cannot be examined, the court shall indicate a fixed date for such purpose. The recording of deposition of witnesses shall then be taken up, after the scheduling exercise is complete. This court has appropriately carried out necessary amendments to the Draft Rules." It has been realised that case management system has universal application for expeditious disposal of all kinds of cases.

The Commercial Courts Act, 2015 has, apparently, adopted the case flow management and brought a new Order with provisions for specific time frame. Order XV- A inserted in the Code of Civil Procedure for setting time lines for each stage of trial after filing of statement of admission and denial of documents by the parties. The Court is required to pass a comprehensive order setting forth in detail the various miles stones in a Commercial Court trial with specific time period and also the consequences of non-compliance of the order of the Court. Various rules go like this

1. **First Case Management Hearing.—The Court shall hold the first Case Management Hearing, not later than four weeks from the date of filing of affidavit of admission or denial of documents by all parties to the suit.**

2. **Orders to be passed in a Case Management Hearing.—In a Case Management Hearing, after hearing the parties, and once it finds that there are issues of fact and law which require to be tried, the Court may pass an order—**

a. framing the issues between the parties in accordance with Order XIV of the Code of Civil Procedure, 1908 (5 of 1908) after examining pleadings, documents and documents produced before it, and on examination conducted by the Court under Rule 2 of Order X, if required;

b. listing witnesses to be examined by the parties;

c. fixing the date by which affidavit of evidence to be filed by parties;

d. fixing the date on which evidence of the witnesses of the parties to be recorded;

e. fixing the date by which written arguments are to be filed before the Court by the parties;

f. fixing the date on which oral arguments are to be heard by the Court; and

g. setting time limits for parties and their advocates to address oral arguments.

3. Time limit for the completion of a trial.—In fixing dates or setting time limits for the purposes of Rule 2 of this Order, the Court shall ensure that the arguments are closed not later than six months from the date of the first Case Management Hearing.

4. Recording of oral evidence on a day-to-day basis.—The Court shall, as far as possible, ensure that the recording of evidence shall be carried on, on a day-to-day basis until the cross-examination of all the witnesses is complete.

5. Case Management Hearings during a trial.—The Court may, if necessary, also hold Case Management Hearings anytime during the trial to issue appropriate orders so as to ensure adherence

by the parties to the dates fixed under Rule 2 and facilitate speedy disposal of the suit.

6. **Powers of the Court in a Case Management Hearing.—**

    1. In any Case Management Hearing held under this Order, the Court shall have the power to—

        a. prior to the framing of issues, hear and decide any pending application filed by the parties under Order XIII-A;

        b. direct parties to file compilations of documents or pleadings relevant and necessary for framing issues;

        c. extend or shorten the time for compliance with any practice, direction or Court order if it finds sufficient reason to do so;

        d. adjourn or bring forward a hearing if it finds sufficient reason to do so;

        e. direct a party to attend the Court for the purposes of examination under Rule 2 of Order X;

        f. consolidate proceedings;

        g. strike off the name of any witness or evidence that it deems irrelevant to the issues framed;

        h. direct a separate trial of any issue;

        i. decide the order in which issues are to be tried;

        j. exclude an issue from consideration;

        k. dismiss or give judgment on a claim after a decision on a preliminary issue;

        l. direct that evidence be recorded by a Commission where necessary in accordance with Order XXVI;

m. reject any affidavit of evidence filed by the parties for containing irrelevant, inadmissible or argumentative material;

n. strike off any parts of the affidavit of evidence filed by the parties containing irrelevant, inadmissible or argumentative material;

o. delegate the recording of evidence to such authority appointed by the Court for this purpose;

p. pass any order relating to the monitoring of recording the evidence by a commission or any other authority;

q. order any party to file and exchange a costs budget;

r. issue directions or pass any order for the purpose of managing the case and furthering the overriding objective of ensuring the efficient disposal of the suit.

2. When the Court passes an order in exercise of its powers under this Order, it may—

   a. make it subject to conditions, including a condition to pay a sum of money into Court; and

   b. specify the consequence of failure to comply with the order or a condition.

3. While fixing the date for a Case Management Hearing, the Court may direct that the parties also be present for such Case Management Hearing, if it is of the view that there is a possibility of settlement between the parties.

7. **Adjournment of Case Management Hearing.—**

   1. The Court shall not adjourn the Case Management Hearing for the sole reason that the advocate appearing on behalf of a party is not present:

Provided that an adjournment of the hearing is sought in advance by moving an application, the Court may adjourn the hearing to another date upon the payment of such costs as the Court deems fit, by the party moving such application.

2. Notwithstanding anything contained in this Rule, if the Court is satisfied that there is a justified reason for the absence of the advocate, it may adjourn the hearing to another date upon such terms and conditions it deems fit.

8. **Consequences of non-compliance with orders.**—Where any party fails to comply with the order of the Court passed in a Case Management Hearing, the Court shall have the power to—

   a. condone such non-compliance by payment of costs to the Court;

   b. foreclose the non-compliant party's right to file affidavits, conduct cross-examination of witnesses, file written submissions, address oral arguments or make further arguments in the trial, as the case may be, or

   c. dismiss the plaint or allow the suit where such non-compliance is wilful, repeated and the imposition of costs is not adequate to ensure compliance."

Compliance of the orders passed by the Court in Case Management is mandatory. The Rule 8 of the Order XV-A provides that the court shall have power to condone such non-compliance by payment of costs to the Court; foreclose the non-compliant party's right to file affidavits, conduct cross-examination of witnesses, file written submissions, address oral arguments or make further arguments in the trial, as the case may be, or dismiss the plaint or allow the suit. These provisions shall override the provision of Or. IX of Code which deals with consequences of non-appearance.

The provisions laid down under Order XV are mandatory and not merely directory to meet the objects of the Commercial Courts Act. The Madras High Court in **M/S. Nexmoo Solutions (India) Pvt. Ltd. v M/S. Nexmo Inc.**[6] held "As pleadings are complete, the process of admission and denial of documents as adumbrated in Order XI Rule 4 of CPC as amended by Act 4 of 2016 shall be completed within three weeks from the delivery of this order. Within a week thereafter i.e., on expiry of four weeks from the date of delivery of this order, the suit shall be listed for Case Management hearing before this Commercial Division as under Order XV-A of CPC which was introduced into CPC by Act 4 of 2016. In the Case Management hearing, issues can be framed and there is no reason why the trial cannot be completed within six weeks as adumbrated in Order XV-A of CPC which was introduced into CPC by Act 4 of 2016. If this is done, judgment will be delivered within 90 days there from by this Commercial Division."

---

6   2018 SCC Online Mad 636 in para 17

7

LEADING EVIDENCE AND ARGUMENT

"Behind every argument is someone's ignorance."

– Louis Brandeis, U S Supreme Court Justice (1916–39)

The unamended Code of Civil Procedure does not prescribe any format for the affidavit of evidence filed as examination-in-chief. Rule 4 of Order XVIII merely provides that the examination-in-chief shall be in an affidavit. Order XIX of Code of Civil Procedure Code has been amended to insert three new rules- 4, 5 and 6. Rule (6) provides the format in which the affidavit of evidence is to be filed. It provides:

6. Format and guidelines of affidavit of evidence.—An affidavit must comply with the form and requirements set forth below:—

a. such affidavit should be confined to, and should follow the chronological sequence of, the dates and events that are relevant for proving any fact or any other matter dealt with;

b. where the Court is of the view that an affidavit is a mere reproduction of the pleadings, or contains the legal grounds of any party's case, the Court may, by order, strike out the affidavit or such parts of the affidavit, as it deems fit and proper;

c. each paragraph of an affidavit should, as far as possible, be confined to a distinct portion of the subject;

d. an affidavit shall state—

   i. which of the statements in it are made from the deponent's own knowledge and which are matters of information or belief; and

   ii. the source for any matters of information or belief;

e. an affidavit should—

   i. have the pages numbered consecutively as a separate document (or as one of several documents contained in a file);

   ii. be divided into numbered paragraphs;

   iii. have all numbers, including dates, expressed in figures; and

   iv. if any of the documents referred to in the body of the affidavit are annexed to the affidavit or any other pleadings, give the annexures and page numbers of such documents that are relied upon."

The use of the word 'must' makes it mandatory to follow the aforesaid format and guidelines while preparing the affidavit. In order to curtail the time consumption in recording of evidence, amendments have been made in Order XVIII of the Code of Civil Procedure in respect of recording of evidence and cross examination of witnesses.

There is a tendency to see an affidavit as a simple document that just sets out the facts and needs no particular care, but sometimes affidavit is important in the tactics and proper presentation of a case, and the chances offered in the drafting of the affidavit should not be thrown away. In fact, the affidavit is a chameleon that turns up in many different forms for different purposes.[1]

---

1   A Practical Approach to Legal Advice & Drafting by Susan Lake at p.209

In respect of commercial trial Order XVIII Rule 4 of the Code of Civil Procedure shall read as follows:

[Recording of evidence.—

(1) In every case, the examination-in-chief of a witness shall be on affidavit and copies thereof shall be supplied to the opposite party by the party who calls him for evidence: Provided that where documents are filed and the parties rely upon the documents, the proof and admissibility of such documents which are filed along with affidavit shall be subject to the orders of the Court.

(1A) The affidavits of evidence of all witnesses whose evidence is proposed to be led by a party shall be filed simultaneously by that party at the time directed in the first Case Management Hearing.

(1B) A party shall not lead additional evidence by the affidavit of any witness (including of a witness who has already filed an affidavit) unless sufficient cause is made out in an application for that purpose and an order, giving reasons, permitting such additional affidavit is passed by the Court.

(1C) A party shall however have the right to withdraw any of the affidavits so filed at any time prior to commencement of cross-examination of that witness, without any adverse inference being drawn based on such withdrawal:

Provided that any other party shall be entitled to tender as evidence and rely upon any admission made in such withdrawn affidavit.]

Rest of the sub rules (2) to (8) of Rule 4 of Order XVIII have been left as it is. Therefore, the evidence (cross-examination and re-examination) of the witness in attendance, whose evidence (examination-in-chief) by affidavit has been furnished to the Court, shall be taken either by the Court or by the Commissioner appointed by it: Provided that the Court may, while appointing a commission under this sub-rule, consider taking into account such relevant factors as it thinks fit.[2] The Court or the Commissioner, as the case may be, shall record evidence either in writing or mechanically in the presence of the Judge or of the Commissioner, as the case may be, and where such evidence is recorded by the Commissioner he shall return such evidence together with his report in writing signed by him to the Court appointing him and the evidence taken under it shall form part of the record of the suit.[3]

However, the unamended provision of this Rule shall be conjointly read with provision of Order XA Rule (2) which provides that **in a Case Management Hearing, after hearing the parties, and once it finds that there are issues of fact and law which require to be tried, the Court may pass an order—**

  b. **listing witnesses to be examined by the parties;**
  c. **fixing the date by which affidavit of evidence to be filed by parties;**
  d. **fixing the date on which evidence of the witnesses of the parties to be recorded;**

It has been further provided that in fixing dates or setting time limits for the purposes of Rule 2 of this Order, the Court shall ensure that the arguments are closed not later than six months from the date of the first Case Management Hearing.[4] The Court shall, as far as possible, ensure that the recording of evidence shall be carried on, on a day-to-day basis until the cross-examination of all the witnesses is complete.[5]

Rule 6 of Order XVA confers certain powers on court while trying a case. Some of the powers in respect of evidence are enumerated as below:

  g. **strike off the name of any witness or evidence that it deems irrelevant to the issues framed;**

---

2   Sub-rule 2 of Rule(4) of Code of Civil Procedure
3   Sub-rule 3 of Rule (4) of Code of Civil Procedure
4   Rule 3 of Order XVA of Code of Civil Procedure Act as amended
5   Rule 4 of Order XVA of Code of Civil Procedure Act as amended

h. direct a separate trial of any issue;

i. decide the order in which issues are to be tried;

j. exclude an issue from consideration;

k. dismiss or give judgment on a claim after a decision on a preliminary issue;

l. direct that evidence be recorded by a Commission where necessary in accordance with Order XXVI;

m. reject any affidavit of evidence filed by the parties for containing irrelevant, inadmissible or argumentative material;

n. strike off any parts of the affidavit of evidence filed by the parties containing irrelevant, inadmissible or argumentative material;

Still further the Commercial Courts Act has amended Order XIX whereby, **after Rule 3, the following Rules shall be inserted, namely:—**

"4. Court may control evidence.—(1) The Court may, by directions, regulate the evidence as to issues on which it requires evidence and the manner in which such evidence may be placed before the Court.

(2) The Court may, in its discretion and for reasons to be recorded in writing, exclude evidence that would otherwise be produced by the parties.

5. Redacting or rejecting evidence.—A Court may, in its discretion, for reasons to be recorded in writing—

i. **redact or order the redaction of such portions of the affidavit of examination-in-chief as do not, in its view, constitute evidence; or**

ii. **return or reject an affidavit of examination-in-chief as not constituting admissible evidence.**

Juxtaposing the aforesaid provision with Sub rule (5) of Rule 4 of Order XVIII which provides that the report of the Commissioner shall be submitted to the Court appointing the commission within sixty days from the date of issue of the commission unless the Court for reasons to be recorded in writing extends the time, there seems to be inconsistencies. But matter can be seen in view of section

16(3) of Commercial Courts Act which provides that where any provision of any Rule of the jurisdictional High Court or any amendment to the Code of Civil Procedure, 1908 (5 of 1908), by the State Government is in conflict with the provisions of the Code of Civil Procedure, 1908, as amended by this Act, the provisions of the Code of Civil Procedure as amended by this Act shall prevail.

Order XVIII carries heading 'Hearing of the suit and examination of witnesses' and it includes hearing of the suit, adducing evidence and tendering arguments.

Hearing of the suit and the trial of the suit are totally two different concepts. Trial would commence the very moment the suit is instituted. "Trial of the suit", therefore, is a comprehensive term. The trial would commence after the filing of suit and it would end with the disposal of the suit. The hearing of the suit is part of the trial process. Hearing relates to examination of witnesses, their cross examination as well as arguments by the counsel. Therefore, hearing is a continuous process not confined to producing and recording evidence. It is therefore, essentially a composite process. The right to begin as mentioned in Rule 1 of Order 18 CPC has to be treated as opening the case, production of evidence followed by arguments. In normal course, the plaintiff has to open the case and he should lead evidence to begin with.[6] This is inextricably related to burden of proof and onus of proof and this rule shall be conjointly read with section 101 and 103 of the Evidence Act.

Order XVIII Rule 2 has been amended by Commercial Courts Act as below:

---

6   Bajaj Auto Ltd. v. TVS Motor Company 2010 SCC Online Mad 5031

Amendment of Order XVIII—In Order XVIII of the Code, in Rule 2, for sub-rules (3A), (3B), (3C), (3D), (3E) and (3F), the following shall be substituted, namely—

"(3A) A party shall, within four weeks prior to commencing the oral arguments, submit concisely and under distinct headings written arguments in support of his case to the Court and such written arguments shall form part of the record.

(3B) The written arguments shall clearly indicate the provisions of the laws being cited in support of the arguments and the citations of judgments being relied upon by the party and include copies of such judgments being relied upon by the party.

(3C) A copy of such written arguments shall be furnished simultaneously to the opposite party.

(3D) The Court may, if it deems fit, after the conclusion of arguments, permit the parties to file revised written arguments within a period of not more than one week after the date of conclusion of arguments.

(3E) No adjournment shall be granted for the purpose of filing the written arguments unless the Court, for reasons to be recorded in writing, considers it necessary to grant such adjournment.

(3F) It shall be open for the Court to limit the time for oral submissions having regard to the nature and complexity of the matter.".

The word 'argument' has not been defined in the Code of Civil Procedure even though this is perhaps the most important task of any lawyer. According to Collins Dictionary "An argument is a statement or set of statements that you use in order to try to convince people that your opinion about something is correct." In Black's Law Dictionary, argument has been defined as, "1. A statement that attempts to persuade; esp. the remarks of counsel in analysing and pointing out or repudiating a desired inference, for the assistance of a decision maker."

Wilson Huhn has introduced the five categories of legal arguments- text, intent, precedent, tradition, and policy. Each category reflects a different value: **text** - clarity and objectivity; **intent** - popular sovereignty (public law) and personal autonomy (private law, e.g., wills, contracts); **precedent** - consistency and stability; **tradition** - social cohesion; and **policy** - flexibility in the face of social change.

To prove a question of fact, lawyers call witnesses and introduce exhibits. To prove a question of law, lawyers create valid legal arguments, drawing on legal text, intent, precedent, traditions, and policy. The different legitimate types of legal argument are the "data" that lawyers use to prove what the law is. The order of these categories corresponds to the order in which they should be considered in a legal argument, and the best argument should weave these into a "cable."[7]

Law Commission in its 99th Report (April, 1984) considered the question of oral and written argument in Higher Courts. Although, the report was not concerned with arguments in district courts, its conclusion is quite relevant on the significance of oral argument as well as written argument. The report concludes, "Having considered all these aspects of the problems, we are not inclined to suggest any rigid or mathematically precise time limits for oral arguments. It may be difficult to lay down any hard and fast rule for determining the minimum time for oral arguments in all cases."

The rule 3A, 3B and 3C as in Code of Civil Procedure was inserted vide amendment Act No 22 of 2002. The amendment *vide* the Commercial Courts Act in substituting 3A to 3F brings time limit and also the content of argument in the Code. Rule 3F provides that it shall be open for the Court to limit the time for oral submissions having regard to the nature and complexity of the matter.

---

7   The Five Types of Legal Argument (Carolina Academic Press 2d ed.) by Wilson R. Huhn

8

JUDGMENT AND DECREE

Justice has nothing to do with what goes on in a courtroom; Justice is what comes out of a courtroom.

– Clarence Darrow

The Commercial Courts Act, 2015 brought amendment in Rule 1 of Order XX of the Code of Civil Procedure only and rest of the rules of this Order have remained unamended. Rule 1 as amended reads as below-

"(1) The [Commercial Court, Commercial Appellate Court], Commercial Division, or Commercial Appellate Division, as the case may be, shall, within ninety days of the conclusion of arguments, pronounce judgment and copies thereof shall be issued to all the parties to the dispute through electronic mail or otherwise." Hence, there is departure under the present Act so as to allow a period of 90 days for pronouncing judgment, copy whereof shall be given by e-mail to the parties.

Contents of judgment and that of decree has been clearly laid in Order XX of the Code of Civil Procedure under Rule 4 Sub Rule (2) which provides that Judgments of other Courts than Small Cause Court shall contain a concise statement of the case, the points for determination, the decision thereon, and the reasons for such decision. Further, Rule 5 provides that in suits in which issues have been framed, the Court shall state its finding or decision, with the reasons therefor, upon each separate issue, unless the finding upon any one or more of the issue is, sufficient for the decision of the suit.

The Supreme Court emphasized on the contents of judgment in **Jalendra Padhiary v Pragati Chhotray** [1] "Time and again, this Court has emphasized on the Courts the need to pass reasoned order in every case, which must contain the narration of the bare facts of the case of the parties to the *lis*, the issues arising in the case, the submissions urged by the parties, the legal principles applicable to the issues involved and the reasons in support of the findings". However, the Courts while passing the judgment cannot travel beyond pleading and form a new case as held by the Supreme Court in **Ishwar Dutt v land Acquisition Collector & Anr**[2] "As has been stated, the defendant traversed that claim in his written statement and pleaded that the business always belonged to him as owner. There was thus no plea that the business was "benami" for Shivanna. We also find that the parties did not join issue on the question that the business was "benami". On the other hand, the point at issue was whether Shivanna was the owner of the business and the tenancy rights of the premises where it was being carried on. It is well-settled, having been laid down by this **Court in Trojan and Co. Ltd. v. RM. N.N. Nagappa Chettiar** and **Raruha Singh v. Achal Singh** that the decision of a case cannot be based on grounds outside the plea of the parties, and that it is the case pleaded which has to be found. The High Court therefore went wrong in ignoring this basic principle of law, and in making out an entirely new case which was not pleaded and was not the subject-matter of the trial." Underlying the need of a reasoned judgment the Bombay High Court held, "......As a Court of first instance, which has an advantage of recording the evidence of parties and witnesses in person, it is expected that the Judgment of the Trial Court

---

1 2018 SCC Online SC 391 in para 16
2 (2005) 7 SCC 190 quoting judgment in In Siddu Venkappa Devadiga v. Smt. Rangu S. Devadiga and Ors., [1977] 3 SCC 532

must reflect the appreciation of evidence and analyzing of submissions advanced before it and, of-course, the reasons for deciding the case in a way or another. "Reasons" are the soul of the Judgment or of any judicial order. Giving of proper reasons serves two fold purposes - of parties being made aware as to why the decision has gone in their favour or against them and, secondly, the recording of reasons assists higher Courts also to test the legality and validity of the Judgment and Order impugned. Recording of reasons in the Judgment helps everyone to know what has transpired in the mind of the Court for decreeing or dismissing a particular Suit. The importance of recording of reasons in the Judgment is that, it guarantees the fundamental principle of justice delivery system that, "justice is not only done, but also appears to have been done", which is the duty of the Court.[3]

In **Joint Commissioner of Income Tax, Surat v. Saheli Leasing & Industries Ltd.**[4] the Supreme Court laid down guidelines on writing judgments and held,

"7. These guidelines are only illustrative in nature, not exhaustive and can further be elaborated looking to the need and requirement of a given case:-

   a. It should always be kept in mind that nothing should be written in the judgment/order, which may not be germane to the facts of the case; It should have a co-relation with the applicable law and facts. The ratio decidendi should be clearly spelt out from the judgment/order.

   b. After preparing the draft, it is necessary to go through the same to find out, if anything, essential to be mentioned, has escaped discussion.

---

3   Manjulaben Shah v Maduriben Meghji Shah 2018 SCC Online Bom 136
4   (2010) 6 SCC 384

c. The ultimate finished judgment/order should have sustained chronology, regard being had to the concept that it has readable, continued interest and one does not feel like parting or leaving it in the midway. To elaborate, it should have flow and perfect sequence of events, which would continue to generate interest in the reader.

d. Appropriate care should be taken not to load it with all legal knowledge on the subject as citation of too many judgments creates more confusion rather than clarity. The foremost requirement is that leading judgments should be mentioned and the evolution that has taken place ever since the same were pronounced and thereafter, latest judgment, in which all previous judgments have been considered, should be mentioned. While writing judgment, psychology of the reader has also to be borne in mind, for the perception on that score is imperative.

e. Language should not be rhetoric and should not reflect a contrived effort on the part of the author.

f. After arguments are concluded, an endeavour should be made to pronounce the judgment at the earliest and in any case not beyond a period of three months. Keeping it pending for long time, sends a wrong signal to the litigants and the society.

g. It should be avoided to give instances, which are likely to cause public agitation or to a particular society. Nothing should be reflected in the same which may hurt the feelings or emotions of any individual or society.

8. Aforesaid are some of the guidelines which are required to be kept in mind while writing judgments. In fact, we are only reiterating what has already been said in several judgments of this Court."

Chief Justice Sabyasachi Mukharji said, "The supreme requirement of a good judgment is reason. Judgment is of value on the strength of its reasons. The weight of a judgment, its binding character or its persuasive character depends on the presentation and articulation of reasons. Reason, therefore, is the soul and spirit of a good judgment."

The Code of Civil Procedure provides that every endeavour shall be made to ensure that the decree is drawn up as expeditiously as possible and, in any case, within fifteen days from the date on which the judgment is pronounced.[5] Decree has been defined as the formal expression of an adjudication which, so far as regards the Court expressing it, conclusively determines the rights of the parties with regard to all or any of the matters in controversy in the suit and may be either preliminary or final.[6] And the judgement has been defines as the statement given by the Judge of the grounds of a decree or order.[7]

Therefore, what has been decided by way of judgment must be formally set out in the decree. The decree shall agree with the judgment: it shall contain the number of the suit, the names and descriptions of the parties, their registered addresses, and particulars of the claim, and shall specify clearly the relief granted or other determination of the suit. [8] The phrase, "shall specify clearly the relief granted" assumes significance in view of the fact that it is the decree which is put for execution. A decree may be executed either by the court which passed it, or by the court to which it is sent for execution.[9] It can conveniently be said that a judgment is followed by decree which forms the operating part. Although the distinction between 'judgment' and 'decree' has been obliterated in U K and other common law countries, it is still maintained in India.

Decree must therefore clearly set out what reliefs have been granted. It is improper and insufficient to render, "The suit is decreed with/without cost" without elucidating what reliefs have been granted. For example, Appendix D, Form No-2 prescribes following content as below:

---

[5] Order XX Rule 6A (1) of Code of Civil Procedure
[6] Sec. 2 (2) of Code of Civil Procedure
[7] Sec. 2 (9) of Code of Civil Procedure
[8] Order XX Rule 6 (1) of Code of Civil Procedure
[9] Sec. 38 of Code of Civil Procedure

"THIS suit coming on this.....................day for final disposal before......... in the presence of............................for the plaintiff and of..............for the defendant; It is ordered that the...............do pay to the..................the sum of Rs..................with interest thereon at the rate of.....................per cent. per annum from..to the date of realization of the said sum and do also pay Rs....................., the costs of this suit, with interest thereon at the rate of...... per cent. per annum from this date to the date of realization. GIVEN under my hand and the seal of the Court, this..........................day of..................19."

Since, in many suits, there are more than one relief sought and accordingly adjudicated it is necessary that each of such reliefs which has been granted shall be spelt out in the decree.

The Supreme Court examined the aspect of the contents of judgment and decree to lay down clearly the law in this regard in **Lakshmi Ram Bhuyan v Hari Prasad Bhuyan & Ors**[10]. In this case a title suit was filed and reliefs claimed for a decree or decrees for recovery of possession of land, for confirmation of possession with declaration of title; a decree or decrees for cancellation of Khatian; decrees for cancellation of the mutation and decree of the costs of the suit against the defendants etc. The suit was seriously contested. By judgment and decree the Trial Court directed the suit to be dismissed. The dismissal of the suit was upheld in first appeal by learned Additional District Judge. The plaintiffs filed second appeal, which was heard by a learned single Judge of the High Court who formed an opinion that the appeal deserved to be allowed and allowed the same by judgment the operative part whereof was, "From my above discussion the appeal is allowed. Respondents are directed to pay Rs. 500/- as cost to the appellants. The case is sent back to the original court for preparation of the decree accordingly. In the result the appeal is allowed."

As per directions of the High Court, the Trial Court drew up a decree. The said decree mentions costs only. The reliefs claimed by the plaintiffs in

---

10 (2003) 1 SCC 197

the suit were not mentioned therein. Execution was applied for. Therein, it appears, the plaintiffs sought for the same reliefs as they had set out in the plaint, being allowed to them in execution, which was resisted to by the judgment-debtors. On 26.08.1997, the Civil Judge passed two orders. In execution proceedings the Civil Judge held that as no formal decree regarding delivery of khas possession etc. was drawn up, the execution was liable to be stayed till preparation of a proper decree in the suit. The record of the suit was directed to be put up for preparation of necessary decree. On the same date, by a separate order passed in the suit, the Civil Judge set out briefly the operative parts of the judgment of the Trial Court in the original suit and that of the High Court in second appeal (referred to hereinabove) and then concluded that the decree should be prepared by this court granting all the reliefs claimed by the plaintiffs/appellants. The earlier decree prepared by this Court was only in respect of the cost granted by the High Court, the decree should have contained all the reliefs claimed in the plaint. The orders were challenged in Revision by the judgment-debtors. Incidentally, the Civil Revision came to be heard by the same Single Judge who had disposed of the second appeal. The Single Judge directed the Civil Revision to be dismissed forming an opinion that there was no infirmity or illegality in the orders of the Civil Judge and there was no jurisdictional error therein.

The judgment-debtors preferred special leave petition against the order of the High Court. It was held by the Supreme Court, "Certain provisions of the Code of Civil Procedure, 1908 may be noticed. Order VII Rule 1 of the CPC requires the plaintiff to give sufficient particulars of the relief, which the plaintiff claims. Order XX requires a judgment to contain all the issues and findings or decision thereon with the reasons therefor. The judgment has to state the relief allowed to a party. The preparation of decree follows the judgment. The decree shall agree with the judgment. The decree shall contain, inter alia, particulars of the claim and shall specify clearly the relief granted or other determination of the suit. The decree shall also state the amount of costs incurred in the suit and by whom or out of what property and in what proportions such costs are to be paid. Rules 9 to 19 of Order XX are illustrative of contents of decrees in certain specified categories of suits. The very obligation cast by the Code that the decree shall agree with the judgment spells out an obligation on the part of the author of the judgment to clearly indicate the relief or reliefs to which a party, in his opinion, has been found entitled to enable decree being framed in such a manner that it agrees with the judgment and specifies clearly the relief granted or other determination of the suit. The operative part of the judgment should be so clear and precise that in the event of an objection being laid, it should not be difficult to find out by a bare reading of the judgment and decree whether the latter agrees with the former and is in conformity therewith. A self-contained decree drawn up in conformity with the judgment would exclude objections and complexities arising at the stage of execution.

The obligation is cast not only on the Trial Court but also on the Appellate Court. In the event of the suit having been decreed by the Trial Court if the Appellate Court interferes with the judgment of the Trial Court, the judgment of the Appellate Court should precisely and specifically set out the reliefs granted and the modifications, if any, made in the original decree explicitly and with particularity and precision. Order XLI Rule 31 of the CPC casts an obligation on the author of the appellate judgment to state the points for determination, the decision thereon, the reasons for the decision and when the decree appealed from is reversed or varied, the relief to which the appellant is entitled. If the suit was dismissed by the Trial Court and in appeal the decree of dismissal is reversed, the operative part of the judgment should be so precise and clear as it would have been if the suit was decreed by the Trial Court to enable a self-contained decree being drawn up in conformity therewith. The plaintiff, being dominus litus, enjoys a free hand in couching the relief clause in the manner he pleases and cases are not wanting where the plaintiff makes full use of the liberty given to him. It is for the Court, decreeing the suit, to examine the reliefs and then construct the operative part of the judgment in such manner as to bring the reliefs granted in conformity with the findings arrived at on different issues and also the admitted facts. The Trial Court merely observing in the operative part of the judgment that the suit is decreed or an appellate Court disposing of an appeal against dismissal of suit observing the appeal is allowed, and then staying short at that, without specifying the reliefs to which the successful party has been found entitled tantamount to a failure on the part of the author of judgment to discharge obligation cast on the Judge by the provisions of Code of Civil Procedure.

In the case at hand, a perusal of the reliefs prayed for in the plaint shows that the reliefs are not very happily worded. There are some reliefs which may not be necessary or may be uncalled for though prayed. The reliefs may have been considered capable of being recast or redefined so as to be precise and specific. May be that the Court was inclined to grant some other relief so as to effectually adjudicate upon the controversy and bring it to an end. Nothing is spelled out from the appellate judgment. The Trial Court, on whom the obligation was cast by second appellate judgment to draw up a decree, was also, as its order shows, not very clear in its mind and thought it safe to proceed on an assumption that all the reliefs sought for in the plaint were allowed to the plaintiffs. The learned single Judge allowing the second appeal, should have clearly and precisely stated the extent and manner of reliefs to which the plaintiffs were found to be entitled in his view of the findings arrived at during the course of the appellate judgment. The parties, the draftsman of decree and the executing Court cannot be left guessing what was transpiring in the mind of the Judge decreeing the suit or allowing the appeal without further placing on record the reliefs to which the plaintiffs are held entitled in the opinion of the Judge."

In **Om Prakash v. State of A.P. & Ors.**[11] The Supreme Court re-iterated the aforesaid position of law in para 61 and 62, "61: To meet the above contentions, learned Attorney General has made an elaborate argument

---

11 (2010) 13 SCC 158

by drawing our attention to the decree prepared by the Registry. In fact, we also summoned the original decree drafted by the Registry. A judgment comprises three segments (i) the facts and the point at issue; (ii) the reasons for the decision and (iii) the final order containing the decision. Order XX CPC requires a judgment to contain all the issues and findings or decision thereon with the reasons therefor. The judgment has to state the relief allowed to a party. The preparation of decree follows the judgment. The decree shall agree with the judgment. The decree shall contain, inter alia, particulars of the claim and shall specify clearly the relief granted or other determination of the suit. 62: The very obligation cast by the Code that the decree shall agree with the judgment spells out an obligation on the part of the author of the judgment to clearly indicate the relief or reliefs to which a party, in his opinion, has been found entitled to enable decree being framed in such a manner that it agrees with the judgment and specifies clearly the relief granted. The operative part of the judgment should be so clear and precise that in the event of an objection being laid, it should not be difficult to find out by a bare reading of the judgment and decree whether the latter agrees with the former and is in conformity therewith. The obligation is cast not only on the trial court but also on the appellate court. Order 41 Rule 31 CPC casts an obligation on the author of the appellate judgment to state the points for determination, the decision thereon, the reasons for the decision and when the decree appealed from is reversed or varied, the relief to which the appellant is entitled."

9

INTEREST AND COST

> *"There is one panacea which heals every sore in litigation, and that is costs" and that there can seldom be an instance where amendments would cause "such a disadvantage as that it cannot be cured by that healing medicine".*
>
> – Lord Justice Bowen in his dissenting judgment in Cropper v. Smith (1884) 26 Ch D 700

Interest and cost are two distinct heads of reliefs which may be awarded to a litigant. While interest means the compensation fixed by agreement or allowed by law for the use and detention of money, or for the loss of money by one who is entitled to its use esp. the amount owed to a lender in a return for the use of borrowed money[1]; the cost is the amount paid or charged for something, price or expenditure.[2] Although not damages in any sense, mention should be made of contractual rights to interest. Many contracts provide expressly or impliedly for a right to interest for late payment of debt. Breach of such an obligation is a non-payment of a debt, enforceable either by the remedy of an action for a debt or by claiming damages equal to the amount of debt.[3] The cost of litigation disputing the breach of contract

---

1   Black's Law Dictionary at p.829
2   Ibid at p.371
3   The Law of Contract Damages by Adam Cramer at p. 216

itself (Including lawyers' fees, disbursements to experts, and expenses) are a loss caused by the breach. But for the breach, the claimant would not have had to embark upon the litigation against the defendant. However, under English law the costs of proceedings are dealt with by the Civil Procedure Rules 44 to 48. these procedural rules have exclusive jurisdiction over the costs of the dispute before the court (including of lawyers, expert reports etc) and mean that ordinary rules of contract damages do not apply.[4] The same principles are applicable in India also.

Section 34 of the Code of Civil Procedure deals with interest for the decree for the payment of money. Rate of interest may be ordered to be paid as the court deems reasonable on the principal sum from the date of the suit to the date of the decree, in addition to amounts for any period prior to the institution of the suit and from the date of decree to the date of payment. Any interest adjudged for any period prior to the institution of the suit shall be at the rate not exceeding six percent *per anum*. In case of commercial transaction the rate of interest may exceed six percent *per anum* but shall not exceed the contractual rate of interest or where there is no contractual rate, the rate at which money is lent or advanced by nationalized bank in relation to commercial transactions.

However, Rule 2A in Order VII as applicable for commercial dispute, provides as follows:

"2A. Where interest is sought in the suit,—

1. **Where the plaintiff seeks interest, the plaint shall contain a statement to that effect along with the details set out under sub-rules (2) and (3).**

2. **Where the plaintiff seeks interest, the plaint shall state whether the plaintiff is seeking interest in relation to a commercial transaction within the meaning of section 34 of the Code of Civil Procedure, 1908 (5 of 1908) and, furthermore, if the plaintiff is doing so under the terms of a contract or under an Act, in which**

---

[4] Ibid at p.558

case the Act is to be specified in the plaint; or on some other basis and shall state the basis of that.

3. Pleadings shall also state—
    a. the rate at which interest is claimed;
    b. the date from which it is claimed;
    c. the date to which it is calculated;
    d. the total amount of interest claimed to the date of calculation; and
    e. the daily rate at which interest accrues after that date."

The combined effect of section 34 read with rule 2A of Order VII is that there is no fetter on rate of interest in a suit of commercial dispute but the same has to be stated in the plaint and proved according to law. The interest shall also be governed by specific provision of law applicable to the specific kind of contract or the parties involved. In the book Civil Procedure Code by M.P. Jain it has been elucidated this way- Interest that may be awarded to a plaintiff in a suit for money may be divided into three heads, according to the period for which it is allowed, namely-

i. interest accrued due prior to the institution of the suit on the principal sum adjudged (as distinguished from the principal sum claimed);

ii. additional interest on the principal sum adjudged, from the date of the suit to the date of the decree, "at such rate as the Court deems reasonable;

iii. further interest on the principal sum adjudged from the date of the decree to the date of the Court thinks fit, at a rate not exceeding 6 per cent, per annum.

There are certain statues governing rate of interest to be awarded to the litigants. The Micro, Small And Medium Enterprises Development Act, 2006 provides that where any buyer fails to make payment of the amount to the supplier, as required under section 15, the buyer shall, notwithstanding anything contained in any agreement between the buyer and the supplier or in any law for the time being in force, be liable to pay compound interest with monthly rests to the supplier on that amount from the appointed day or, as the case may be, from the date immediately following the date agreed upon, at three times of the bank rate notified by the Reserve Bank.[5] Here the word "supplier" means a micro or small enterprise, which has filed a memorandum with the authority referred to in sub-section (1) of section 8.[6] As stated above, section 34 of the Code of Civil Procedure was amended vide Amending Act of 1976 by which it was provided that where the liability in relation to the sum adjudged by the Court has arisen out of a commercial transaction the rate of interest may exceed six percent per annum. However, such rate shall not exceed the contractual rate of interest, or where is there is no contractual rate, the rate at which money is lent or advanced by nationalized banks in relation to commercial transactions.

Cost has been a contentious issue in civil litigation. Black's Law dictionary defines costs as "The expense of litigation, prosecution, or other legal transaction, esp. those allowed in favour of one party against the other." "Costs are certain allowances authorized by statute to reimburse the successful party for expenses incurred in prosecuting or defending an action or special proceeding[7]. The common thread running through all these cases is the reiteration of three salutary principles: (i) costs should ordinarily follow the event; (ii) realistic costs ought to be awarded keeping in view the ever increasing litigation expenses; and (iii) the cost should serve the purpose of curbing frivolous and vexatious litigation.[8] It is generally accepted that a successful party in litigation is entitled to his costs in the case unless he is guilty of misconduct, or there is sufficient cause to deprive him of it. Section 35 of the Code has been substituted with a new provision,

---

5 Section 16
6 Section 2(n)
7 P. Ramanatha Aiyar's Major Law Lexicon, 4 th Edn. At p. 1571,
8 Law Commission 240th Report

sub section (2) of 35 A has been omitted and section 35B is applicable to the commercial dispute as well.

Sec 35:

1. In relation to any commercial dispute, the Court, notwithstanding anything contained in any other law for the time being in force or Rule, has the discretion to determine:

   a. whether costs are payable by one party to another;

   b. the quantum of those costs; and

   c. when they are to be paid.

   Explanation.—For the purpose of clause (*a*), the expression "costs" shall mean reasonable costs relating to—

   i. the fees and expenses of the witnesses incurred;

   ii. legal fees and expenses incurred;

   iii. any other expenses incurred in connection with the proceedings.

2. If the Court decides to make an order for payment of costs, the general rule is that the unsuccessful party shall be ordered to pay the costs of the successful party:

   Provided that the Court may make an order deviating from the general rule for reasons to be recorded in writing.

   Illustration

   The Plaintiff, in his suit, seeks a money decree for breach of contract, and damages. The Court holds that the Plaintiff is entitled to the money decree. However, it returns a finding that the claim for damages is frivolous and vexatious. In such circumstances the Court may impose costs on the Plaintiff, despite the Plaintiff being the successful party, for having raised frivolous claims for damages.

3. In making an order for the payment of costs, the Court shall have regard to the following circumstances, including—

   a. the conduct of the parties;

   b. whether a party has succeeded on part of its case, even if that party has not been wholly successful;

   c. whether the party had made a frivolous counterclaim leading to delay in the disposal of the case;

   d. whether any reasonable offer to settle is made by a party and unreasonably refused by the other party; and

   e. whether the party had made a frivolous claim and instituted a vexatious proceeding wasting the time of the Court.

4. The orders which the Court may make under this provision include an order that a party must pay—

   a. a proportion of another party's costs;

   b. a stated amount in respect of another party's costs;

   c. costs from or until a certain date;

   d. costs incurred before proceedings have begun;

   e. costs relating to particular steps taken in the proceedings;

   f. costs relating to a distinct part of the proceedings; and

   g. interest on costs from or until a certain date.'

Bombay High Court in **Harmony Lifestyle Structures Pvt. Ltd v. Morya Infrastructural Pvt. Ltd** held "Sub section 2 of section 35 of the CPC as amended by the Commercial Courts Act, 2015 requires that costs must be awarded to the successful party and reasons are required to be given if costs are not to be awarded. The explanation to sub section 1 of section 35 of the CPC clarifies that the expression costs includes legal fees and expenses incurred and all other expenses incurred in connection with the proceedings. In my assessment of it this would therefore include reasonable fees and costs of institution i.e. court fees and attendance cost as also all legal fees. These are set out in a statement tendered by plaintiffs[9].

Under section 35A of the Code of Civil Procedure, the court can award the compensatory costs only in a case where defendant objects that the claim is false or vexatious to the knowledge of the plaintiff and the same was ultimately found to be false or vexatious. The costs awarded under section 35A of the Code are compensatory only and not penal. Sub section (2) has been omitted and as such the limit of cost has been done away with.

Section 35B of the Code of Civil Procedure provides that the costs of and incident to all suits shall be determined at the discretion of the court. A court lacking jurisdiction to try suit can also burden a party with costs. It provides for costs for causing delay in hearing of a suit or for taking any step therein. The delay may be caused by a party on any of the two grounds- the party fails to take the step which he was required under law to take on the date fixed, and the party obtains an adjournment for taking such step or for producing evidence or any other ground.

Order XVII of the Code deals with adjournments and the costs, it has to be read with section 35B. It is obligatory for the court to record reason for granting adjournments, which cannot be more than three times to a party during hearing of the suit. It also provides that the fact that the pleader of a party is engaged in another court, shall not be a ground for adjournment. In addition to the above, The Commercial Courts Act provides for imposition of costs for failure of a party to comply with at different stages of a commercial dispute trial:-

Written statement

Or. V R. 1 and Or. VIII R. 1, *proviso* provide that where the defendant fails to file written statement within the said period of thirty days, he shall be allowed to file the written statement on payment of such costs as court deems fit within one hundred twenty days from date of service of summons.

---

9 2018 SCC Online Bom 19973

Interrogatories

Or.XI R.2(3) provides that in adjusting the costs of the suit inquiry shall at the instance of any party be made into the propriety of exhibiting such interrogatories, and if it is the opinion of the taxing officer or of the court, either with or without an application for inquiry, that such interrogatories have been exhibited unreasonably, vexatiously, or at improper length, the costs occasioned by the said interrogatories and the answers thereto shall be paid in any event by the party in fault.

Inspection

Or.XI R.3(6) provides that the Court may impose exemplary costs against a defaulting party, who wilfully or negligently failed to disclose all documents pertaining to a suit or essential for a decision therein and which are in their power, possession, control or custody or where a Court holds that inspection or copies of any documents had been wrongfully or unreasonably withheld or refused.

Admission & denial of documents:

Or XI R. 4 (6) provides that in the event that the Court holds that any party has unduly refused to admit a document under any of the above criteria,–costs (including exemplary costs) for deciding on admissibility of a document may be imposed by the Court on such party.

Production

Or. XI R. 5 (4) The Court may draw an adverse inference against a party refusing to produce such document after issuance of a notice to produce and where sufficient reasons for such non-production are not given and order costs.

Case Management Hearing

Or. XV-A R. 7 (1) provides that the Court shall not adjourn the Case Management Hearing for the sole reason that the advocate appearing on behalf of a party is not present:

Provided that an adjournment of the hearing is sought in advance by moving an application, the Court may adjourn the hearing to another date upon the payment of such costs as the Court deems fit, by the party moving such application.

R.8. provides that where any party fails to comply with the order of the Court passed in a Case Management Hearing, the Court shall have the power to (*a*) condone such non-compliance by payment of costs to the Court.

The Arbitration and Conciliation Act, 1996 (as amended in 2015) has also made extensive provision to deal with the cost for both arbitral tribunal as well as court. The costs of an arbitration shall be fixed by the arbitral tribunal in accordance with section 31A.[10]

531A. Regime for costs.

1. In relation to any arbitration proceeding or a proceeding under any of the provisions of this Act pertaining to the arbitration, the Court or arbitral tribunal, notwithstanding anything contained in the Code of Civil Procedure, 1908, shall have the discretion to determine –

   a. Whether costs are payable by one party to another;

   b. The amount of such costs;

   c. When such costs are to be paid. Explanation – For the purpose of this sub-section, "costs" means reasonable costs relating to –

      i. The fees and expenses of the arbitrators, Courts and witnesses;

      ii. Legal fees and expenses;

      iii. Any administration fees of the institution supervising the arbitration; and

      iv. Any other expenses incurred in connection with the arbitral or Court proceedings and the arbitral award.

---

10   Sec 31 (8) of Arbitration & Conciliation Act, 1996

2. If the Court or arbitral tribunal decides to make an order as to payment of costs, (a) The general rule is that the unsuccessful party will be ordered to pay the costs of the successful party; or (b) The Court or the arbitral tribunal may make a different order for reasons to be recorded in writing.

3. In determining the costs, the Court or the arbitral tribunal shall have regard to all the circumstances, including –

   a. The conduct of all the parties;

   b. Whether a party has succeeded partly in the case;

   c. Whether the party had made a frivolous counter claim leading to delay in the disposal of the arbitral proceedings; and

   d. Whether any reasonable offer to settle the dispute is made by a party and refused by the other party.

4. The Court or the arbitral tribunal may make any order under this section including the order that a party shall pay–

   i. A proportion of another party's costs;

   ii. A stated amount in respect of another party's costs;

      i. Costs from or until a certain date only;

      ii. Costs incurred before proceedings have begun;

      iii. Costs relating to particular steps taken in the proceedings;

      iv. Costs relating only to a distinct part of the proceedings; and

      v. Interest on costs from or until a certain date.

5. An agreement which has the effect that a party is to pay the whole or part of the costs of the arbitration in any event shall be only valid if such agreement is made after the dispute in question has arisen.

10

SUMMARY PROCEDURE

"....by the way, although it is important that judicial business management by engineering, not tinkering, so as to produce efficient expedition, is in urgent, high-priority item on the agenda of court reform, to be radically undertaken none too soon."

– Justice V R Krishna Aiyer in Babu Singh
v. State of U P, AIR 1978 SC 527

Summary, is a short application to a Court without the formality of a full procedure. Summary judgment is a judgment on a claim or defence about which there is no genuine issue of material fact and upon which the movant is entitled to prevail a matter of law. The court considers the contents of the pleadings, the motions, and additional evidence adduced by the parties to determine whether there is a genuine issue of material fact rather than one of law. This procedural device allows the speedy disposition of a controversy without the need of trial. It may be referred to show cause proceedings.

The object of provision of Or. XXXVII of Code of Civil Procedure is that when there is a written document which ex facie, in itself, without any further factual events to be pleaded as a cause of action in the suit, admits and acknowledges liability and obligation of the defendant to pay to the plaintiff and only then a suit can be filed under summary procedure. This provision is with respect to filing of the suits either on the basis of a negotiable instrument or a written contract of guarantee or a written contract obliging payment of liquidated amount as contained in Rule 1 of this Order.

The Supreme Court in **Milkhiram (India) Private Ltd. v Chamanlal Bros.**[1] held, "'Taken by and large, the object is to see that the defendant does not unnecessarily prolong the litigation and prevent the plaintiff from obtaining an early decree by raising untenable and frivolous defences in a class of cases where speedy decisions are desirable in the interests of trade and commerce. In general, therefore, the test is to see whether the defence raises a real Issue and not a sham one, in the sense that, if the facts alleged by the defendant are established, there would be a good, or even a plausible, defence on those facts."

It appears that this Order XXXVII is meant for addressing commercial disputes so that the plaintiff may be saved from lengthy litigation. In an old judgment of Supreme Court in **Santosh Kumar v Bhai Mool Singh**[2] High Court decision arising out of a suit instituted in the Court of Commercial Subordinate Judge, Delhi in Suit No. 264 of 1956 under Order XXXVII, C.P.C. was being considered. However, this provision is applicable to very limited kind of suits as listed in R.1.

The Commercial Courts Act, 2015 has not done away with this Order but in addition to the same has inserted an Order XIII-A which empowers the court to decide a claim pertaining to commercial dispute without recording oral evidence.

---

1 AIR 1965 SC 1698
2 1958 AIR 321, 1958 SCR 1211

ORDER XIII-A

SUMMARY JUDGMENT

1. **Scope of and classes of suits to which this Order applies.—**

   1. This Order sets out the procedure by which Courts may decide a claim pertaining to any Commercial Dispute without recording oral evidence.

   2. For the purposes of this Order, the word "claim" shall include—

      a. part of a claim;

      b. any particular question on which the claim (whether in whole or in part) depends; or

      c. a counterclaim, as the case may be.

   3. Notwithstanding anything to the contrary, an application for summary judgment under this Order shall not be made in a suit in respect of any Commercial Dispute that is originally filed as a summary suit under Order XXXVII.

2. **Stage for application for summary judgment.—**An applicant may apply for summary judgment at any time after summons has been served on the defendant:

   Provided that, no application for summary judgment may be made by such applicant after the Court has framed the issues in respect of the suit.

3. **Grounds for summary judgment.—**The Court may give a summary judgment against a plaintiff or defendant on a claim if it considers that—

   a. the plaintiff has no real prospect of succeeding on the claim or the defendant has no real prospect of successfully defending the claim, as the case may be; and

   b. there is no other compelling reason why the claim should not be disposed of before recording of oral evidence.

4. Procedure.—

1. An application for summary judgment to a Court shall, in addition to any other matters the applicant may deem relevant, include the matters set forth in sub-clauses (*a*) to (*f*) mentioned hereunder:—

    a. the application must contain a statement that it is an application for summary judgment made under this Order;

    b. the application must precisely disclose all material facts and identify the point of law, if any;

    c. in the event the applicant seeks to rely upon any documentary evidence, the applicant must,—

        i. include such documentary evidence in its application, and

        ii. identify the relevant content of such documentary evidence on which the applicant relies;

    d. the application must state the reason why there are no real prospects of succeeding on the claim or defending the claim, as the case may be;

    e. the application must state what relief the applicant is seeking and briefly state the grounds for seeking such relief.

2. Where a hearing for summary judgment is fixed, the respondent must be given at least thirty days' notice of:—

    a. the date fixed for the hearing; and

    b. the claim that is proposed to be decided by the Court at such hearing.

3. The respondent may, within thirty days of the receipt of notice of application of summary judgment or notice of hearing (whichever is earlier), file a reply addressing the matters set forth in clauses *(a)* to *(f)* mentioned hereunder in addition to any other matters that the respondent may deem relevant:—

a. the reply must precisely—
   i. disclose all material facts;
   ii. identify the point of law, if any; and
   iii. state the reasons why the relief sought by the applicant should not be granted;
b. in the event the respondent seeks to rely upon any documentary evidence in its reply, the respondent must—
   i. include such documentary evidence in its reply; and
   ii. identify the relevant content of such documentary evidence on which the respondent relies;
c. the reply must state the reason why there are real prospects of succeeding on the claim or defending the claim, as the case may be;
d. the reply must concisely state the issues that should be framed for trial;
e. the reply must identify what further evidence shall be brought on record at trial that could not be brought on record at the stage of summary judgment; and
f. the reply must state why, in light of the evidence or material on record if any, the Court should not proceed to summary judgment.

5. **Evidence for hearing of summary judgment.—**
   1. Notwithstanding anything in this Order, if the respondent in an application for summary judgment wishes to rely on additional documentary evidence during the hearing, the respondent must:—
      a. file such documentary evidence; and
      b. serve copies of such documentary evidence on every other party to the application at least fifteen days prior to the date of the hearing.

2. Notwithstanding anything in this Order, if the applicant for summary judgment wishes to rely on documentary evidence in reply to the defendant's documentary evidence, the applicant must:—

   a. file such documentary evidence in reply; and

   b. serve a copy of such documentary evidence on the respondent at least five days prior to the date of the hearing.

3. Notwithstanding anything to the contrary, sub-rules (*1*) and (*2*) shall not require documentary evidence to be:—

   a. filed if such documentary evidence has already been filed; or

   b. served on a party on whom it has already been served.

6. **Orders that may be made by Court.—**

   1. On an application made under this Order, the Court may make such orders that it may deem fit in its discretion including the following:—

      a. judgment on the claim;

      b. conditional order in accordance with Rule 7 mentioned hereunder;

      c. dismissing the application;

      d. dismissing part of the claim and a judgment on part of the claim that is not dismissed;

      e. striking out the pleadings (whether in whole or in part); or

      f. further directions to proceed for case management under Order XV-A.

   2. Where the Court makes any of the orders as set forth in sub-rule (*1*) (*a*) to (*f*), the Court shall record its reasons for making such order.

7. Conditional order.—

1. Where it appears to the Court that it is possible that a claim or defence may succeed but it is improbable that it shall do so, the Court may make a conditional order as set forth in Rule 6 (*1*) (*b*).

2. Where the Court makes a conditional order, it may:—

   a. make it subject to all or any of the following conditions:—

      i. require a party to deposit a sum of money in the Court;

      ii. require a party to take a specified step in relation to the claim or defence, as the case may be;

      iii. require a party, as the case may be, to give such security or provide such surety for restitution of costs as the Court deems fit and proper;

      iv. impose such other conditions, including providing security for restitution of losses that any party is likely to suffer during the pendency of the suit, as the Court may deem fit in its discretion; and

   b. specify the consequences of the failure to comply with the conditional order, including passing a judgment against the party that have not complied with the conditional order.

8. **Power to impose costs.**—The Court may make an order for payment of costs in an application for summary judgment in accordance with the provisions of sections 35 and 35A of the Code.'.

11
ARBITRATION MATTER

'There was a refreshing absence of that forensic chauvinism which sometimes disfigures international debates in this field. Nevertheless, it must be recognised that the distinguished people who took part, whether they were professors of law or senior officials in government departments or executives of national arbitration institutions, were in the main more acquainted with the theory than with the practice of arbitration. Again, the majority of those who did have direct personal experience of arbitration had acquired it in the field of large-scale, formal, heavily-documented and very expensive arbitrations of a kind quite different from those with which this present Congress is concerned.'

– Lord Mustill

The Commercial arbitration is becoming more and more preferred mode of dispute resolution for complex commercial disputes. The arbitration clauses in standard form/adhesion contracts are used mostly in government entities and public sector undertakings, its prominent use can be seen in Non- Banking Finance Companies' contracts. Recent trends in Arbitration are to include provision with regard to time limits and less time taken in resorting the dispute, encouraging Institutional arbitration, discouraging filing frivolous applications challenging arbitral awards, narrowing the court intervention and making arbitration cost effective. The executive has also sought to bring about efficiencies in arbitration involving government entities by encouraging ministries to comply with arbitration awards. At the same time, arbitrary use of the arbitration clause has made the role of courts more relevant and a greater scrutiny of malpractices involved can be done by the court.

An arbitration clause is a part of the contract. It being a part of collateral terms need not, in all situations, perish with coming to an end of the contract. It may survive. This concept of separability of the arbitration clause is now widely accepted. In line with this thinking, the UNICITRAL Model Law on International Commercial Arbitration incorporates the doctrines of separability in Article 16(1). The Indian law-The Arbitration and Conciliation Act, 1996, which is based on the UNICITRAL Model Law, also explicitly adopts this approach in Section 16(1)(b). But this must be distinguished from the situation where the claim itself was to be raised during the subsistence of a contract.[1]

Commercial Courts Act, 2015 does confer jurisdiction upon Commercial Courts to decide such matters as brought before it.

10. Jurisdiction in respect of arbitration matters.—Where the subject-matter of an arbitration is a commercial dispute of a Specified Value and—(1) If such arbitration is an international commercial arbitration, all applications or appeals arising out of such arbitration under the provisions of the Arbitration and Conciliation Act, 1996 (26 of 1996) that have been filed in a High Court, shall be heard and disposed of by the Commercial Division where such Commercial Division has been constituted in such High Court.

---

1   P. Manohar Reddy & Bros. v. Maharastra Krishna Valley Development Corpn. (2009) 2 SCC 494

(2) If such arbitration is other than an international commercial arbitration, all applications or appeals arising out of such arbitration under the provisions of the Arbitration and Conciliation Act, 1996 (26 of 1996) that have been filed on the original side of the High Court, shall be heard and disposed of by the Commercial Division where such Commercial Division has been constituted in such High Court.

(3) If such arbitration is other than an international commercial arbitration, all applications or appeals arising out of such arbitration under the provisions of the Arbitration and Conciliation Act, 1996 (26 of 1996) that would ordinarily lie before any principal civil court of original jurisdiction in a district (not being a High Court) shall be filed in, and heard and disposed of by the Commercial Court exercising territorial jurisdiction over such arbitration where such Commercial Court has been constituted.

Section 12(2) of Commercial Courts Act deals with valuation of an application arising out of arbitral award. It provides, **"(2) The aggregate value of the claim and counter claim, if any as set out in the statement of claim and the counterclaim, if any, in an arbitration of a commercial dispute shall be the basis for determining whether such arbitration is subject to the jurisdiction of a Commercial Division, Commercial Appellate Division or Commercial Court, as the case may be."**

The Arbitration and Conciliation Act, 1996 defines "courts" under section 2(1)(e) as, "Court" means –

i. In the case of an arbitration other than international commercial arbitration, the principal Civil Court of original jurisdiction in a district, and includes the High Court in exercise of its ordinary original civil jurisdiction, having jurisdiction to decide the questions forming the subject-matter of the arbitration if the same had been the subject-matter of a suit, but does not include any civil court of a grade inferior to such principal Civil Court, or any Court of Small Causes;

ii. In the case of international commercial arbitration, the High Court in exercise of its ordinary original civil jurisdiction, having jurisdiction to decide the questions forming the subject-matter of the arbitration if the same had been the subject matter of a suit, and in other cases, a High Court having jurisdiction to hear appeals from decrees of courts subordinate to that High Court;

The Arbitration and Conciliation Act, 1996 has defined role of courts at different stages of arbitration proceeding right from pre-arbitration proceeding to that of post-award proceeding including challenges to the award as well as enforcement of award by the courts. Disputes within the defined specified value limits shall be dealt with by the Commercial court, subject to other factors like territorial jurisdiction. The provisions in the Arbitration and Conciliation Act providing different roles to court is examined below:

Section 5 of the Arbitration and Conciliation Act, 1996 provides that notwithstanding anything contained in any other law for the time being in force, in matters governed by this Part, no judicial authority shall intervene except where so provided in this Part. The power of judicial review vested in the superior courts undoubtedly has wide amplitude but when there exists an arbitration agreement, the writ court ordinarily would not exercise its discretionary jurisdiction to enter into the dispute.[2]

The expression "judicial authority" as used in section 5 of has not been defined in the Arbitration and Conciliation Act, 1996. What is defined in section 2(1)(e) thereof is "court". In its ordinary parlance "judicial authority" would comprehend a court defined under the 1996 Act but also courts which would either be a civil court or other authorities which perform judicial functions or quasi-judicial functions. The expression "judicial authority" must be interpreted having regard to the purport and object for which the 1996 Act was enacted.[3]

---

2   Sanjana M Wig v. Hindustan Petroleum Corpn Ltd. (2005) 8 SCC 242
3   Morgan Securities & Credit (P) Ltd. v. Modi Rubber Ltd. (2006) 12 SCC 642

Section 8 of Arbitration and Conciliation Act, 1996 again uses the expression "judicial authority" in respect of power to refer parties to arbitration where there is an arbitration agreement. It provides:

1. A judicial authority, before which an action is brought in a matter which is the subject of an arbitration agreement shall, if a party to the arbitration agreement or any person claiming through or under him, so applies not later than the date of submitting his first statement on the substance of the dispute, then, notwithstanding any judgment, decree or order of the Supreme Court or any court, refer the parties to arbitration unless it finds that prima facie no valid arbitration agreement exists.

2. The application referred to in sub-section (1) shall not be entertained unless it is accompanied by the original arbitration agreement or a duly certified copy thereof.

Provided that where the original arbitration agreement or a certified copy thereof is not available with the party applying for reference to arbitration under sub-section (1), and the said agreement or certified copy is retained by the other party to that agreement, then, the party so applying shall file such application along with a copy of the arbitration agreement and a petition praying the Court to call upon the other party to produce the original arbitration agreement or its duly certified copy before that Court.

In section 9 of the of Arbitration and Conciliation Act, 1996, the expression "Court" has been used to deal with interim measures.

1. A party may, before, or during arbitral proceedings or at any time after the making of the arbitral award but before it is enforced in accordance with section 36, apply to a court –

    i. For the appointment of a guardian for a minor or person of unsound mind for the purposes of arbitral proceedings; or

    ii. For an interim measure or protection in respect of any of the following matters, namely:

a. The preservation, interim custody or sale of any goods which are the subject matter of the arbitration agreement;

b. Securing the amount in dispute in the arbitration;

c. The detention, preservation or inspection of any property or thing which is the subject-matter of the dispute in arbitration, or as to which any question may arise therein and authorising for any of the aforesaid purposes any person to enter upon any land or building in the possession of any party, or authorising any samples to be taken or any observation to be made, or experiment to be tried, which may be necessary or expedient for the purpose of obtaining full information or evidence;

d. Interim injunction or the appointment of a receiver;

e. Such other interim measure of protection as may appear to the Court to be just and convenient, And the Court shall have the same power for making orders as it has for the purpose of, and in relation to, any proceedings before it.

2. Where, before the commencement of the arbitral proceedings, a Court passes an order for any interim measure of protection under sub-section (1), the arbitral proceedings shall be commenced within a period of ninety days from the date of such order or within such further time as the Court may determine. (3) Once the arbitral tribunal has been constituted, the Court shall not entertain an application under sub-section (1), unless the Court finds that circumstances exists which may not render remedy provided under Section 17 efficacious. Section 27 of the of Arbitration and Conciliation Act, 1996 provides that the Arbitral tribunal, or a party with the approval of the arbitral tribunal, may apply to the Court for assistance in taking evidence[4]. Section 29A(4) Arbitration

---

[4] Sec. 27(1) of Arbitration and Conciliation Act, 1996

and Conciliation Act, 1996 provides that if the award is not made within the period specified in sub-section (1) or the extended period specified under sub-section (3), the mandate of the arbitrator(s) shall terminate unless the Court has, either prior to or after the expiry of the period so specified, extend the period. Recourse to a court against an arbitral award may be made only by an application for setting aside such award in accordance with sub section (2) and (3). Section 36 provides that an application for enforcement shall be filed in the court which shall enforce it as if a court of decree.

13. Challenge procedure.—(1) Subject to sub-section (4), the parties are free to agree on a procedure for challenging an arbitrator. (2) Failing any agreement referred to in sub-section (1), a party who intends to challenge an arbitrator shall, within fifteen days after becoming aware of the constitution of the arbitral tribunal or after becoming aware of any circumstances referred to in sub-section (3) of section 12, send a written statement of the reasons for the challenge to the arbitral tribunal. (3) Unless the arbitrator challenged under sub-section (2) withdraws from his office or the other party agrees to the challenge, the arbitral tribunal shall decide on the challenge. (4) If a challenge under any procedure agreed upon by the parties or under the procedure under sub-section (2) is not successful, the arbitral tribunal shall continue the arbitral proceedings and make an arbitral award. (5) Where an arbitral award is made under sub-section (4), the party challenging the arbitrator may make an application for setting aside such an arbitral award in accordance with section 34. (6) Where an arbitral award is set aside on an application made under sub-section (5), **the Court may decide as to whether the arbitrator who is challenged is entitled to any fees.**

14. Failure or impossibility to act.—(1) 3 [The mandate of an arbitrator shall terminate and he shall be substituted by another arbitrator, if]— (a) he becomes de jure or de facto unable to perform his functions or for other reasons fails to act without undue delay; and

(b) he withdraws from his office or the parties agree to the termination of his mandate. (2) If a controversy remains concerning any of the grounds referred to in clause (a) of sub-section (1), a party may, **unless otherwise agreed by the parties, apply to the Court to decide on the termination of the mandate.** (3) If, under this section or sub-section (3) of section 13, an arbitrator withdraws from his office or a party agrees to the termination of the mandate of an arbitrator, it shall not imply acceptance of the validity of any ground referred to in this section or sub-section (3) of section 12.

Sec. 27. Court assistance in taking evidence.—

1. The arbitral tribunal, or a party with the approval of the arbitral tribunal, may apply to the Court for assistance in taking evidence.
2. The application shall specify— (a) the names and addresses of the parties and the arbitrators; (b) the general nature of the claim and the relief sought; (c) the evidence to be obtained, in particular,— (i) the name and address of any person to be heard as witness or expert witness and a statement of the subject-matter of the testimony required; (ii) the description of any document to be produced or property to be inspected. (3) The Court may, within its competence and according to its rules on taking evidence, execute the request by ordering that the evidence be provided directly to the arbitral tribunal. (4) The Court may, while making an order under sub-section (3), issue the same processes to witnesses as it may issue in suits tried before it. (5) Persons failing to attend in accordance with such process, or making any other default, or refusing to give their evidence, or guilty of any contempt to the arbitral tribunal during the conduct of arbitral proceedings, shall be subject to the like disadvantages, penalties and punishments by order of the Court on the representation of the arbitral tribunal as they would incur for the like offences in suits tried before the Court. (6) In this section the expression "Processes" includes summonses and

commissions for the examination of witnesses and summonses to produce documents.

29A. **Time limit for arbitral award.**—(1) The award shall be made within a period of twelve months from the date the arbitral tribunal enters upon the reference. Explanation.—For the purpose of this sub-section, an arbitral tribunal shall be deemed to have entered upon the reference on the date on which the arbitrator or all the arbitrators, as the case may be, have received notice, in writing, of their appointment. (2) If the award is made within a period of six months from the date the arbitral tribunal enters upon the reference, the arbitral tribunal shall be entitled to receive such amount of additional fees as the parties may agree. (3) The parties may, by consent, extend the period specified in sub-section (1) for making award for a further period not exceeding six months. (4) If the award is not made within the period specified in sub-section (1) or the extended period specified under sub-section (3), the mandate of the arbitrator(s) shall terminate unless the Court has, either prior to or after the expiry of the period so specified, extended the period: Provided that while extending the period under this sub-section, if the Court finds that the proceedings have been delayed for the reasons attributable to the arbitral tribunal, then, it may order reduction of fees of arbitrator(s) by not exceeding five per cent. for each month of such delay. (5) The extension of period referred to in sub-section (4) may be on the application of any of the parties and may be granted only for sufficient cause and on such terms and conditions as may be imposed by the Court. (6) While extending the period referred to in sub-section (4), it shall be open to the Court to substitute one or all of the arbitrators and if one or all of the arbitrators are substituted, the arbitral proceedings shall continue from the stage already reached and on the basis of the evidence and material already on record, and the arbitrator(s) appointed under this section shall be deemed to have received the said evidence and material. (7) In the event of arbitrator(s) being appointed under this section, the arbitral tribunal thus reconstituted shall be deemed to be in continuation of the previously appointed arbitral tribunal. (8) It shall be open to the Court to impose actual or exemplary costs upon any of the parties under this section. (9) An application filed under sub-section (5) shall be disposed of by the Court as expeditiously as possible and endeavour shall be made to dispose of the matter within a period of sixty days from the date of service of notice on the opposite party.

31A. Regime for costs.—(1) In relation to any arbitration proceeding or a proceeding under any of the provisions of this Act pertaining to the arbitration, the Court or arbitral tribunal, notwithstanding anything contained in the Code of Civil Procedure, 1908 (5 of 1908), shall have the discretion to determine— (a) whether costs are payable by one party to another; (b) the amount of such costs; and (c) when such costs are to be paid. Explanation.—For the purpose of this sub-section, "costs" means reasonable costs relating to— (i) the fees and expenses of the arbitrators, Courts and witnesses; (ii) legal fees and expenses; (iii) any administration fees of the institution supervising the arbitration; and (iv) any other expenses incurred in connection with the arbitral or Court proceedings and the arbitral award. (2) If the Court or arbitral tribunal decides to make an order as to payment of costs,— (a) the general rule is that the unsuccessful party shall be ordered to pay the costs of the successful party; or (b) the Court or arbitral tribunal may make a different order for reasons to be recorded in writing. (3) In determining the costs, the Court or arbitral tribunal shall have regard to all the circumstances, including— (a) the conduct of all the parties; (b) whether a party has succeeded partly in the case; (c) whether the party had made a frivolous counterclaim leading to delay in the disposal of the arbitral proceedings; and (d) whether any reasonable offer to settle the dispute is made by a party and refused by the other party. (4) The Court or arbitral tribunal may make any order under this section including the order that a party shall pay— (a) a proportion of another party's costs; (b) a stated amount in respect of another party's costs; (c) costs from or until a certain date only; (d) costs incurred before proceedings have begun; (e) costs relating to particular steps taken in the proceedings; (f) costs relating only to a distinct part of the proceedings; and (g) interest on costs from or until a certain date. (5) An agreement which has the effect that a party is to pay the whole or part of the costs of the arbitration in any event shall be only valid if such agreement is made after the dispute in question has arisen.]

34. Application for setting aside arbitral award.—(1) Recourse to a Court against an arbitral award may be made only by an application for setting aside such award in accordance with sub-section (2) and sub-section (3). 20 (2) An arbitral award may be set aside by the Court only if— (a) the party making the application furnishes proof that— (i) a party was under some incapacity, or (ii) the arbitration agreement is not valid under the law to which the parties have subjected it or, failing any indication thereon, under the law for the time being in force; or (iii) the party making the application was not given proper notice of the appointment of an arbitrator or of the arbitral proceedings or was otherwise unable to present his case; or (iv) the arbitral award deals with a dispute not contemplated by or not falling within the terms of the submission to arbitration, or it contains decisions on matters beyond the scope of the submission to arbitration: Provided that, if the decisions on matters submitted to arbitration can be separated from those not so submitted, only that part of the arbitral award which contains decisions on matters not submitted to arbitration may be set aside; or (v) the composition of the arbitral tribunal or the arbitral procedure was not in accordance with the agreement of the parties, unless such agreement was in conflict with a provision of this Part from which the parties cannot derogate, or, failing such agreement, was not in accordance with this Part; or (b) the Court finds that— (i) the subject-matter of the dispute is not capable of settlement by arbitration under the law for the time being in force, or (ii) the arbitral award is in conflict with the public policy of India. 1 [Explanation 1.—For the avoidance of any doubt, it is clarified that an award is in conflict with the public policy of

India, only if,— (i) the making of the award was induced or affected by fraud or corruption or was in violation of section 75 or section 81; or (ii) it is in contravention with the fundamental policy of Indian law; or (iii) it is in conflict with the most basic notions of morality or justice. Explanation 2.— For the avoidance of doubt, the test as to whether there is a contravention with the fundamental policy of Indian law shall not entail a review on the merits of the dispute.] 2 [(2A) An arbitral award arising out of arbitrations other than international commercial arbitrations, may also be set aside by the Court, if the Court finds that the award is vitiated by patent illegality appearing on the face of the award: Provided that an award shall not be set aside merely on the ground of an erroneous application of the law or by reappreciation of evidence.] (3) An application for setting aside may not be made after three months have elapsed from the date on which the party making that application had received the arbitral award or, if a request had been made under section 33, from the date on which that request had been disposed of by the arbitral tribunal: Provided that if the Court is satisfied that the applicant was prevented by sufficient cause from making the application within the said period of three months it may entertain the application within a further period of thirty days, but not thereafter. (4) On receipt of an application under sub-section (1), the Court may, where it is appropriate and it is so requested by a party, adjourn the proceedings for a period of time determined by it in order to give the arbitral tribunal an opportunity to resume the arbitral proceedings or to take such other action as in the opinion of arbitral tribunal will eliminate the grounds for setting aside the arbitral award. 1 [(5) An application under this section shall be filed by a party only after issuing a prior notice to the other party and such application shall be accompanied by an affidavit by the applicant endorsing compliance with the said requirement. (6) An application under this section shall be disposed of expeditiously, and in any event, within a period of one year from the date on which the notice referred to in sub-section (5) is served upon the other party.]

Section 37 of the Act says an appeal shall lie from the specific orders as provided (and from no others) to the Court authorized by law to hear appeals from original decrees of the Court passing the order.

Neither the UNICITRAL (Model) law nor the Arbitration and Conciliation Act, 1996 use the words, "venue" or "seat" in respect of arbitration proceeding but the twin concept is the crux to define the jurisdiction of courts.

The Commercial Courts Act, 2015 confers jurisdiction on Commercial Court in sec. 10 as follows:

Sec. 42. Jurisdiction-Notwithstanding anything contained elsewhere in this Part or in any other law for the time being in force, where with respect to an arbitration agreement any application under this Part has been made in a Court, that Court alone shall have jurisdiction over the arbitral proceedings and all subsequent applications arising out of that agreement and the arbitral proceedings shall be made in that Court and in no other Court.

Sec.50.

Prior to Amendment Act of 2015 in Arbitration & Conciliation Act, the word "court" means and includes only two courts- Districts Courts and High Courts having original civil jurisdiction. After the amendment, it depends on the kind of arbitration. For international commercial arbitration it is only the High Courts, and for other arbitration it is Districts Courts and High Courts having original civil jurisdiction.

Prior to Amendment in 2015, the Supreme Court examined the definition of 'court' and 'jurisdiction' and laid down the law, "Our conclusions therefore on Section 2(1)(e) and Section 42 of the Arbitration Act, 1996 are as follows:

a. Section 2(1)(e) contains an exhaustive definition marking out only the Principal Civil Court of original jurisdiction in a district or a High Court having original civil jurisdiction in the State, and no other court as "court" for the purpose of Part-I of the Arbitration Act, 1996.

b. The expression "with respect to an arbitration agreement" makes it clear that Section 42 will apply to all applications made whether before or during arbitral proceedings or after an Award is pronounced under Part-I of the 1996 Act.

c. However, Section 42 only applies to applications made under Part-I if they are made to a court as defined. Since applications made Under Section 8 are made to judicial authorities and since applications Under Section 11 are made to the Chief Justice or his designate, the judicial authority and the Chief Justice or his designate not being court as defined, such applications would be outside Section 42.

d. Section 9 applications being applications made to a court and Section 34 applications to set aside arbitral awards are applications which are within Section 42.

e. In no circumstances can the Supreme Court be "court" for the purposes of Section 2(1)(e), and whether the Supreme Court does or does not retain seisin after appointing an Arbitrator, applications will follow the first application made before either a High Court having original jurisdiction in the State or a Principal Civil court having original jurisdiction in the district as the case may be.

f. Section 42 will apply to applications made after the arbitral proceedings have come to an end provided they are made under Part-I.

g. If a first application is made to a court which is neither a Principal Court of original jurisdiction in a district or a High Court exercising original jurisdiction in a State, such application not being to a court as defined would be outside Section 42. Also, an application made to a court without subject matter jurisdiction would be outside Section 42.[5]

Section 29-A of Arbitration & Conciliation Act provides limit for arbitral award.—

1. The award in matters other than international commercial arbitration shall be made by the arbitral tribunal within a period of twelve months from the date of completion of pleadings under sub-section (4) of Section 23:

   Provided that the award in the matter of international commercial arbitration may be made as expeditiously as possible and endeavour may be made to dispose of the matter within a period of twelve months from the date of completion of pleadings under sub-section (4) of Section 23.]

2. If the award is made within a period of six months from the date the arbitral tribunal enters upon the reference, the arbitral tribunal shall be entitled to receive such amount of additional fees as the parties may agree.

3. The parties may, by consent, extend the period specified in sub-section (1) for making award for a further period not exceeding six months.

4. If the award is not made within the period specified in sub-section (1) or the extended period specified under sub-section (3), the mandate of the arbitrator(s) shall terminate unless the court has, either prior to or after the expiry of the period so specified, extended the period:

   Provided that while extending the period under this sub-section, if the court finds that the proceedings have been delayed for the reasons attributable to the arbitral tribunal, then, it may order

---

5 State of West Bengal v. Associated Contractors (10.09.2014 - SC): MANU/SC/0793/2014

reduction of fees of arbitrator(s) by not exceeding five percent for each month of such delay:

[2] [Provided further that where an application under sub-section (5) is pending, the mandate of the arbitrator shall continue till the disposal of the said application:

Provided also that the arbitrator shall be given an opportunity of being heard before the fees is reduced.]

5. The extension of period referred to in sub-section (4) may be on the application of any of the parties and may be granted only for sufficient cause and on such terms and conditions as may be imposed by the court.

6. While extending the period referred to in sub-section (4), it shall be open to the court to substitute one or all of the arbitrators and if one or all of the arbitrators are substituted, the arbitral proceedings shall continue from the stage already reached and on the basis of the evidence and material already on record, and the arbitrator(s) appointed under this section shall be deemed to have received the said evidence and material.

7. In the event of arbitrator(s) being appointed under this section, the arbitral tribunal thus reconstituted shall be deemed to be in continuation of the previously appointed arbitral tribunal.

8. It shall be open to the court to impose actual or exemplary costs upon any of the parties under this section.

9. An application filed under sub-section (5) shall be disposed of by the court as expeditiously as possible and endeavour shall be made to dispose of the matter within a period of sixty days from the date of service of notice on the opposite party.

By virtue of the Arbitration and Conciliation (Amendment) Act, 2019 ('**2019 Amendment Act**'), a further period of up to six months was added for the purpose of completion of pleadings, thereby effectively requiring an award to be passed within a period of eighteen months from the date on which the arbitral tribunal was constituted, subject to a further extension of a maximum period of six months by consent between the parties.

The only avenue for the revival and/or continuation of the arbitral proceedings in this regard would be to approach the competent Court with an application under Section 29A(5) of the Arbitration and Conciliation Act, 1996 ('**Arbitration Act**') seeking extension of time for completion of the arbitral proceedings ('**application for extension**'). While adjudicating upon such a request, a Court is competent to impose costs on a party as also direct a reduction in the professional fees of the arbitral tribunal, if it were to specifically attribute responsibility for the delay in the conduct of the arbitral proceedings to the concerned entity(s), while ultimately extending the time for completion of the arbitration proceedings.

However, in a case where the Court finds the arbitration proceedings conducted by the arbitral tribunal to be completely unconducive to a structured and timely completion of the arbitration process, the Court may very well exercise an option to substitute one or all of the arbitrators, and if one or all of the arbitrators are so substituted by the Court, then the arbitration proceedings would continue from the stage already reached and on the basis of the evidence and material already on record.

As would be evident from the above, when the time for rendering the award has expired, the adjudication of the application for extension is critical for the continuation of the proceedings. At the said stage, the parties would have invested significantly in the arbitration proceedings in the form of financial expenditure and man-hours, and an adverse decision in the form of the substitution of the arbitral tribunal, particularly when the proceedings are at an advanced stage such as the parties having already commenced oral arguments, could effectively set the arbitration back by many months as also lead to the attendant wastage of resources.

Though the further amendment to Section 29(A)(4) by the 2019 Amendment Act now mandates that the arbitration proceedings shall continue during the pendency of an application for extension before the Court has provided some succour by ensuring that the arbitration proceedings are not unnecessarily paused and derailed for the period when an application for extension is pending consideration before the Court, the ultimate fate of the continuing proceedings would still rest on the result of the final adjudication by the Court.

Considering the stakes involved, and the very real statutory possibility of the Court substituting the arbitral tribunal, it is but natural for a disgruntled party that has serious reservations about continuing with the arbitration proceedings to attempt to utilize this opportunity to get rid of an ostensibly unfavourable arbitral tribunal or arbitrator on issues completely unrelated to the aspect of delay.

For instance, a party apprehending that a particular arbitrator or the arbitral tribunal as a whole is biased against it, or that any decision taken by the arbitral tribunal in matters of procedure or on the merits at an interim stage may seriously disadvantage it, would attempt to use this as an opportunity to try and have the unpalatable arbitral tribunal or arbitrator substituted by the Court.

In the aforesaid background, what is of significance for the purpose of the present piece is the scope of the adjudication which the Court undertakes while considering an application for extension, and which scope is seemingly articulated in Section 29(A)(5) of the Arbitration Act as under:

"(5) The extension of period referred to in sub-section (4) may be on the application of any of the parties and **may be granted only for sufficient cause** and on such terms and conditions as may be imposed by the Court."

As is evident, the usage of the somewhat nebulous term "sufficient cause" in the context of the extension of time results in some ambiguity. Would the term "sufficient cause" refer only to the aspect of delay or would it also encompass within itself other elements which may give the Court serious food for thought as to the manner in which the arbitral tribunal has conducted the proceedings?

It is evident that adopting the latter approach could, in many cases, result in an application for extension resulting in a mini-trial pertaining to the conduct of the arbitration proceedings by the arbitral tribunal till the date of the filing of the application for extension before the Court. This would inevitably be coupled with a minute examination of each and every action or decision taken by the arbitral tribunal during the course of the proceedings, all from the prism of whether the Court, on an overall conspectus of the proceedings, is satisfied that "sufficient cause" has been demonstrated to extend the tenure of the arbitral tribunal.

In the aforesaid background, if one were to undertake a review of the judicial precedents on the issue, the Courts appear to have unanimously veered towards an extremely restrictive understanding of the term "sufficient cause" as appearing in Section 29A by inter-linking it with the element of delay alone. The High Court of Delhi in **NCC Ltd. v. Union of India**[6] has unequivocally held that Section 29A of the Arbitration Act is intended to counter the delay in the conclusion of arbitration proceedings alone, and cannot be sought to be utilized for the achievement of objectives that are alien to the said purpose in the following words:

"11. Section 29A of the Act is intended to sensitize the parties as also the Arbitral Tribunal to aim for culmination of the arbitration proceedings expeditiously. It is with this legislative intent, Section 29A was introduced in the Act by way of the Arbitration and Conciliation (Amendment) Act, 2015. This provision is not intended for a party to seek substitution of an Arbitrator only because the party has apprehension about the conduct of the arbitration proceedings by the said Arbitrator. The only ground for removal of the Arbitrator under Section 29A of the Act can be the failure of the Arbitrator to proceed expeditiously in the adjudication process."

---

6   2018 Scc Online 12699

The Court then further went on to observe that an allegation that the arbitral tribunal was biased against the resisting party would not be a relevant factor which would detain the Court while considering an application for extension in the following words:

"14. As far as the grievance of the respondents that the conduct of the arbitration proceedings are biased is concerned, the same cannot be the subject matter of the present proceedings. The respondents have also filed an application under Section 13 of the Act before the Arbitrator, which is pending adjudication. This Court, therefore, refrains from making an y observation on the said application. Even otherwise, in term of Section 13(4) of the Act, in case the said application is decided against the respondents, the remedy provided to the respondents would be to challenge the same alongwith the ultimate Award passed by the Arbitrator."

In a similar vein, in a unreported decision in **Orissa Concrete and Allied Industries Ltd. v. Union of India & Anr.**[7], the High Court of Delhi observed as under while brushing aside the resistance to an application for extension on the ground that the arbitral tribunal had allegedly not afforded the resisting party a sufficient opportunity of hearing:

"In my view, any issue with respect to the conduct of the Arbitration Proceedings, except the one relating to the expeditious disposal of the Arbitration Proceedings, cannot be raised by the respondent at this stage. These contentions can be raised by the respondent before the Arbitrator himself or in an application under Section 34 of the Act while challenging the award passed by the Arbitrator, if the respondent is aggrieved of the same. In exercise of power under Section 29A(5) of the Act, the Court is only to see if there is sufficient cause shown to extend the time for making of the award."

Various other High Courts have also arrived at a similar conclusion. To elucidate with a few examples, the High Court of Bombay in **FCA**

---

7   2016 SCC Online Delhi 3463

India Automobiles Pvt. Ltd. v. Torque Motor Cars Pvt. Ltd. & Anr[8], while granting the extension prayed for, refused to examine the correctness of various orders passed by the arbitral tribunal relating to fixation of fees and rejection of the application for termination of mandate filed by the resisting party under Sections 12 and 13 of the Arbitration Act, by holding the same to be beyond the purview of examination under Section 29A. Further, on a related note, the High Court of Gujarat in **Nilesh Ramanbhai Patel & Ors. v. Bhanubhai Ramanbhai Patel**[9] has pertinently observed that Section 29A of the Arbitration Act represents a complete code in itself.

An examination of the aforesaid precedents would categorically demonstrate that the scope of adjudication in an application for extension under Section 29A pertains only to the aspect of delay.

Insofar as other issues such as alleged bias and/or incorrect decisions on the merits or on matters of procedure by the arbitral tribunal are concerned, the applicable relevant provisions of the Arbitration Act would have to be taken recourse to by the parties, and these grievances cannot be sought to be dovetailed into and made part of the arsenal when seeking to resist an application for extension. It is evident that such an approach is not only in line with the legislative intent behind the incorporation of Section 29(A), which was to eschew delay rather than to enable a review by the Court of the conduct of the proceedings by the arbitral tribunal at the said stage.[6]

---

8 2018 SCC Online Bom 4371
9 Miscellaneous Civil Application (O J) No. 1 of 2018

12

APPEAL, REVISION & CIVIL WRIT

What is the argument on the other side? Only this, that no case has been found in which it has been done before. That argument does not appeal to me in the least.

If we never do anything which has not been done before, we shall never get anywhere. The law will stand still while the rest of the world goes on, and that will be bad for both

– Lord Denning 1899-1999.

The Commercial Courts Act, 2015 provides for appeal against the judgment or order passed by a Commercial Court, whereas the Code of Civil Procedure which provides that an appeal shall lie from every decree passed by any Court exercising original jurisdiction to the Court authorized to hear appeals from the decisions of such Court.[1] The memorandum shall be accompanied by a copy of the Judgment.[2] The Heading of section, however, is 'Appeals from decrees of Commercial Courts and Commercial Divisions'. The same is as below:

13. Appeals from decrees of Commercial Courts and Commercial Divisions.—(1) Any person aggrieved by the judgment or order of a

---

1 Sec 96
2 Order XLI Rule 1 of Code of Civil Procedure

Commercial Court below the level of a District Judge may appeal to the Commercial Appellate Court within a period of sixty days from the date of judgment or order.

(1A) Any person aggrieved by the judgment or order of a Commercial Court at the level of District Judge exercising original civil jurisdiction or, as the case may be, Commercial Division of a High Court may appeal to the Commercial Appellate Division of that High Court within a period of sixty days from the date of the judgment or order:

Provided that an appeal shall lie from such orders passed by a Commercial Division or a Commercial Court that are specifically enumerated under Order XLIII of the Code of Civil Procedure, 1908 (5 of 1908) as amended by this Act and section 37 of the Arbitration and Conciliation Act, 1996 (26 of 1996).]

(2) Notwithstanding anything contained in any other law for the time being in force or Letters Patent of a High Court, no appeal shall lie from any order or decree of a Commercial Division or Commercial Court otherwise than in accordance with the provisions of this Act.

14. Expeditious disposal of appeals—The Commercial Appellate Court and the Commercial Appellate Division shall endeavour to dispose of appeals filed before it within a period of six months from the date of filing of such appeal.

Further, there is bar against revision against interlocutory orders.

8. Bar against revision application or petition against an interlocutory order.—Notwithstanding anything contained in any other law for the time being in force, no civil revision application or petition shall be entertained against any interlocutory order of a Commercial Court, including an order on the issue of jurisdiction, and any such challenge, subject to the provisions of section 13, shall be raised only in an appeal against the decree of the Commercial Court.

An appeal against judgment and decree of a Commercial Court shall be preferred under section 13 of this Act and not under section 96 of the Code of Civil Procedure. Appeal against an order of Commercial Court on interlocutory application is also governed by section 13 of the Act. The procedure in such appeals shall be governed under Or.41 and Or.43 of the Code so far as they are not inconsistent with any provision of this Act. In respect to the appeal against 'orders' the Commercial Courts Act is very clear that only those 'orders' are appealable which are made so under Order XLIII. A Division Bench of the Bombay High Court considered the provision in detail in **Shailendra Bhaduria & Ors v. Matrix Partners India Investment Holdings LLP & Ors**[3] and held, "A combined reading of these two definitions would denote that an order means the formal expression of any decision of a civil court which is not a decree, whereas a decree means the formal expression of an adjudication but has finality or conclusiveness attached to it. Sub section(2) of section 2 defines the word decree in such a way that an adjudication which conclusively determines right of the parties with regard to all or any of the matters in controversy in the suit may be preliminary or finally, is termed a decree. By the deeming fiction, it includes rejection of plaint and any question within meaning of section 144 but does not include what is specifically from its purview." The Court further held, "Now the Commercial Courts (Amendment) Act, 2018 amends the Act 4 of 2016 and deletes the word "decision" from section 13. We have already reproduced it above. Thus the earlier view in Hubtowm Limited (*supra*) and Sigmarg Technologies (*supra*) will have to give way and all the more after the judgment of Hon'ble Supreme Court delivered in the case of Fuerst Day Lawson Limited v. Jindal Exports Limited reported in (2011) 8 SCC 33 and the authoritative and binding pronouncement in Kandla Export Corporation(*supra*). The statute has to confer a right to appeal. That has to be conferred in clear words. We cannot as suggested by Mr. Adhyaarjuna, by an interpretative process carve out a right of appeal when the law is not

---

3   2018 SCC Online 13804 (decided on 25.09.2018)

creating it." This judgment was subsequently relied upon by the Bombay High court in Base Industries Group v. Mahesh P Raheja[4]. Sub-Section (1) of Section 13 not only provides the forum of appeal (i.e., Commercial Appellate Division of a High Court) but also prescribes a period of limitation for an appeal from a decision of the Commercial Court or the Commercial Division of a High Court.[5]

Kandla Export Corporation v M/S. OCI Corporation[6] is the authority on the subject where the Supreme Court considered the question as to whether an appeal, not maintainable Under Section 50 of the Arbitration and Conciliation Act, 1996 is nonetheless maintainable Under Section 13(1) of the Commercial Courts, Commercial Division and Commercial Appellate Division of High Courts Act, 2015 (hereinafter referred to as "the Commercial Courts Act"). It was held, "22. However, the question still arises as to why Section 37 of the Arbitration Act was expressly included in the proviso to Section 13(1) of the Commercial Courts Act, which is equally a special provision of appeal contained in a self-contained code, which in any case would be outside Section 13(1) of the Commercial Courts Act. One answer is that this was done *ex abundanti cautela*. Another answer may be that as Section 37 itself was amended by the Arbitration Amendment Act, 2015, which came into force on the same day as the Commercial Courts Act, Parliament thought, in its wisdom, that it was necessary to emphasise that the amended Section 37 would have precedence over the general provision contained in Section 13(1) of the Commercial Courts Act. Incidentally, the amendment of 2015 introduced one more category into the category of appealable orders in the Arbitration Act, namely, a category where an order is made Under Section 8 refusing to refer parties to arbitration. Parliament may have found it necessary to emphasize the fact that an order referring parties to arbitration Under Section 8 is not appealable Under Section

---

4 SCC Online 2018 Bom 6575 decided on 2012.2018
5 Hpl (India) Limited & Ors v Qrg Enterprises And Anr ;2017 SCC Online Del 6955
6 (2018) 14 SCC 715

37(1)(a) and would, therefore, not be appealable Under Section 13(1) of the Commercial Courts Act. Whatever may be the ultimate reason for including Section 37 of the Arbitration Act in the proviso to Section 13(1), the ratio decidendi of the judgment in Fuerst Day Lawson (supra) would apply, and this being so, appeals filed Under Section 50 of the Arbitration Act would have to follow the drill of Section 50 alone.

23. This, in fact, follows from the language of Section 50 itself. In all arbitration cases of enforcement of foreign awards, it is Section 50 alone that provides an appeal. Having provided for an appeal, the forum of appeal is left "to the Court authorized by law to hear appeals from such orders". Section 50 properly read would, therefore, mean that if an appeal lies under the said provision, then alone would Section 13(1) of the Commercial Courts Act be attracted as laying down the forum which will hear and decide such an appeal.

28. The matter can be looked at from a slightly different angle. Given the objects of both the statutes, it is clear that arbitration itself is meant to be a speedy resolution of disputes between parties. Equally, enforcement of foreign awards should take place as soon as possible if India is to remain as an equal partner, commercially speaking, in the international community. In point of fact, the *raison d'etre* for the enactment of the Commercial Courts Act is that commercial disputes involving high amounts of money should be speedily decided. Given the objects of both the enactments, if we were to provide an additional appeal, when Section 50 does away with an appeal so as to speedily enforce foreign awards, we would be turning the Arbitration Act and the Commercial Courts Act on their heads. Admittedly, if the amount contained in a foreign award to be enforced in India were less than Rs. one crore, and a Single Judge of a High Court were to enforce such award, no appeal would lie, in keeping with the object of speedy enforcement of foreign awards. However, if, in the same fact circumstance, a foreign award were to be for Rs. one crore or more, if the Appellants are correct, enforcement of such award would be further delayed by providing an appeal Under

Section 13(1) of the Commercial Courts Act. Any such interpretation would lead to absurdity, and would be directly contrary to the object sought to be achieved by the Commercial Courts Act, viz., speedy resolution of disputes of a commercial nature involving a sum of Rs. 1 crore and over. For this reason also, we feel that Section 13(1) of the Commercial Courts Act must be construed in accordance with the object sought to be achieved by the Act. Any construction of Section 13 of the Commercial Courts Act, which would lead to further delay, instead of an expeditious enforcement of a foreign award must, therefore, be eschewed. Even on applying the doctrine of harmonious construction of both statutes, it is clear that they are best harmonized by giving effect to the special statute i.e. the Arbitration Act, vis-à-vis the more general statute, namely the Commercial Courts Act, being left to operate in spheres other than arbitration." It is quite evident that the legislative or Parliamentary intent, was to confer upon the Commercial Appellate Courts and Commercial appellate Division Bench of a High Court, extremely limited jurisdiction and circumscribe the appellate jurisdiction. Thus, in interlocutory matters, as it were, Commercial Appellate Division possesses jurisdiction in matters enumerated in the Order XLIII Rule 1 - no less no more. Likewise, with respect to the appeals against orders made in the course of proceedings under the Arbitration Act, the Court's power is delineated to what is enumerated in Section 37 of CPC (it ought to be Arbitration & Conciliation Act).[7]

Since it is indisputable that the present suit pertains to a commercial dispute and has to be regarded as a commercial suit, whether or not the interlocutory Court was alive to such aspect when the application for rejection of the plaint was decided, the Court and the parties remain bound by the Act of 2015 to act in accordance therewith. As a consequence, no appeal can be entertained from an order rejecting an application under Order VII Rule 11 of the Code as the Civil Procedure Code of 1908 does not provide for an appeal therefrom. Since an appeal is a creature of a

---

7   South Delhi Municipal ... v M/S Tech Mahindra 2019 SCC Online Del 11863

statute and there is no statute that the appellant can cite which authorises the present appeal are found to be incompetent and dismissed as not maintainable.[8]

Writ jurisdiction of High Courts

Article 227 of the Constitution confers power of superintendence over all courts and tribunals within its jurisdiction except those which are constituted by or under a law relating to armed forces. This power of superintendence and control over all subordinate courts and tribunals is both administrative and judicial in nature. This jurisdiction cannot be limited or fettered by any act of State Legislature. They can be used to interfere with an interlocutory order.[9] However, this power is discretionary and must be exercised sparingly and only to keep subordinate courts and tribunals within the bounds of their authority and not to correct mere errors.[10] In Sneh Gupta v. Devi Sarup[11], it was held, "The High Court moreover was exercising its jurisdiction under Article 227 of the Constitution of India. While exercising the said jurisdiction, the High Court had a limited role to play. It is not the function of the High court while exercising its supervisory jurisdiction to enter into the disputed question of fact. It has not been found by the High Court that the findings arrived at by the learned Additional District Judge were perverse and/ or in arriving the said findings, the learned Additional District Judge failed and/ or neglected to take into consideration the relevant factors or based its decision on irrelevant factors not germane therefor. It could intervene, if there existed an error apparent on the face of the record or, if any other well known principle of judicial review was found to be applicable.[See Yeshwant Sakhalkar and Another v. Hirabat Kamat Mhamai and Another [(2004) 6 SCC 71]"

---

8   Surajit Sen v The Royal Bank Of Scotland Nv 2019 SCC Online Cal 3215
9   Indian Constitution Law by M P Jain p.421
10 Ibid
11 (2009) 6 SCC 194

In **Jai Singh & Ors. V. Municipal Corporation of Delhi**[12] it was held, "15. .....Undoubtedly the High Court, under this Article, has the jurisdiction to ensure that all subordinate courts as well as statutory or quasi judicial tribunals, exercise the powers vested in them, within the bounds of their authority. The High Court has the power and the jurisdiction to ensure that they act in accordance with well established principles of law. The High Court is vested with the powers of superintendence and/or judicial revision, even in matters where no revision or appeal lies to the High Court. The jurisdiction under this Article is, in some ways, wider than the power and jurisdiction under Article 226 of the Constitution of India. It is, however, well to remember the well known adage that greater the power, greater the care and caution in exercise thereof. The High Court is, therefore, expected to exercise such wide powers with great care, caution and circumspection. The exercise of jurisdiction must be within the well recognized constraints. It cannot be exercised like a `bull in a china shop', to correct all errors of judgment of a court, or tribunal, acting within the limits of its jurisdiction. This correctional jurisdiction can be exercised in cases where orders have been passed in grave dereliction of duty or in flagrant abuse of fundamental principles of law or justice.

16. The High Court cannot lightly or liberally act as an appellate court and re-appreciate the evidence. Generally, it can not substitute its own conclusions for the conclusions reached by the courts below or the statutory/quasi judicial tribunals. The power to re-appreciate evidence would only be justified in rare and exceptional situations where grave injustice would be done unless the High Court interferes. The exercise of such discretionary power would depend on the peculiar facts of each case, with the sole objective of ensuring that there is no miscarriage of justice." The jurisdiction of the High Court while deciding the writ Petition under Article 227 is not akin to appeal and nor it can decide the writ petition like

---

12 (2010) 9 SCC 385

an Appellate Court.[13] The power of superintendence conferred by Article 227 is supervisory and not appellate jurisdiction. The High Court will usually interfere under Article 227, if a court or tribunal acts arbitrarily, or declines to do what is legally incumbent on it to do and thereby refuses to exercise jurisdiction vested in it by law, or exceeds its jurisdiction, or assumes erroneous jurisdiction.[14] However, the jurisdiction under Article 226/227 upon High Courts and upon the Supreme Court under Article 32 of the Constitution is part of the inviolable basic structure of the Constitution.[15] The Supreme Court formulated following principles on the exercise of High Court's jurisdiction under Article 227 of the Constitution in Shalini Shyam Shetty & Anr. v. Rajendra Shanker Patil[16]:

a. A petition under Article 226 of the Constitution is different from a petition under Article 227. The mode of exercise of power by High Court under these two Articles is also different.

b. In any event, a petition under Article 227 cannot be called a writ petition. The history of the conferment of writ jurisdiction on High Courts is substantially different from the history of conferment of the power of Superintendence on the High Courts under Article 227 and have been discussed above.

c. High Courts cannot, on the drop of a hat, in exercise of its power of superintendence under Article 227 of the Constitution, interfere with the orders of tribunals or Courts inferior to it. Nor can it, in exercise of this power, act as a Court of appeal over the orders of Court or tribunal subordinate to it. In cases where an alternative statutory mode of redressal has been provided, that would also operate as a restrain on the exercise of this power by the High Court.

---

13 Dr.Kazimunnisa (Dead) by L.R. v. Zakia Sultana (Dead) By L.R.& Ors. (2018) 11 SCC 208
14 Indian Constitutional Law by M P Jain at p. 422
15 L. Chandra Kumar v. Union of India (1997) 3 SCC 261 (Constitution Bench)
16 (2010) 8 SCC 329

d. The parameters of interference by High Courts in exercise of its power of superintendence have been repeatedly laid down by this Court. In this regard the High Court must be guided by the principles laid down by the Constitution Bench of this Court in Waryam Singh (supra) and the principles in Waryam Singh (supra) have been repeatedly followed by subsequent Constitution Benches and various other decisions of this Court.

e. According to the ratio in Waryam Singh (supra), followed in subsequent cases, the High Court in exercise of its jurisdiction of superintendence can interfere in order only to keep the tribunals and Courts subordinate to it, `within the bounds of their authority'.

f. In order to ensure that law is followed by such tribunals and Courts by exercising jurisdiction which is vested in them and by not declining to exercise the jurisdiction which is vested in them.

g. Apart from the situations pointed in (e) and (f), High Court can interfere in exercise of its power of superintendence when there has been a patent perversity in the orders of tribunals and Courts subordinate to it or where there has been a gross and manifest failure of justice or the basic principles of natural justice have been flouted.

h. In exercise of its power of superintendence High Court cannot interfere to correct mere errors of law or fact or just because another view than the one taken by the tribunals or Courts subordinate to it, is a possible view. In other words the jurisdiction has to be very sparingly exercised.

i. High Court's power of superintendence under Article 227 cannot be curtailed by any statute. It has been declared a part of the basic structure of the Constitution by the Constitution Bench of this Court in the case of L. Chandra Kumar v. Union of India &

others, reported in (1997) 3 SCC 261 and therefore abridgement by a Constitutional amendment is also very doubtful.

j. It may be true that a statutory amendment of a rather cognate provision, like Section 115 of the Civil Procedure Code by the Civil Procedure Code (Amendment) Act, 1999 does not and cannot cut down the ambit of High Court's power under Article 227. At the same time, it must be remembered that such statutory amendment does not correspondingly expand the High Courts jurisdiction of superintendence under Article 227.

k. The power is discretionary and has to be exercised on equitable principle. In an appropriate case, the power can be exercised *suo motu*.

l. On a proper appreciation of the wide and unfettered power of the High Court under Article 227, it transpires that the main object of this Article is to keep strict administrative and judicial control by the High Court on the administration of justice within its territory.

m. The object of superintendence, both administrative and judicial, is to maintain efficiency, smooth and orderly functioning of the entire machinery of justice in such a way as it does not bring it into any disrepute. The power of interference under this Article is to be kept to the minimum to ensure that the wheel of justice does not come to a halt and the fountain of justice remains pure and unpolluted in order to maintain public confidence in the functioning of the tribunals and Courts subordinate to High Court.

n. This reserve and exceptional power of judicial intervention is not to be exercised just for grant of relief in individual cases but should be directed for promotion of public confidence in the administration of justice in the larger public interest whereas Article 226 is meant for protection of individual grievance. Therefore, the power under

Article 227 may be unfettered but its exercise is subject to high degree of judicial discipline pointed out above.

o. An improper and a frequent exercise of this power will be counter-productive and will divest this extraordinary power of its strength and vitality.

Relying on the aforesaid judgment the Delhi High Court in a very recent judgment in Commerzbank Aktiengesellschaft v State Bank Of India & Ors[17] observed in para 13- "On 01.09.2020, when the writ petition came up for adjudication, we had expressed our reservation about the maintainability of the petition, particularly when the Statute provides for a remedy of an appeal before the learned DRAT under Section 20 of the Recovery of Debts Due to Banks and Financial Institutions Act, 1993 (for short ‹RDDBFI Act›) and then held in para 25- "Section 21 of the RDDBFI Act postulates that when an appeal is preferred by a person against whom the amount of debt is due to a bank or financial institution, then an appeal shall not be entertained by the Appellate Tribunal unless such a person has deposited 75% of the amount so due from him, as determined by the Tribunal. The fact that judgment has been pronounced by the DRT after a period of two years, and the Appellate Tribunal will also in all likelihood remand the matter back to the DRT for a fresh consideration of the case in the light of the judgment of the Supreme Court, existence of an alternative remedy which mandates deposit of 75% of the amount determined, cannot be an impediment on exercising jurisdiction under Article 227 of the Constitution of India by this court. We are of the opinion that if the petitioner is relegated to avail of the alternate remedy, grave prejudice will be caused to it."

In **Vaijanath Dayanand Kale And Ors. v Nerkar Properties LLP And Ors**[18] the Bombay High Court held, "The scheme of the Commercial Courts Act, as indicated by Section 8, envisages that no civil revision application

---

17 2020 SCC Online Del 1666
18 2020 SCC Online Bom 906

or petition shall be entertained against any interlocutory order of a commercial court, including an order on an issue of jurisdiction; any such challenge, subject to the provisions of Section 13 of the Act, shall be raised only in an appeal against the decree of the commercial court. Section 8 is a non-obstante provision and has an overriding effect over other provisions of law. The bar exists evidently to ensure that no suit, filed as a commercial suit, is obstructed in its hearing before the commercial court by filing of challenges from interlocutory orders including, of course, an order on the issue of jurisdiction. This bar, obviously, would not apply to the jurisdiction of this court under Article 226 or 227, but the writ court, equally obviously, would restrict its interference with interlocutory orders of commercial courts only to those exceptional cases, where the courts have made patent jurisdictional errors. The present challenge involves an interlocutory or miscellaneous order passed by a commercial court concerning its jurisdiction on a fair assessment of the Plaintiff's case and there is no reason why the matter should be treated by this court as a special matter for making an exception for interfering in its writ jurisdiction. After all, if the defendants are right in their objection to the jurisdiction of the court, the same may well form part of their appeal from the final decree passed by the commercial court." The Court allowed cost of Rs. 50000/- to be paid by the petitioner to the respondent.

13

EXECUTION OF DECREE AND AWARD

The rule of law requires that all judgments should be implemented promptly, fully and effectively. Prompt execution of domestic court decisions is one of the hallmarks of a democratic society. The same should apply for execution of international judgments.

– Commissioner for Human Rights-Council of Europe

Execution means the act of carrying out or putting into effect (as a court order) execution of the court's decree; judicial enforcement of a money judgment, usu. by seizing and selling the judgment debtor's property; a court order directing a sheriff or other officer to enforce a judgment, usu. by seizing and selling the judgment debtor's property[1]. A writ of execution is an authorization to an executive officer, issued from a court in which a final judgment has been rendered, for the purpose of carrying such judgment into force and effect. It is founded upon the judgment, must generally be conformed to it in every respect, and the plaintiff is also entitled to it to obtain a satisfaction of his claim, unless his right has been suspended by proceedings in the nature of an appeal or by his own agreement.[2]

---

1   Black's Law Dictionary at p. 609
2   Ibid at p. 609 quoting Benjamin J. Shipman, Handbook of Common-Law Pleading

Sections between 36 and 74 and Order XXI of the Code of Civil Procedure Code deal with the execution of decrees. The word execution is not defined in the Code. It means enforcement of decrees or orders by the process of the court so as to enable the decree holder to realise the fruits of the decree, judgment or order.

In commercial suits, expeditious execution of decree assumes special significance because without the timely execution of a decree of commercial court, the entire object of the Commercial Courts Act would get defeated. The question of delay in execution process is neither new nor unacknowledged in this country. Since, the Commercial Courts Act, 2015 does not bring any amendment in Order XXI of the Code of Civil Procedure, it would be important to see how time - efficient is the Commercial Court in conducting the execution process.

A three Judges Bench of the Supreme Court in **Satyawati v Rajinder Singh And Anr**[3] held, "It is really agonizing to learn that the appellant-decree holder is unable to enjoy the fruits of her success even today i.e. in 2013 though the appellant- plaintiff had finally succeeded in January, 1996. As stated hereinabove, the Privy Council in the case of The **General Manager of the Raj Durbhnga under the Court of Wards v. Maharajah Coomar Ramaput Sing** had observed that the difficulties of a litigant in India begin when he has obtained a Decree. Even in 1925, while quoting the afore stated judgment of the Privy Council in the case of **Kuer Jang Bahadur v. Bank of Upper India Ltd., Lucknow**[4], the Court was constrained to observe that "Courts in India have to be careful to see that process of the Court and law of procedure are not abused by the judgment-debtors in such a way as to make Courts of law instrumental in defrauding creditors, who have obtained decrees in accordance with their rights." Very recently, the Supreme Court held in Rahul S. Shah v. Jinendra Kumar Gandhi reported in 2021 SCC Online SC 341, "All Courts dealing with suits and execution proceedings shall mandatorily follow the below-mentioned directions:

---

3   (2013) 9 SCC 491
4   AIR 1925 Oudh 448

1. In suits relating to delivery of possession, the court must examine the parties to the suit under Order X in relation to third

2. Party interest and further exercise the power under Order XI Rule 14 asking parties to disclose and produce documents, upon oath, which are in possession of the parties including declaration pertaining to third party interest in such properties.

3. In appropriate cases, where the possession is not in dispute and not a question of fact for adjudication before the Court, the Court may appoint Commissioner to assess the accurate description and status of the property.

4. After examination of parties under Order X or production of documents under Order XI or receipt of commission report, the Court must add all necessary or proper parties to the suit, so as to avoid multiplicity of proceedings and also make such joinder of cause of action in the same suit.

5. Under Order XL Rule 1 of CPC, a Court Receiver can be appointed to monitor the status of the property in question as custodia legis for proper adjudication of the matter.

6. The Court must, before passing the decree, pertaining to delivery of possession of a property ensure that the decree is unambiguous so as to not only contain clear description of the property but also having regard to the status of the property.

8. In a money suit, the Court must invariably resort to Order XXI Rule 11, ensuring immediate execution of decree for payment of money on oral application.

9. In a suit for payment of money, before settlement of issues, the defendant may be required to disclose his assets on oath, to the extent that he is being made liable in a suit. The Court may further, at any stage, in appropriate cases during the pendency of suit, using powers under Section 151 CPC, demand security to ensure satisfaction of any decree.

10. The Court exercising jurisdiction under Section 47 or under Order XXI of CPC, must not issue notice on an application of third-party claiming rights in a mechanical manner. Further, the Court should refrain from entertaining any such application(s) that has already been considered by the Court while adjudicating the suit or which raises any such issue which otherwise could have been raised and determined during adjudication of suit if due diligence was exercised by the applicant.

11. The Court should allow taking of evidence during the execution proceedings only in exceptional and rare cases where the question of fact could not be decided by resorting to any other expeditious method like appointment of Commissioner or calling for electronic materials including photographs or video with affidavits.

12. The Court must in appropriate cases where it finds the objection or resistance or claim to be frivolous or mala fide, resort to Sub-rule (2) of Rule 98 of Order XXI as well as grant compensatory costs in accordance with Section 35A.

13. Under section 60 of CPC the term "...in name of the judgment-debtor or by another person in trust for him or on his behalf" should be read liberally to incorporate any other person from whom he may have the ability to derive share, profit or property.

14. The Executing Court must dispose of the Execution Proceedings within six months from the date of filing, which may be extended only by recording reasons in writing for such delay.

The Supreme Court further held, " 45. We further direct all the High Courts to reconsider and update all the Rules relating to Execution of Decrees, made under exercise of its powers under Article 227 of the Constitution of India and Section 122 of CPC, within one year of the date of this Order. The High Courts must ensure that the Rules are in consonance with CPC and the above directions, with an endeavour to expedite the process of execution with the use of Information Technology tools. Until such time these Rules are brought into existence, the above directions shall remain enforceable."

More than one mode of execution has been provided under the Code of Civil Procedure. The decree can be executed in any of the following modes-

a. by delivery of any property specifically decreed,
b. by attachment and sale of property,
c. by sale without attachment of any property,
d. by arrest and detention in prison,
e. by appointing receiver
f. by such other mode or manner as the nature of relief granted may require.

However, it is well settled that the decree holder may chose which mode or manner he wants for executing the decree. It is a matter of common knowledge that far too many obstacles are placed in the way of a decree-holder who seeks to execute his decree against the property of the judgment-debtor. Perhaps because of that there is no statutory provision against a number of execution: proceedings continuing concurrently. Section 51 of the Code gives an option to the creditor, of enforcing the decree either against the person or the property of the debtor; and nowhere it has been laid down that execution against the person of the debtor shall not be allowed unless and until the decree-holder has exhausted his remedy against the property. Order 21, Rule 30 of the Code provides that "every decree for payment of money, including a decree for the payment of money as the alternative to some other relief, may be executed by the detention in the civil prison of the Judgment-debtor, or by the attachment and sale of his property, or by both."[5]

In case of money decree, the same can be put for execution by attachment and sale of the property of the judgment debtor. A person can

---

[5] Shyam Singh v Collector, District Hamirpur, (1993) Supp 1 SCC 693

be arrested and detained in civil prison in execution of money decree in any of the circumstances mentioned below:

a. The judgment debtor has dishonestly transferred, concealed or removed his property

b. The judgment debtor has means to pay the amount of the decree and refuses or neglects to pay the same, or

c. The decretal dues are such that the judgment debtor is bound in fiduciary capacity to account.

The Arbitration and Conciliation Act provides for enforcement of award passed by the arbitral tribunal under the Code of Civil Procedure as if it were a decree. Section 36 of Arbitration and Conciliation Act, 1996 as it stood before amendment in 2015, it was evident that an arbitral award could be executed in two situations: (i) when the time of filing an application for setting aside had expired and no application had been filed; (ii) where such application having been made has been refused. The first situation arose when the limitation for filing an application under section 34 had run out, and no application was filed. And second situation arose when award became executable is when such application having been made has been refused.[6]

Now the amending Act of 2015 provides section 36 as below:

[7]36. Enforcement.—

1. Where the time for making an application to set aside the arbitral award under section 34 has expired, then, subject to the provisions of sub-section (2), such award shall be enforced in accordance with the provisions of the Code of Civil Procedure, 1908 (5 of 1908), in the same manner as if it were a decree of the court.

2. Where an application to set aside the arbitral award has been filed in the Court under section 34, the filing of such an application shall

---

6 Law & Practice of Arbitration and Conciliation by O P Malhotra at p. 1250
7 Subs. by s. 19, of Act 3 of 2016 , for section 36 (w.e.f. 23-10-2015)

not by itself render that award unenforceable, unless the Court grants an order of stay of the operation of the said arbitral award in accordance with the provisions of sub-section (3), on a separate application made for that purpose.

3. Upon filing of an application under sub-section (2) for stay of the operation of the arbitral award, the Court may, subject to such conditions as it may deem fit, grant stay of the operation of such award for reasons to be recorded in writing:

Provided that the Court shall, while considering the application for grant of stay in the case of an arbitral award for payment of money, have due regard to the provisions for grant of stay of a money decree under the provisions of the Code of Civil Procedure, 1908 (5 of 1908).

The first and foremost effect of this amendment is the removal of the automatic stay on execution proceeding once application under section 34 is filed.

A question arose whether section 36, as amended by the Amendment Act, 2015 would apply in its original form or in its amended form to the pending cases under section 34 of the before the date of amendment i.e. 23.10.201. In **Board Of Control For Cricket In India Versus Kochi Cricket Pvt. Ltd. And Etc.**[8] the Supreme Court was considering the questions raised in various appeals about only a few important dates. In four of these appeals, Section 34 applications under the Arbitration and Conciliation Act, 1996 (hereinafter referred to as the "1996 Act") *were all filed prior to the coming into force of the Amendment Act w.e.f. 23rd October, 2015.* In the other four appeals, the Section *34 applications were filed after the Amendment Act came into force.* The question which was put for the decision before the Supreme Court was as to whether Section 36, which was substituted by the Amendment Act, would apply in its amended form or in its original form to the appeals in question. The Supreme Court held,

---

8 (2018) 6 SCC 287

"**39** From a reading of Section 26 as interpreted by us, it thus becomes clear that in all cases where the Section 34 petition is filed after the commencement of the Amendment Act, and an application for stay having been made under Section 36 therein, will be governed by Section 34 as amended and Section 36 as substituted. But, what is to happen to Section 34 petitions that have been filed before the commencement of the Amendment Act, which were governed by Section 36 of the old Act? Would Section 36, as substituted, apply to such petitions? To answer this question, we have necessarily to decide on what is meant by "enforcement" in Section 36. On the one hand, it has been argued that "enforcement" is nothing but "execution", and on the other hand, it has been argued that "enforcement" and "execution" are different concepts, "enforcement" being substantive and "execution" being procedural in nature.

40. At this stage, it is necessary to set out the scheme of the 1996 Act. An arbitral proceeding commences under Section 21, unless otherwise agreed by parties, when a dispute arises between the parties for which a request for the dispute to be referred to arbitration is received by the respondent. The arbitral proceedings terminate under Section 32(1) by the delivery of a final arbitral award or by the circumstances mentioned in Section 32(2). The mandate of the arbitral tribunal terminates with the termination of arbitral proceedings, save and except for correction and interpretation of the award within the bounds of Section 33, or the making of an additional arbitral award as to claims presented in the proceedings, but omitted from the award. Once this is over, in cases where an arbitral award is delivered, such award shall be final and binding on the parties and persons claiming under them, under Section 35 of the 1996 Act. Under Section 36, both pre and post amendment, such award shall be "enforced" in accordance with the provisions of the Code of Civil Procedure, 1908, in the same manner as if it were a decree of the Court. It is clear that the scheme of the 1996 Act is materially different from the scheme of the 1940 Act. Under Section 17 of the 1940 Act, once an award was delivered, the Court had to pronounce judgment in accordance with the award, following which a decree would be drawn up, which would then be executable under the Code of Civil Procedure. Under Section 36 of the 1996 Act, the Court does not have to deliver judgment in terms of the award, which is then followed by a decree, which is the formal expression of the adjudication between the parties. Under Section 36 of the 1996 Act, the award is deemed to be a decree and shall be enforced under the Code of Civil Procedure as such.

41. This brings us to the manner of enforcement of a decree under the Code of Civil Procedure. A decree is enforced under the Code of Civil Procedure only through the execution process - see Order XXI of the Code of Civil Procedure. Also, Section 36(3), as amended, refers to the provisions of the Code of Civil Procedure for grant of stay of a money decree. This, in turn, has reference to Order LXI, Rule 5 of the Code of Civil Procedure, which appears under the Chapter heading, "Stay of Proceedings and of Execution". This being so, it is clear that Section 36 refers to the execution of an award as if it were a decree, attracting the provisions of Order XXI and Order LXI, Rule 5 of the Code of Civil Procedure and would, therefore, be a provision dealing with the execution of arbitral awards. This being the case, we need to refer to some judgments in order to determine whether execution proceedings and proceedings akin thereto give rise to vested rights, and whether they are substantive in nature." It was further held,"... Since it is clear that execution of a decree pertains to the realm of procedure, and that there is no substantive vested right in a judgment debtor to resist execution, Section 36, as substituted, would apply even to pending Section 34 applications on the date of commencement of the Amendment Act."

Similar question once again reached to Supreme Court in **Hindustan Construction Company Ltd. V. Union of India**[9] where a set of Writ Petitions were filed seek to challenge the constitutional validity of Section 87 of the Arbitration and Conciliation Act, 1996 as inserted by Section 13 of the Arbitration and Conciliation (Amendment) Act, 2019 and brought

---

9 AIR 2020 SC 122

into force with effect from 30.08.2019. They also seek to challenge the repeal (with effect from 23.10.2015) of Section 26 of the Arbitration and Conciliation (Amendment) Act, 2015 (hereinafter referred to as the "2015 Amendment Act") by Section 15 of the 2019 Amendment Act. It was held by the Supreme Court

"53 In the present case, the challenge is not to the fixing of 23.10.2015 as a cut-off date, as the aforesaid date is the date on which the 2015 Amendment Act came into force. For this reason, the aforesaid judgments have no application. Instead, what has been found to be manifestly arbitrary is the non-bifurcation of court proceedings and arbitration proceedings with reference to the aforesaid date, resulting in improvements in the working of the Arbitration Act, 1996 being put on a backburner. This argument of the learned Attorney General for India also therefore must be rejected.

54 The result is that the BCCI judgment (supra) will therefore continue to apply so as to make applicable the salutary amendments made by the 2015 Amendment Act to all court proceedings initiated after 23.10.2015."

The Hindustan Construction in para 54, therefore, leaves the question open and the BCCI judgment shall be applicable only to the proceeding initiated after 23.10.2015. This author confronted one such situation where it was argued that para 54 of the judgment contains some mistakes as the Supreme Court, once held that salutary principles of *BCCI* shall apply, setting cut off date as 23.10.2015 can only be typing mistake.

The Arbitration and Conciliation (Amendment) Act, 2021 seeks to bring amendment in section 36 of the Arbitration and Conciliation Act, 1996, in section 36, in sub-section (3), after the proviso, the following shall be inserted and shall be deemed to have been inserted with effect from the 23rd day of October, 2015, namely:— "Provided further that where the Court is satisfied that a prima facie case is made out that, — (a) the arbitration agreement or contract which is the basis of the award; or (b) the making of the award, Short title and commencement. Amendment of section 36. 26 of 1996 as induced or effected by fraud or corruption, it shall stay the award unconditionally pending disposal of the challenge under section 34 to the award.

Explanation.—For the removal of doubts, it is hereby clarified that the above proviso shall apply to all court cases arising out of or in relation to arbitral proceedings, irrespective of whether the arbitral or court proceedings were commenced prior to or after the commencement of the Arbitration and Conciliation (Amendment) Act, 2015.".

Prior to that the Arbitration and Conciliation (Amendment) Ordinance, 2020 was promulgated on November 4, 2020. It seeks to amend the Arbitration and Conciliation Act, 1996. The Act contains provisions to deal with domestic and international arbitration and defines the law for conducting conciliation proceedings. Key features of the Ordinance include:

Automatic stay on awards: The 1996 Act allowed a party to file an application to set aside an arbitral award (i.e., the order given in an arbitration proceeding). Courts had interpreted this provision to mean that an automatic stay on an arbitral award was granted the moment an application for setting aside an arbitral award was made before a court. In 2015, the Act was amended to state that an arbitral award would not be automatically stayed merely because an application is made to a court to set aside the arbitral award.

The Ordinance specifies that a stay on arbitral award can be provided (even during the pendency of the setting aside application) if the court is satisfied that: (i) the relevant arbitration agreement or contract, or (ii) the making of the award, was induced or effected by fraud or corruption. This change will be effective from October 23, 2015.[10]

Another aspect of enforcement of arbitral award is the distinction between the enforcement of domestic award and international award as classified in the Arbitration and Conciliation Act.

---

10 https://prsindia.org/

Part II of the Arbitration and Conciliation Act, 1996 deals with enforcement of certain foreign awards. It depends on the convention and framework agreed upon and the same has been defined under section 44 and 53 of the Arbitration and Conciliation Act, 1996. Section 44 provides as follows:

New York Convention Awards

44. Definition.—In this Chapter, unless the context otherwise requires, "foreign award" means an arbitral award on differences between persons arising out of legal relationships, whether contractual or not, considered as commercial under the law in force in India, made on or after the 11th day of October, 1960— (a) in pursuance of an agreement in writing for arbitration to which the Convention set forth in the First Schedule applies, and (b) in one of such territories as the Central Government, being satisfied that reciprocal provisions have been made may, by notification in the Official Gazette, declare to be territories to which the said Convention applies.

Section 48 of the Arbitration and Conciliation Act, 1996 provides the conditions which have to be complied with:

48. (1) Enforcement of a foreign award may be refused, at the request of the party against whom it is invoked, only if that party furnishes to the court proof that—

   a. the parties to the agreement referred to in section 44 were, under the law applicable to them, under some incapacity, or the said agreement is not valid under the law to which the parties have subjected it or, failing any indication thereon, under the law of the country where the award was made; or

   b. the party against whom the award is invoked was not given proper notice of the appointment of the arbitrator or of the arbitral proceedings or was otherwise unable to present his case; or

c. the award deals with a difference not contemplated by or not falling within the terms of the submission to arbitration, or it contains decisions on matters beyond the scope of the submission to arbitration: Provided that, if the decisions on matters submitted to arbitration can be separated from those not so submitted, that part of the award which contains decisions on matters submitted to arbitration may be enforced; or

d. the composition of the arbitral authority or the arbitral procedure was not in accordance with the agreement of the parties, or, failing such agreement, was not in accordance with the law of the country where the arbitration took place; or

e. the award has not yet become binding on the parties, or has been set aside or suspended by a competent authority of the country in which, or under the law of which, that award was made.

2. Enforcement of an arbitral award may also be refused if the Court finds that—

a. the subject-matter of the difference is not capable of settlement by arbitration under the law of India; or

b. the enforcement of the award would be contrary to the public policy of India. 2

[Explanation 1.—For the avoidance of any doubt, it is clarified that an award is in conflict with the public policy of India, only if,— (i) the making of the award was induced or affected by fraud or corruption or was in violation of section 75 or section 81; or (ii) it is in contravention with the fundamental policy of Indian law; or (iii) it is in conflict with the most basic notions of morality or justice.

Explanation 2.—For the avoidance of doubt, the test as to whether there is a contravention with the fundamental policy of Indian law shall not entail a review on the merits of the dispute.] (3) If an application for the setting aside or suspension of the award has been made to a competent authority referred to in clause (e) of sub-section (1) the Court may, if it considers it proper, adjourn the decision on the enforcement of the award and may also, on the application of the party claiming enforcement of the award, order the other party to give suitable security. The Supreme Court in **Vijay Karia v. Versus Prysmian Cavi E Sistemi Srl & Ors.**[11] held, "Given the fact that the object of Section 48 is to enforce foreign awards subject to certain well-defined narrow exceptions, the expression "was otherwise unable to present his case" occurring in Section 48 (1)(b) cannot be given an expansive meaning and would have to be read in the context and colour of the words preceding the said phrase. In short, this expression would be a facet of natural justice, which would be breached only if a fair hearing was not given by the arbitrator to the parties. Read along with the first part of Section 48 (1)(b), it is clear that this expression would apply at the hearing stage and not after the award has been delivered, as has been held in **Ssangyong** (supra). A good working test for determining whether a party has been unable to present his case is to see whether factors outside the party's control have combined to deny the party a fair hearing. Thus, where no opportunity was given to deal with an argument which goes to the root of the case or findings based on evidence which go behind the back of the party and which results in a denial of justice to the prejudice of the party; or additional or new evidence is taken which forms the basis of the award on which a party has been given no opportunity of rebuttal, would, on the facts of a given case, render a foreign award liable to be set aside on the ground that a party has been unable to present his case. This must, of course, be with the caveat that such breach be clearly made out on the facts of a given case, and that awards must always be read supportively with an inclination to uphold rather than destroy, given the minimal interference possible with foreign awards under Section 48."

---

11   2020 (11) SCC 1

It may be noted that while section 34 of the Arbitration and Conciliation Act, 1996 differentiates the domestic arbitration and international commercial arbitration held in India, the position has become uniform so far as the grounds of 'public policy of India' is concerned in view of the identical provision made in section 34 and 48 on this ground.

Section 53 of the Arbitration and Conciliation Act, 1996, however, defines provision relating to international commercial arbitration under Geneva Convention. It provides-

Interpretation.—In this Chapter "foreign award" means an arbitral award on differences relating to matters considered as commercial under the law in force in India made after the 28th day of July, 1924,—

a. in pursuance of an agreement for arbitration to which the Protocol set forth in the Second Schedule applies, and

b. between persons of whom one is subject to the jurisdiction of some one of such Powers as the Central Government, being satisfied that reciprocal provisions have been made, may, by notification in the Official Gazette, declare to be parties to the Convention set forth in the Third Schedule, and of whom the other is subject to the jurisdiction of some other of the Powers aforesaid, and

c. in one of such territories as the Central Government, being satisfied that reciprocal provisions have been made, may, by like notification, declare to be territories to which the said Convention applies, and for the purposes of this Chapter an award shall not be deemed to be final if any proceedings for the purpose of contesting the validity of the award are pending in the country in which it was made.

In **Government Of India Versus Vedanta Limited (Formerly Cairn India Ltd.), And Others**[12] the Supreme Court was considering a Civil Appeal filed by the Government of India to challenge the Judgment and Order

---

12 (2020) 10 SCC 1

passed by the Delhi High Court, wherein the application under Section 48 of the Arbitration and Conciliation Act, 1996 filed by the Government of India had been dismissed; the Application filed under Section 47 read with 49 for the enforcement of the foreign award by the Respondents, and the for condonation of delay in filing the execution petition by the Respondents were allowed. After setting out the entire facts and law, the Supreme Court held, ".. that the period of limitation for filing a petition for enforcement of a foreign award under Sections 47 and 49, would be governed by Article 137 of the Limitation Act, 1963 which prescribes a period of three years from when the right to apply accrues."

It was further held, "The application under Sections 47 and 49 for enforcement of the foreign award, is a substantive petition filed under the Arbitration Act, 1996. It is a well-settled position that the Arbitration Act is a self-contained code[13]. The application under Section 47 is not an application filed under any of the provisions of Order XXI of the CPC, 1908. The application is filed before the appropriate High Court for enforcement, which would take recourse to the provisions of Order XXI of the CPC only for the purposes of execution of the foreign award as a deemed decree. The bar contained in Section 5, which excludes an application filed under any of the provisions of Order XXI of the CPC, would not be applicable to a substantive petition filed under the Arbitration Act, 1996. Consequently, a party may file an application under Section 5 for condonation of delay, if required in the facts and circumstances of the case."

On the point of foreign award and foreign decree, the Supreme Court held, "A foreign award is not a decree by itself, which is executable as such under Section 49 of the Act. The enforcement of the foreign award takes place only after the court is satisfied that the foreign award is enforceable under Chapter 1 in Part II of the 1996 Act. After the stages of Sections 47 and 48 are completed, the award becomes enforceable as a deemed decree, as provided by Section 49. The phrase "that court" refers to the Indian

---

13 Fuerst Day Law son Ltd. v. Jindal Exports Ltd. (2011) 8 SCC 333

court which has adjudicated on the petition filed under Section 47, and the application under Section 48.

In contrast, the procedure for enforcement of a foreign decree is not covered by the 1996 Act, but is governed by the provisions of Section 44A read with Section 13 of the CPC."

PART- II

PART-II

14

ENFORCEMENT AND BREACH OF CONTRACT

Promises are like the full moon, if they are not kept at once they diminish day by day.

– German Proverb

In Act I of the play Merchant of Venice, Shylock lends 3000 ducats to Bassino but a contract (The Private Code) is entered into between the friend of Bassino namely Antonio with a stipulation that if the 3000 ducats are not returned within three months, Antonio forfeits a pound of his flesh. The Code is sealed at Notary's. Thus do the seasoned businessman, acting at arm's length and fully cognizant of the Code's Terms, set in motion a series of events that eventually finds them in a Vatican Court. The three months have passed, Antonio has defaulted and Shylock demands his pound of flesh or to put it better demands of the court that it place its formal imprimatur on the Private Code. It subsequently unfolds that Portia invokes Public Code indeed to save Antonio.[1]

Intention to create legal relations is dependent upon parties' intentions, objectively judged. The traditional starting point for determining this

---

1   Shakespeare & the Law   at p.291

intention is the use of different presumption for domestic and commercial agreements. There is a presumption in the case of domestic and social agreements that there is no intention to create legal relations. There is a presumption of an intention to create legal relations in commercial agreements.[2] **Bowerman v. Association of British Travel Agents Ltd**[3] is an authority on this point.

BLUE PENCIL RULE

However, it may so happen that a contract may include some clauses which are not enforceable in which case can the entire contract be rendered as un-enforceable? In **Attwood v. Lamont**[4], the plaintiff was carrying on business as a draper, tailor and general outfitter at Kidderminster. By a contract for employment, the defendant agreed with the plaintiff that he would not, at any time thereafter "either on his own account or on that of any wife of his or in partnership with or as assistant, servant or agent to any other person, persons or company carry on or be in any way directly or indirectly concerned in any of the following grades or businesses, that is to say, the trade or business of a tailor, dressmaker, general draper, milliner, hatter, haberdasher, gentlemen's, ladies' or children's outfitter at any place within a radius of ten miles of" Kidderminster. The defendant, however, subsequently set up business as a tailor at Worcester, outside the ten miles limit, but obtained and executed tailoring orders in Kidderminster. When the plaintiff brought an action, it was contended by the defendant that the agreement was illegal and could not be enforced. The Court, however, held that various parts of the contract were severable and valid part thereof could be enforced. Upholding the argument of the plaintiff and granting relief in his favour, the Court observed that the Courts would sever in a proper case, where the severance can be made by using a 'blue pencil'. But it could be done only in those cases where the part so enforceable is clearly

---

2   A casebook on Contract Law by Jill Poole, Oxford University Press at p. 179, 184
3   [1996] CLC 451 (CA)
4   [1920] 2 KB 146

severable and not where it could not be severed. By such process, main purport and substance of the clause cannot be ignored or overlooked. Thus, a covenant "not to carry on business in Birmingham or within 100 miles" may be severed so as to reduce the area to Birmingham, but a covenant "not to carry on business within 100 miles of Birmingham" will not be severed so as to read "will not carry on business in Birmingham". Therefore, Blue Pencil Rule is a legal concept, where the courts may find a portion of contract as void or illegal still proceed to hold other parts enforceable. This rule has found acceptance in India and the courts do apply the same in appropriate case.[5] The Supreme Court in **Beed District Central... v State Of Maharashtra**[6] explained the rule in following words,

"The `doctrine of blue pencil' was evolved by the English and American Courts. In Halsbury's Laws of England (4th Edn. Vol.9), p.297, para 430, it is stated:

"430. Severance of illegal and void provisions - A contract will rarely be totally illegal or void and certain parts of it may be entirely lawful in themselves. The question therefore arises whether the illegal or void parts may be separated or "severed" from the contract and the rest of the contract enforced without them. Nearly all the cases arise in the context of restraint of trade, but the following principles are applicable to contracts in general"

In P. Ramanatha Aiyar's Advanced Law Lexicon, 3rd Edn. 2005, Vol. l,p.553-554, it is stated:

"Blue pencil doctrine (test). A judicial standard for deciding whether to invalidate the whole contract or only the offending words. Under this standard, only the offending words are invalidated if it would be possible to delete them simply by running a blue pencil through them, as opposed to changing, adding, or rearranging words. (Black, 7th Edn., 1999) This doctrine holds that if Courts can render an unreasonable restraint reasonable by scratching out the offensive portions of the covenant, they

---

5   Shin Satellite Public Co. Ltd. v. M/s Jain Studios Ltd. (2006) 2 SCC 628
6   (2006) 8 SCC 514

should do so and then enforce the remainder. Traditionally, the doctrine is applicable only if the covenant in question is applicable, so that the unreasonable portions may be separated. E.P.I, of Cleveland, Inc. v. Basler, 12 Ohio App2d 16:230 NE2d 552, 556.

Blue pencil rule/test. - Legal theory that permits a judge to limit unreasonable aspects of a covenant not to compete.

Severance of contract. - "severance can be effected when the part severed can be removed by running a blue pencil through it without affording the remaining part. Attwood v. Lamont, (1920) 3 K 571 (Banking) A rule in contracts a Court may strike parts of a covenant not to compete in order to make the covenant reasonable. (Merriam Webster) Phrase referring to severance (q.v.) of contract. "Severance can be effected when the part severed can be removed by running a blue pencil through it" without affording the remaining part. Attwood v. Lamont, (1920) 3 KB 571. (Banking)"

Enforcement of contract *aka* legal promise is *sine qua non* for viable commercial regime. Courts have a bounden duty to ensure that promises are made for their fructification. Historically, law did not concern itself at first with agreements or breaches of agreements. Its function was to keep the peace by regulating or preventing private war and this only required to deal with personal violence and with disputes over the possession of property.[7] The proposition of Hippodamus in the fifth century BC that there were three subjects of lawsuits, namely insult, injury and homicide. If a dispute over breach of agreement led to an assault and breach of peace, tribunals might be called on to act. But it was the assault not the breach of agreement with which they were concerned.[8]

Enforcement of contract is the most important facet of contract as it is the enforcement which serves the purpose of contract if it is executed in its natural way whereof both the parties proceed to fructify the reciprocal

---

7   An Introduction to Law by Roscoe Pounds at p.136
8   Ibid

promises. Economists often assert that law serves a market economy when it concentrates on the principal task enforcing contract, defining property rights, and punishing fraud.[9] Roscoe Pound further examined the gradual development of the enforcement of contract to finally reaching to the contemporary era. Putting them in order of their currency, we may call them- the will theory, the bargain theory, the equivalent theory and the injurious-reliance theory. In a liberal society recognizing a far reaching freedom of contract it would be difficult for a court to invalidate an agreement (in the absence of a positive prohibition) on the ground of repugnancy to public policy and justice unless a strong case can be made out to show that basic notions of collecting morality were violated by the agreement, or that the integrity of the social fabric would be jeopardized by its enforcement.[10] Under the Indian Contract act, a person *sui juris* has the freedom to enter into a contract. This freedom of contract available to a citizen cannot be curtailed or curbed relying on the fundamental rights enshrined in Part III of the Constitution against the state action. A right to enforce a fundamental right into contract giving up an absolute right in oneself in the interest of an association to be formed or in the interest of the members in general of that association.[11]

After formation of contract, the next stage is reached, namely, the fulfillment of the object the parties had in their minds. When the object is fulfilled, the liability of either party under the Contract comes to an end. The contract is then said to be discharged. But 'performance' is not the only way in which a contract is discharged. A contract may be discharged by performance, by impossibility of performance, by agreement and by breach.[12] In simplest words, the parties to a contract may either chose

---

9   Contracts in Modern Supreme Court by G. Richard Shelf; California Law Review Vol 81 March 1993 No-2
10 Jurisprudence, Edgar Bodenheimer at p. 141
11 Zorastrian Co-op. Housing Society Ltd. v District registrar Co-op. Society (Urban) ; (2005) 5 SCC 632 also Daman Singh v State of Punjab (1985) 2 SCC 670
12 Contract and Specific Relief by Avtar Singh at p.351

to perform the contract or break it. The breaking of contract by a party thereto is called breach of contract. Failure to perform as contemplated under the contract is called actual breach. Not performing at the time fixed for performance is also actual breach[13]. A breach of contract occurs when a party thereto renounces his liability under it, or by his own acts make it impossible that he should perform his obligation under it totally or partially fails to perform such obligations.[14]

The word breach means a violation or infraction of a law or obligation.[15] A breach may be one by non-performance, or by repudiation, or by both. Every breach give rise to other remedies. Even if the injured party sustains no pecuniary loss or is unable to show such loss with sufficient certainty, he has at least a claim of nominal damages. If a court choose to ignore a trifling departure, there is no breach and no claim arises.[16]

ANTICIPATORY BREACH

An anticipatory breach occurs where, before the time of performance, one party informs the other that they will not perform their contractual obligations. This type of breach will normally be repudiatory, since the contract is renounced or the party incapacitates himself from performing the obligations under the contract.

When a party has refused to perform or disabled himself from performing his promise in its entirety, the promissee may put an end to the contract, unless his acquiescence in its continuation.[17] Section 39 of Contract Act only means to enact what was the law in England and the law here before an act was passed, namely that where a party to a contract refuses altogether to perform it or disable from performing his party of

---

13   Contract I :Cases and Materials by V Keshva Rao at p. 669
14   Associated Cinemmas of America Inc. v. World Amusement Company (1937) 201 Min 94 as quoted in Contract & specific Relief by Avtar Singh
15   Black's Law dictionary
16   Ibid
17   Sec 39 of Indian Contract Act, 1872

it the other side has a right to rescind it.[18] In this case (**Sooltan Chund v. Schiller**[19]) the plaintiff had filed a suit for damages for the non-delivery of linseed, upon a contract payment under which cash made in cash on delivery(COD). Part delivery had been made by the defendant and a sum of Rs. 1000 had been paid on account by the plaintiff. The plaintiff then made a claim against the defendants for excess refraction, and the defendant thereupon refused to deliver the remainder of the linseed unless the plaintiffs paid full amount owing for the portion that had been delivered. The plaintiff declined to accept these terms, and the defendants cancelled the contract. The question before the Bench was whether the defendants were justified in cancelling the contract. It was argued that the plaintiff not having paid for the goods on delivery, they have refused to perform the contract in its entirety; and that the defendants had, therefore, a right to cancel it. But Garth, C.J. held that the plaintiffs never refused to perform any part of their contract. They were willing to pay the sum due as soon as their claims were adjusted; and their default consisted in not paying for linseed on delivery. Applicability of section 51 of Contract act was also ruled out. The defendants were bound to deliver, the plaintiff to pay for, the linseed. If the plaintiff had been unwilling or unable to pay, the defendants would have been justified in refusing to deliver but the defendants did deliver the seed, the neglect to pay in this instance was after delivery; and there is reciprocity of obligation had ceased; and there is clearly no evidence here that the plaintiff were unwilling or unable to pay for the deliveries which the defendants refused to make.

Breach is one of the methods of discharge but every breach of contract does not discharge the innocent party from performance of his part of contract. The expression 'discharge by breach' is not very accurate.[20] Referring to Chitty on Contract, Mulla says "any breach of contract gives

---

18 Sooltan Chund v. Schiller (1879-80) ILR 4-5 Cal 161
19 Ibid
20 Mulla on Contract and Specific Relief at p. 1006

rise to a cause of action, not every breach discharges from liability. A discharge may follow at the option of one party where the other party has repudiated the contract. Repudiation does not discharge the contract, thereby automatically terminating the obligations of the innocent party. It gives an option to the innocent party to regard itself as 'discharged'. If the innocent party rescinds the contract, the primary obligations of both parties are over, but the defaulting party becomes liable for payment of compensation for the breach. If the innocent party elects not to end the contract, it continues. The innocent party may also waive the defective performance and elect to accept damages instead of ending the contract"[21].

The word 'discharge' assumes significance because of its varied meaning in different branch of law. Black's Law Dictionary defines discharge as 1. Any method by which a legal duty is extinguished esp. the payment of a debt or satisfaction of some other obligation; 2. The release of debtor from monetary obligation upon adjudication of bankruptcy. A contract that has been fully performed is also termed discharges contract. Not only is the term void contract in itself technically inaccurate, but a contract is sometimes said to be void, not because it was destitute of legal defect from its commencement but because it has been fully performed, and so has ceased to have legal operation. It would be more proper to describe such contract discharged.[22] A breach of contract occurs where-

a. A party expressly repudiates the contract, that is states explicitly that he will not perform his promise; or

b. A party fails to perform his obligation upon the date fixed for performance by the contract; or

c. A party does some act which disables him from performing his obligation, that is, makes the performance of his part performance.[23]

---

21 Ibid
22 Black's law Dictionary at p. 350
23 Law Relating to Contract Act by Sanjiva Row's 12th Ed. P. 1151

The party at fault must either show an intention no longer to be bound by the contract, or by some act or default break some stipulation so essential to the continuance of the contractual relation that the facts and circumstances of each case. The test is whether the breach prevents substantial performance.[24] Section 39 does not apply to executed contract. It applies to executory contract.[25] The section according to its true meaning refers to either refused to perform or self created disability in the promisor to perform a possible act. The plaintiff here by parting with his oxen and wagons had disabled himself from carting the timber at all. Did the defendant then (the promise) put an end to the contract? Was the letter of October 20th, a determination? In their Lordship's opinion it was.[26]

---

24 Ibid at p.1152
25 Sheikh Sultan Ahmad v. Syed Masked Hussain 1943 SCC Online Pat 154
26 John Usher Jones v. Edward Scott GroganAIR 1919 PC 190

15

INTERPRETATION OF CONTRACTS

"But words are things,
and a small drop of ink,
Falling, like dew, upon a thought produces
That which makes thousands,
perhaps millions think."

– Lord George Gordon Byron

Answering the question, what is interpretation, Catherine Mitchell says, "this basic question is perhaps the most difficult one to answer at the outset, since 'interpretation' is, by nature, an elusive concept. It is difficult to advance any widely accepted view of what interpretation is and how it should be conducted since almost everything claimed in relation to interpretation is disputed."[1] The word interpretation means, as per Black's Law Dictionary, the process of determining what something, esp. the law or a legal document, means; the ascertainment of meaning to be given to words or other manifestations of intention. Meaning of the word 'interpretation' sometimes depends on how 'interpretation' is done by courts. Debates in interpretation generally manifest themselves between

---

1 Interpretation of Contracts (Current Controversies in Law)

different 'camps.' Thus, there is the 'textualist' (or literalist), who approaches the interpretative task with a belief that the text is largely self sufficient and can be interpreted without reference to any extrinsic evidence. The textualist may be at odds with both 'contextualists' and 'intentionalists' in interpretation. Contextualism is broadly the position that material other than the text is important to the interpretative task, and the intentionalism is the position that interpretation involves the search for author's intent.[2]

Many interpretative difficulties arise not from problems of drafting and ambiguous word meaning, but the over-and under inclusiveness of rules and contract terms. An illustration is provided by the Court of Appeal decisions in **Hayward v Norwich Union Insurance**[3]. In this case the claimant's car had been stolen. The car had been left unlocked with the keys in the ignition. The car was fitted with an immobiliser, which was armed, but the thief had managed to override its operation. The defendant insurance company refused to indemnify the claimant for the theft, since the insurance policy excluded 'Loss or damage arising from theft whilst the ignition keys of your car have been left in or on the car'. On the face of it, the claimant had certainly left his keys in the car. However, the first instance judge thought there was ambiguity and interpreted the exception as meaning the car had been 'left unattended'. He accepted the claimant's argument that although the keys had been left in the car, the car had not been left unattended. The Court of Appeal overturned this, adopting the plain meaning of the words. But Peter Gibson LJ did note how changing the factual situation or context could change the interpretation of 'left in the car':

"............ the driver leaves the key in the ignition while he fills up and pays for petrol at a time when there is a passenger in the car. Whether the keys have been left in those circumstances must, in my view, depend on the circumstances. If the passenger is an adult in whose charge the keys have

---

2   Ibid
3   [2001] 1 ALL ER 545

been left so that such person stands in for the driver, then on the plain and ordinary meaning of the words of the Exception the keys have not been left in the car. But if the passenger is, for example, a small child, then the presence of the passenger will not prevent the keys from having been left. A second situation is where there is hijacking, the driver for example being pulled out of the car while the keys are in the ignition. In my judgment such duress prevents the keys from being left in the car.[4]

Most judges use the terms 'construction' and 'interpretation' interchangeably, but some commentators have regarded these as qualitatively different processes. Interpretation may be regarded as being limited to fixing on the meaning of the expressed words in the agreement in instances of ambiguity or vagueness, whereas 'construction' describes the next step of determining the parties' obligations based on that interpretation. Paden, for example, draws the following distinction: "Interpretation" describes the process whereby courts determine the meaning of words, and "construction" describes the process of determining their legal effect. Interpretation may therefore be part of construction.[5] Interpretation of agreement (at least in context of litigation) is regarded as a role for the court, not the parties. Interpretation is question of law, not fact. Since almost every interpretation problem is unique, precedents have a limited role in settling interpretative disputes.[6]

Lord Hoffman in the landmark case **Investors Compensation Scheme v. West Bromwich Building Society**[7] said, "But I think I should preface my explanation of my reasons with some general remarks about the principles by which contractual documents are nowadays construed... The principles may be summarised as follows:

---

[4] Interpretation of Contracts (Current Controversies in Law) at p.22
[5] Ibid at p.22
[6] Ibid at p.31
[7] [1998] 1 WLR 896

1. Interpretation is the ascertainment of the meaning which the document would convey to a reasonable person having all the background knowledge which would reasonably have been available to the parties in the situation in which they were at the time of the contract.

2. The background was famously referred to by Lord Wilberforce as the "matrix of fact," but this phrase is, if anything, an understated description of what the background may include. Subject to the requirement that it should have been reasonably available to the parties and to the exception to be mentioned next, it includes absolutely anything which would have affected the way in which the language of the document would have been understood by a reasonable man.

3. The law excludes from the admissible background the previous negotiations of the parties and their declarations of subjective intent. They are admissible only in an action for rectification. The law makes this distinction for reasons of practical policy and, in this respect only, legal interpretation differs from the way we would interpret utterances in ordinary life. The boundaries of this exception are in some respects unclear. But this is not the occasion on which to explore them.

4. The meaning which a document (or any other utterance) would convey to a reasonable man is not the same thing as the meaning of its words. The meaning of words is a matter of dictionaries and grammars; the meaning of the document is what the parties using those words against the relevant background would reasonably have been understood to mean. The background may not merely enable the reasonable man to choose between the possible meanings of words which are ambiguous but even (as occasionally happens in ordinary life) to conclude that the parties must, for whatever reason, have used the wrong words or syntax. (see

Mannai Investments Co. Ltd. v. Eagle Star Life Assurance Co. Ltd. [1997] 2 WLR 945

5. The "rule" that words should be given their "natural and ordinary meaning" reflects the common sense proposition that we do not easily accept that people have made linguistic mistakes, particularly in formal documents. On the other hand, if one would nevertheless conclude from the background that something must have gone wrong with the language, the law does not require judges to attribute to the parties an intention which they plainly could not have had. Lord Diplock made this point more vigorously when he said in **The Antaios Compania Neviera S.A. v. Salen Rederierna A.B.** 1985 1 A.C. 191, 201:

"... if detailed semantic and syntactical analysis of words in a commercial contract is going to lead to a conclusion that flouts business common sense, it must be made to yield to business common sense." But these principles have on the one hand hailed as pathbreaking in searching for true meaning of contracts, the fact that there was a dissenting voice in the Bench itself suggest that the debate has revived rather than settled.

The question as to how law of evidence deals with the use of external aid in interpretation of contract or any of its terms has been provided under Chapter VI of Indian Evidence Act. When the terms of a contract, or of a grant, or of any other disposition of property, have been reduced to the form of a document, and in all cases in which any matter is required by law to be reduced to the form of a document, no evidence shall be given in proof of the terms of such contract, grant or other disposition of property, or of such matter, except the document itself, or secondary evidence of its contents in cases in which secondary evidence is admissible under the provisions hereinbefore contained.[8] Section 91 is thus based on the best evidence principle and it excludes extrinsic evidence of the terms.[9]

---

8   Sec. 91 Evidence Act
9   2014 SCC Online Bom 1348

At common law this is referred to as the Parole Evidence which Rule provides that where a contract is made wholly in writing, evidence is not admissible to add to, vary or contradict the written terms. In **Jacobs v Batavia**[10] this rule has been stated as, " It is firmly established as a rule of law that parol evidence cannot be admitted to add, vary or contradict a deed or other written statement. Accordingly, it has been held that (except in cases of fraud or rectification, and except, in certain circumstances, as a defence to an action for specific performance) parol evidence will not be admitted to prove that some particular term, which had been verbally agreed upon, had been omitted (by design or otherwise) from a written instrument constituting a valid and operative contract between the parties.

Section 92 of Evidence Act provides that when the terms of any such contract, grant or other disposition of property, or any matter required by law to be reduced to the form of a document, have been proved according to the last section, no evidence of any oral agreement or statement shall be admitted, as between the parties to any such instrument or their representatives in interest, for the purpose of contradicting, varying, adding to, or subtracting from, its terms. *Proviso* 1 to this section provides that Any fact may be proved which would invalidate any document, or which would entitle any person to any decree or order relating thereto; such as fraud, intimidation, illegality, want of due execution, want of capacity in any contracting party, 3[want or failure] of consideration, or mistake in fact or law. *Proviso* 4 to section 92 provides that the existence of any distinct subsequent oral agreement to rescind or modify any such contract, grant or disposition of property, may be proved, except in cases in which such contract, grant or disposition of property is by law required to be in writing, or has been registered according to the law in force for the time being as to the registration of documents. The Bombay High Court drawn up the distinction between the proviso (1) and proviso (2) as follows:

---

10   [1924] 1 Ch. 287

"12. The distinction between proviso (1) and (4) below Section 92 is required to be noticed. The proviso (1) permits leading of parol evidence of any fact which would invalidate any document, at the instance of any party to such document or their representatives in interest. The proviso illustrates such facts as fraud, intimidation, illegality, want of due execution, want of capacity in any contracting party, want or failure of consideration, or mistake in fact or law, which induces the party to enter into the terms contained in the document. It applies to all kinds of documents, the terms of which are required by law to be reduced in writing, irrespective of the fact whether such document is required to be compulsorily, by law, registered or not. The applicability of proviso (1) does not, therefore, depend upon the fact whether the document in question is required by law to be registered.

13. Proviso (4), does not deal with the question of invalidating any document, but it relates to the existence of any distinct subsequent oral agreement to rescind or modify any such contract, grant or disposition of property. Thus, it makes the parol evidence admissible to show that the prior written contract has been waived or replaced by subsequent oral agreement with a rider that, if a matter has been reduced into writing because the law requires it to be in writing for its validity, no oral evidence can be given of any subsequent agreement, rescinding or modifying it. It can only be waived, rescinded, modified or altered by another written agreement of equally solemn character. The rule applies to all registered instruments, whether or not, registration is compulsory under the law. So when writing embodying the contract has been registered, parol evidence of any subsequent agreement, modifying or rescinding the registered instrument is not

admissible, unless the modification, alteration or waiver is by another registered instrument.[11]

In an old case Laxmibai Versus Keshav Annaji Pokharkar[12] the Bombay High Court dealt with the distinction between the English law and Indian law in respect of parol evidence. it held, "The difficulties created by Section 92 of our Evidence Act appear to me to be obvious. In the English Courts, in somewhat analogous if not exactly similar cases, they have been surmounted by processes of reasoning which, with great respect to the very eminent and learned Judges using them, do not appear to me to be adequate. Nothing could well be plainer than the provisions of Section 92 of the Indian Evidence Act. Where Courts have to deal with a written contract, the law of this country absolutely prohibits parol evidence being given except within the limits very carefully laid down in Section 92 itself. Although, no doubt, the law of England was intended to be in substance the same as the law to which expression has thus hem given in Section 92,; the Judges had no definitely worded Statute to interpret and by which to be bound as the Courts in India have. Speaking generally, the rule laid down in England and considered to be settled by the decision in the leading case of Biggins V/s. Senior (1841) 8 M. & W. 831 : 11 L.J. Ex. 199 : 58 R.R. 884 was that where there was a written agreement or contract not under seal, the obligor might not give parol evidence to evade his liability even though the facts upon which he relied were within the plaintiff's knowledge: while, on the other hand, the plaintiff might pass over the actual obligor of the contract if he chose to do so and seek the real maker behind him. In other words, if A contracted as an agent in such a form as to make himself personally liable, his principal being B, the plaintiff might, at his option, show by parol, notwithstanding what appeared on the face of the document, that his contract was really with B, A, however, could not by way of defence prove by parol that he was not, as he appeared to be on

---

11 2014 SCC Online Bom 1348
12 1916 SCC Online Bom 239

the face of the document, liable under it. So far the distinction is perfectly intelligible, though I think it would be extremely difficult to reconcile it with the strict language of Section 92 of the Indian Evidence Act.

Proviso 6 of section 92 of Evidence Act, however, provides that any fact may be proved which shows in what manner the language of a document is related to existing facts. Section 94 Evidence Act provides that when language used in a document is plain in itself, and when it applies accurately to existing facts, evidence may not be given to show that it was not meant to apply to such facts. The subsequent three sections- 95, 96 and 97 of Evidence Act provide as to when evidence may be given in respect of meaning and application of language. The Supreme Court in **Pandit Chunchun Jha v. Sheikh Ebadat Ali**[13] held that as in every other case where a document has to be construed the intention must be gathered, in the first place, from the document itself. If the words are express and clear., effect must be given to them and any extraneous enquiry into what was thought or intended is ruled out. the real question in such a case is not what the parties intended or meant but what is the legal effect of the words which they used. If, however, there is ambiguity in the language employed, then it is permissible to look to the surrounding circumstances to determine what was intended. In **Mukul Sharma v. Orion India(P) Ltd.**[14], it was held that extrinsic evidence to determine the effect of an instrument is permissible where there remains a doubt as to its true meaning. Evidence of the acts done under it is a guide to the intention of the parties in such a case and particularly when acts are done shortly after the date of the instrument. What the courts are required to see in such cases of disputes about meaning and purport of the documents in question is to look for surrounding circumstances to decipher the true meaning. Yet in other case, by Constitution Bench of the Supreme Court, it was held, "We agree that when a contract has been reduced to writing we must look

---

13   AIR 1954 SC 345
14   (2016) 12 SCC 623

only to that writing for ascertaining the terms of the agreement between the parties but it does not follow from this that it is only what is set out expressly and in so many words in the document that can constitute a term of the contract between the parties. If on a reading of the document as a whole, it can fairly be deduced from the words actually used therein that the parties had agreed on a particular term, there is nothing in law which prevents them from setting up that term. The terms of a contract can be expressed or implied from what has been expressed. It is in the ultimate analysis a question of construction of the contract. And again it is well established that in construing a contract it would be legitimate to take into account surrounding circumstances. Therefore, on the question whether there was an agreement between the parties that the contract was to be non-transferable, the absence of a specific clause forbidding transfer is not conclusive. What has to be seen is whether it could be held on a reasonable interpretation of the contract, aided by such considerations as can legitimately be taken into account that the agreement of the parties was that it was not to be transferred. When once a conclusion is reached that such was the understanding of the parties, there is nothing in law which prevents effect from being given to it."[15]

UNIDROIT has worked extensively in the area of contract law and adopted a variety of instruments intended to offer harmonised and effective rules to respond to the evolving needs of modern transactions.[16] It provides:

ARTICLE 4.1

1. A contract shall be interpreted according to the common intention of the parties.

2. If such an intention cannot be established, the contract shall be interpreted according to the meaning that reasonable persons

---

15 Khardah Company Ltd v Raymon & Co. (India) Private, 1962 AIR 1810
16 www.unidroit.org

of the same kind as the parties would give to it in the same circumstances.

ARTICLE 4.2 (Interpretation of statements and other conduct)

1. The statements and other conduct of a party shall be interpreted according to that party's intention if the other party knew or could not have been unaware of that intention.
2. If the preceding paragraph is not applicable, such statements and other conduct shall be interpreted according to the meaning that a reasonable person of the same kind as the other party would give to it in the same circumstances.

ARTICLE 4.3 (Relevant circumstances)

In applying Articles 4.1 and 4.2, regard shall be had to all the circumstances, including

a. preliminary negotiations between the parties;
b. practices which the parties have established between themselves;
c. the conduct of the parties subsequent to the conclusion of the contract;
d. the nature and purpose of the contract;
e. the meaning commonly given to terms and expressions in the trade concerned;
f. usages.

Catherine Mitchel examines as to the way the contracting parties can control the 'interpretation' of the contracts. She says, "The next task is to consider how the parties might exercise greater interpretative control over their agreement, or how they might be able to reduce the scope of context to influence the meaning placed on their agreement. The kind of contextual material of interest here is that which may have the effect of altering, or adding to, the agreed statement of terms. This might be material from previous contracts, oral conversations prior, or subsequent, to the contract, previous negotiations, trade customs, or understandings generated by the market in which the parties conduct business.[17]

She quotes Katz who suggests three possible ways that contracting parties can influence interpretative method: merger (or entire agreement) clauses, choice of law clauses and choice of forum clauses. Choice of law clauses may enable parties to choose a regime characterised by more or less formality, depending on their own particular preferences.[18] In relation to choice of forum, parties may choose arbitration or mediation over courts if they believe that either forum will be more, or less, formal and less expensive. Commercial parties often prefer to have their disputes settled by arbitration and include clauses in their contracts directing that disputes should be resolved by this method in preference to litigation (although the effect of such clauses is often itself the obligations).

An 'Entire Agreement Clause' is usually phrased along the following lines: 'This contract comprises the entire agreement between the parties, as detailed in the various Articles and Annexures and there are not any agreements, understandings, promises or conditions, oral or written, expressed or implied, concerning the subject matter which are not merged into this contract and superseded hereby.'[19] This has, in principle, approval in *proviso* (5) of section 92 of Indian Evidence Act which provides that any usage or custom by which incidents not expressly mentioned in any contract are usually annexed to contracts of that description, may be proved: Provided that the annexing of such incident would not be repugnant to, or inconsistent with, the express terms of the contract.

The cynical truth about interpretation in England seems to be that the Bench has been provided with some dozens of 'principles' from which a judicious selection can be made to achieve substantial justice in each individual case. From time to time, all the relevant principles point in

---

17   Interpretation of Contracts at pp. 125
18   Ibid
19   Ibid at pp.127

the same direction and leave the court no choice, but in most of the cases susceptible of any real dispute, the function of counsel is merely to provide sufficient material for the court to perform its task of selection.[20] These principles are referred to as the Canons of Construction. Kim Lewison has outlined following canons-

1. **Construing the document as a whole**: In Order to arrive at the true interpretation of a document, but must be considered in the context of the whole of the document.

2. **Giving effect to all parts of a contract**: In construing a contract all parts of it must be given effect where possible, and no part of it should be treated as inoperative or surplus.

3. **Standard printed terms and special terms**: Where the contract is a standard form of contract to which the parties have added special conditions, then unless the contract otherwise provides, greater weight must be given to the special conditions, and in case of conflict between the general conditions and special conditions, the latter will prevail. However, in interpreting a standard form there is less room for the influence of the special background applicable to any particular transaction.

4. **General Provisions and special provisions**: Where a contract contains general provisions and specific provisions, the specific provisions will be given greater weight than the general provisions where the facts to which the contract is to be applied fall within the scope of the specific provisions.

5. **Express mention of part of subject matter**: Where the contract expressly mentions some things, it is often to be inferred that other things of the same general category which are not expressly mentioned were deliberately omitted. Similar principles apply to

---

20 Megarry, Review (1945) 61 LQR 102 as quoted in Interpretation of Contracts by Kim Lewison at p. 335

the express inclusion of obligations dealing with a particular area of application.

6. **Express terms negative implied terms**: An express term in a contract excludes the possibility of implying any term dealing with the same subject-matter as the express term.

7. **Construction contra proferentum**: Where there is doubt about the meaning of a contract, the words will be construed against the person who put them forward. However, the rule is reversed in the case of a grant by the Crown, but not in the case of a commercial contract to which the Crown is a party.

8. **Construction in favour of consumer**: If there is doubt about the meaning of a written term in a consumer contract, the interpretation which is most favourable to the consumer prevails.

9. **Party not to take advantage of own wrong**: A contract will be construed so far as possible in such a manner as not permit one party to it to take advantage of his own wrong.

10. **Contract to be construed so as to be lawful**: Where the words of a contract are capable of two meanings, one of which is lawful and the other unlawful, the former construction should be preferred.

11. **Expression of terms implied by law**: The expression of a term which the law implies as a necessary part of the contract has no greater effect than the implied term would have had.

12. **The ejusdem generis principle**: If it is found that things described by particular words have some common characteristic which constitutes them a genus, the general words which follow them ought to be limited to things of that genus.

13. **Meaning is known by context**: The meaning of an unclear word is known by its context.

14. **Distributive construction**: In an appropriate case where a plural subject is followed by a plural predicate the plurals may be

distributively construed, thereby breaking down the plural into its component singulars.

15. **Saving the document**: Where two constructions of an instrument are equally plausible, upon one of which the instrument is valid, and upon the other of which it is invalid, the court should lean towards that construction which validates the instrument.

16. **The reasonableness of the result**: The reasonableness of the result of any particular construction is a relevant consideration in choosing between rival constructions.

17. **The clear words principle**: Where a construction would produce an unfair result, the court will often require clear words to support the construction in question.

18. **Presumption against impossibility**: There is a presumption of interpretation that a contract does not require performance of the impossible, but this may be rebutted by clear words.

16

FRUSTRATION OF CONTRACT

> *"In secret we met -*
> *In silence I grieve,*
> *That thy heart could forget,*
> *Thy spirit deceive.*
> *If I should meet thee*
> *After long years,*
> *How should I greet thee? -*
> *With silence and tears"*
>
> – Lord Byron

If the parties entered into a contract under the same mistaken assumption, that contract may be void for 'common mistake', if the mistake is so fundamental that it 'nullifies' consent. This is often referred to as 'initial impossibility' because the impossibility already exists when the contract is made. The impossibility maybe subsequent, i. e. after the formation of the contract, events occur, without the fault of either party, which render further performance of the contract either impossible, illegal, or radically different from what was originally envisaged. In this situation the contract may be automatically discharged on the grounds of frustration and the parties will be excused further performance of the their contractual obligations.[1] So, there is an initial impossibility to perform and there is a subsequent impossibility to perform. The latter comes within the doctrine of frustration of contract. Section 56, second paragraph, the Indian Contract Act provides, "A contract to do an act which, after the contract is made, becomes impossible, or, by reason of some event which the promisor could not prevent, unlawful, becomes void when the act becomes void when the act becomes impossible or unlawful." The doctrine of frustration is, truly speaking, a mode of discharge from the performance of the contract. Its story starts from the day the contract is made, but remains dormant till certain event outside the framework of the contract takes place, all of its own without any cause or fault of either of the parties to the contract.[2]

Section 56 of the Indian Contract Act does not explain as to what is meant by 'becomes impossible' but there may be several grounds which can lead to invocation of the doctrine. *Firstly*, destruction of the subject matter when the contract becomes impossible. In **Taylor v. Caldwell**[3], on 27 May 1862, the plaintiffs entered into a contract with the defendants by which the defendants agreed to let the plaintiffs have the use of Surrey Gardens and Music Hall on 17 June, 15 July, and 5 and 19 August for the purpose of giving a series of four grand concerts and fetes. On 11 June (before the first of these dates on which a concert was to be given), the Hall was destroyed by fire, without the fault of either party. The concerts could not be given as intended. The plaintiffs argued that the defendants were in breach of contract in failing to supply the Hall and they sought damages for their wasted advertising expenditure. It was held that the continuation of the contract was subject to an implied condition that the parties would be excused if the subject matter was destroyed. Therefore, the contract was discharged by frustration and both parties were

---

1 Casebook on Contract Law by Jill Poole at p. 495
2 Doctrine of Frustration in Law of Contract by Dr. G.K. Tripathi at p. 7
3 122 ER 309 (QB)

released. But in Indian context, this would not mean physical or literal impossibility alone.[4] In **Satyabrata Ghosh v. Mugnee Ram**[5] it was held by the Supreme Court,

"15. These differences in the way of formulating legal theories really do not concern us so long as we have a statutory provision in the Indian Contract Act, 1872. In deciding cases in India, the only doctrine that we have to go by is that of supervening impossibility or illegality as laid down in sec. 56 of the Contract Act taking the word 'impossible' in its practical and not literal sense. It must be borne in mind, however, that sec. 56 lays down a rule of positive law and does not leave the matter to be determined according to the intention of the parties.

16 In the latest decision of the House of Lords referred to above, the Lord Chancellor puts the whole doctrine upon the principle of construction. But the question of construction may manifest itself in two totally different ways. In one class of cases the question may simply be, as to what the parties themselves had actually intended; and whether or not there was a condition in the contract itself, express or implied, which operated, according to the agreement of the parties themselves, to release them from their obligations; this would be a question of construction pure and simple and the ordinary rules of construction would have to be applied to find out what the real intention of the parties was. According to Indian Contract Act, a promise may be express or implied. In cases, therefore, where the court gathers as a matter of construction that the contract itself contained impliedly or expressly a term, according to which it would stand discharged on the happening of certain circumstances, the dissolution of the contract would take place under the terms of the contract itself and such cases would be outside the purview of sec. 56 altogether. Although in English law these cases are treated as cases of frustration, in India they would be dealt with u/s. 32

---

4   Doctrine of Frustration in Law of Contract by Dr. G.K. Tripathi at p. 25
5   AIR 1954 SC 44

of the Indian Contract Act, 1872 which deals with contingent contracts or similar other provisions contained in the Act.

In the large majority of cases however the doctrine of frustration is applied not on the ground that the parties themselves agreed to an implied term which operated to release them from the performance of the contract. The relief is given by the court on the ground of subsequent impossibility when it finds that the whole purpose or basis of a contract was frustrated by the intrusion or occurrence of an unexpected event or change of circumstances which was beyond what was contemplated by the parties at the time when they entered into the agreement. Here there is no question of finding out an implied term agreed to by the parties embodying a provision for discharge, because the parties did not think about the matter at all nor could possibly have any intention regarding it.

When such an event or change of circumstance occurs which is so fundamental as to be regarded by law as striking at the root of the contract as a whole, it is the court which can pronounce the contract to be frustrated and at an end. The court undoubtedly has to examine the contract and the circumstances under which it was made. The belief, knowledge and intention of the parties are evidence, but evidence only on which the court has to form its own conclusion whether the changed circumstances destroyed altogether the basis of the adventure and its underlying object. This may be called a rule of construction by English Judges but it is certainly not a principle of giving effect to the intention of the parties which underlies all rules of construction. This is really a rule of positive law and as such comes within the purview of sec. 56 of the Indian Contract Act, 1872.

This judgment has been consistently relied upon by the Courts in India. In **South East Asia Marine Engineering And Constructions Ltd. (Seamec Ltd.) v. Oil India Limited**[6] the Supreme Court held, "When the

---

6   2020 (5) SCC 164

parties have not provided for what would take place when an event which renders the performance of the contract impossible, then Section 56 of the Contract Act applies. When the act contracted for becomes impossible, then under Section 56, the parties are exempted from further performance and the contract becomes void. As held by this Court in Satyabrata Ghose v. Mugneeram Bangur & Co., AIR 1954 SC 44:"

The *second* ground may be where the contract becomes impossible of the performance in cases concerning non-occurrence of an agreed event. In **Krell v. Henry**[7] on 20 June 1902, the defendant agreed to hire a flat in Pall Mall from the plaintiff for £75. The hire was for 26 and 27 June, which were the days on which coronation procession of Edward VII was due to take place pass along Pall Mall. The £25 deposit was paid and the balance was due on 24 June. The contract contained no express reference to the coronation procession or to any other purpose for which the flat was taken. it was announced on 24 June that the procession would not take place on those days because the coronation had been postponed due to King's illness. The defendant refused to pay the balance of the agreed rent. Darling J (at first instance) relying on Taylor v. Caldwell, held that there was an implied condition in the contract that the procession should take place. It was held in appeal, from the circumstances it was clear that the procession actually taking place on these days along the advertised route was regarded by both contracting parties as being of the foundation of the contract, and hence the contract was frustrated. The doctrine of frustration has been stated to have developed by the law as an expedient to escape from injustice, where such would result from enforcement of a contract in its literal terms after a significant change in circumstances.[8] However, the Supreme Court has emphasized that so far as courts in this country are concerned they must look primarily to the law as embodied in sections 32 and 56 of the

---

7   [1903] 2 KB 740(CA)
8   National Carriers Ltd v. Panalpina (Northern) Ltd [1981] 1 All ER 161

Contract Act.[9] The doctrine of frustration is not available where a party has simply failed to take adequate contractual steps to protect itself against a foreseeable risk.

The *third* ground is where the performance of the contract depends on the act of third parties. The Courts in India have not accepted this as act of impossibility. In **Ganga Ram v. Ram Charan**[10] the Supreme Court held, "......... it seems to us that the considerations which prevailed with them must govern the construction of the agreement with which we are concerned in this case. The agreement does not seem to us to convey the meaning that the delivery of the goods was made contingent on their being supplied to the respondent-firm by the Victoria Mills. We find it difficult to hold that the parties ever contemplated the possibility of the goods not being supplied at all. The words "prepared by the Mill" are only a description of the goods to be supplied, and the expressions "as soon as they are prepared" and "as soon as they are supplied to us by the said Mill" simply indicate the process of delivery. It should be remembered that what we have to construe is a commercial agreement entered into in a somewhat common form, and, to use the words of Lord Sumner in the case to which reference has been made, "there is nothing surprising in a merchant's binding himself to procure certain goods at all events, it being a matter of price and of market expectations." Since the true construction of an agreement must depend upon the import of the words used and not upon what the parties choose to say afterwards, it is unnecessary to refer to what the parties have said about it."

The *fourth* ground is where transport facilities are not available. In **Seth Mohan Lal v. Grain Chambers Ltd., Muzaffarnagar**[11], the Supreme Court held, "The plea that there was frustration of the contracts, and on that account the Company was liable to refund all the amounts

---

9 Ganga Saran v. Firm Ram Charan Ram Gopal AIR 1952 SC 9
10 AIR 1952 SC 9
11 AIR 1968 SC 772

which it had received, has no substance. As we have already held, the outstanding contracts were not at all affected by the Government Order. Imposition by the Central Government of a prohibition by its notification dated 01.03.1950 restraining persons from offering and the Railway Administration from accepting for transportation by rail any gur, except with the permit of the Central Government from any station outside the State of Uttar Pradesh which was situated within a radius of thirty miles from the border of Uttar Pradesh does not lead to frustration of the contracts. Fresh contracts were prohibited: but settlement of the outstanding contracts by payment of differences was not prohibited, nor was delivery of gur in pursuance of the contract and acceptance thereof at the due date by the Company prohibited. The difficulty arising by the Government orders in transporting the goods needed to meet the contract was not an impossibility contemplated by sec. 56 of the Contract Act leading to frustration of the contracts."

The *fifth* ground may arise when there is delayed performance. It may fairly be concluded that delay may defeat the contract only in those cases when time is of essence. If, however, it is of essence, it will operate to frustrate the contract only in that situation when it hits the performance so badly that no reasonable man would demand further performance keeping in view the object of the contract, the time, the cost and the alternatives involved.[12] Whether time is of essence or not is governed by provision of section 55 of Indian Contract Act.

The contract is discharged by frustration at the time of the frustrating event. For this purpose, the Court must look at the matter on the basis of the facts known to the parties at the time of the event interfering with the contract and the probabilities as they appeared, and not in the light of later events, which may show that the contract might, in fact, have been performed.[13] Where a contract is 'discovered to be void' for impossibility

---

12 The Doctrine of Frustration in Law of Contract by Dr. G.P. Tripathi at p. 41
13 Pollock & Mulla on Contract Act at p.1199

under the first paragraph of this section, or 'becomes void' because of an event occurring after it is made, rendering it impossible or unlawful, the party who has received any advantage under it is bound to restore it or make compensation for it to the other party under section 65.[14]

The third paragraph of Section 56 provides that where one person has promised to do something which he knew, or, with reasonable diligence, might have known, and which the promisee did not know, to be impossible or unlawful, such promisor must make compensation to such promisee for any loss which such promisee sustains through the non-performance of the promise. This is an exception to the doctrine of frustration, where instead of declaring the contract discharged, the promisor is saddled with the liability to pay compensation to the promisee for the non-performance of the promise.[15] There is authority under the English law, that where, by reason of special knowledge, one party foresees the possibility of the event and conceals this from the other, the party with the special knowledge will not be discharged.[16] If a contract is frustrated, but subsequently the work is started again or proceeded with under protest, then in the absence of any express agreement, the contractor would on general principles be entitled to payment for the work done after the frustration on a quantum meruit.[17]

The arbitration clause in the contract survives even after the contract is frustrated. In case of frustration, it is the performance of the contract which comes to an end but the contract would still be in existence for purposes such as the resolution of disputes arising under or in connection with it. The question as to whether the contract becomes impossible of performance and was discharged under the doctrine of frustration would still have to be decided under the arbitration clause which operates in respect of such purposes.[18] According to Russel, "The test in such cases has

---

14 Ibid at p. 1200
15 Satyabrata Ghosh v. Mugneeram Bangur & Co.
16 Walton Harvey Ltd v. Walker and Homfrays Ltd [1930] All ER Rep 465(CA)
17 Hudson, Building & Engineering Contracts Ninth Edition at p.651
18 Naihati Jute Mills Ltd. v Khyaliram Jaggannth AIR 1968 SC 522

been said to be whether the contract is determined by something outside itself, in which case the arbitration clause is determined with it, or by something arising out of the contract, in which case the arbitration clause remains effective and can be enforced.[19]

---

[19] Russel On Arbitration

17

WARRANTIES, CONDITIONS AND TERMS

> *"It was a good strategy but this is where I intended to turn her plans upside-down. In the courtroom there are three things for the lawyer to always consider: the knowns, the known unknowns and the unknown unknowns. Whether at the prosecution or defence table, it is the lawyer's job to master the first two and always be prepared for the third."*
>
> – Michael Connelly, The Fifth Witness

In day-to-day practice, the three words- contractual terms, conditions and warranties are often used interchangeably, rather in pleadings it is customary to use all three words concomitantly to leave it for stages of evidence and final argument to draw finer distinction to buttress plaintiff's or defendant's case. It is not that the lawyers are not aware of the distinction but such drafting is done to camouflage the real case before the stage of evidence. The law on this point, is however, well settled and the courts do not shy away from tearing into the niceties for drawing real intentions. Therefore, a term will be treated as condition of a contract where the parties have provided for it to be so treated either expressly or by necessary implication.

In **Kingston v Preston**, Lord Mansfield is reported as having said that there were three kinds of covenant:

1. Such as are called mutual and independent, where either party may recover damages from the other, for the injury may have received by a breach of the covenants in his favour, and where it is no excuse for the defendant, to allege a breach of the covenants on the part of the plaintiff;

2. Covenants which are conditions and dependent, in which the performance of one depends on the prior performance of another, and, therefore until this prior condition is performed, the other party is not liable to an action on his covenant;

3. Mutual conditions to be performed at the same time; and in these, if one party was ready, and offered to perform his part, and the other neglected or refused to perform his, he who was ready and has offered has fulfilled his engagement, and may maintain an action for the default of the other, though it is not certain that either is obliged to do the first act.

In modern terminology the first category of covenants would be called warranties, and the second and third conditions.[1] Lawyers use conditions in several senses. Sometimes they use it to refer to the term in the agreement that makes the promise conditional... However, lawyers also use condition to refer to an operative fact rather than to a term. According to the Restatement Second a condition is an event, not certain to occur, which must occur, unless occurrence is excused, before performance under a contract becomes due. This use of the word has the support of leading writers. E. Allan Farnsworth, Contracts[2]. A stipulation or prerequisite

---

1 Interpretation of Contracts- Sir Kim Lewison at p.749
2 As quoted in Black's Law Dictionary

in a contract, will, or other instrument, constituting the essence of the instrument is a condition.[3] The Indian Sale of Goods Act[4] provides -

1. A stipulation in a contract of sale with reference to goods which are the subject thereof may be a condition or a warranty.

2. A condition is a stipulation essential to the main purpose of the contract, the breach of which gives rise to a right to treat the contract as repudiated.

3. A warranty is a stipulation collateral to the main purpose of the contract, the breach of which gives rise to a claim for damages but not to a right to reject the goods and treat the contract as repudiated.

4. Whether a stipulation in a contract of sale is a condition or a warranty depends in each case on the construction of the contract. A stipulation may be a condition, though called a warranty in the contract.

The provisions as to when a condition may be treated as warranty have also been dealt with in the Sale of Goods Act.[5]

It is condition *precedent* when an act or event other than a lapse of time, that must exist or occur before a duty to perform something promised arises. A condition that, if it occurs, will bring something else to an end; an event the existence of which, by agreement of parties, discharges a duty of performance that has arisen.[6] If.......... the deed or will uses such words as 'but if', 'on condition that', 'provided', or 'if however' it will generally be assumed that a condition subsequent was intended.[7]

---

[3] Ibid
[4] Sec. 12
[5] Sec. 13
[6] Ibid
[7] Thomus F Bergin & Paul G Haskel, Preface to Estates in Land and Future Interest as quoted in Black's Law Dictionary

The word 'term' means a word or phrase esp. an expression that has a fixed meaning in some field; a contractual stipulation.[8] A fundamental term is a contractual provision that must be included for contract to exist; a contractual provision that specifies an essential purpose of the contract, so that a breach of the provision through inadequate performance makes the performance not only defective but essentially different from what had been promised.[9] From a commercial lawyer point of view, contractual terms may be divided into three broad classes:

1. Terms breach of which will always give rise to a right to bring the contract to an end (conditions);

2. Terms breach of which may or may not give rise to such a right depending on the gravity of the breach (intermediate terms or innominate terms)

3. Terms breach of which will never give rise to a right to bring the contract to an end, but give rise to a claim for compensation (warranties)[10]

In contrast to the fundamental term, there is 'implied term' which means a provision not expressly agreed by the parties but instead read into the contract by a court as being implicit. An implied term should not, in theory, contradict the contract's express terms[11]. One of the curious fields for interpretation is principle of implied terms in contracts. In order for a term to be implied the following criteria are useful guidelines[12].

1. it must be reasonable and equitable;

2. it must be necessary to give business efficacy to the contract so that no term will be implied if the contract is effective without it;

3. it must be so obvious that it goes without saying;

---

8   Black's Law Dictionary
9   Ibid
10 Interpretation of Contracts- Sir Kim Lewison at p.750
11 Ibid
12 Ibid

4. it must be capable of clear expression;

5. it must not contradict any express term of contract

Nabha Power Ltd. v. Punjab State Power Corporation[13] is the latest authority on interpretation of contract *vis a vis* implied terms where the Supreme Court relied upon the aforesaid broad conditions for applicability of implication of term in contract. The facts involved in this case was about interpretation of the pricing coal which were differently claimed. While contractor claimed 'washing' of coal as term implied, the employer refused to accept 'washing' as the same was not mentioned in the contract.

Actual definition in the PPA: FCOAL n is the weighted average actual cost to the Seller of purchasing, transporting and unloading the coal most recently supplied to and at the Project.

PSPCL's Interpretation: FCOAL n is the weighted average actual cost to the Seller of purchasing unwashed coal, transporting washed and unloading the washed coal most recently supplied to and at the Project"

It was held in para 62, "The plea of the first respondent that the fuel supply agreement and the fuel transportation agreement are part of the 'project documents' which does not include the component of 'washing', does not hold much water for the reason that 'washed' coal is a necessity for the project as a quality requirement for the formula envisaging the requisite quality of coal to be obtained at the project site and, thus, including all the relevant costs up to that quality. The mere term 'coal', therefore, would have to mean 'washed' coal, as no other type of coal could be used in the matter at hand."

"Para 63. Now turning to the transportation cost, once again, what is sought to be excluded is taking the coal for 'washing' as well as the last mile to the project, on account of the Railway siding not being located at the project site for a certain specified period of time. It is for that period of time

---

13 (2018) 11 SCC 508

that the actual transportation cost through road is sought to be recovered by the appellant."

"Para 64. We fail to appreciate as to how these costs can be excluded, as the transportation costs to the project site have to be compensated to the appellant. It is not qualified by the methodology of transfer, i.e., railways or road. It is also a matter of necessity, since the railway siding had not reached the project site due to some complications in acquisition of land. It is really the transportation cost from point to point which would be involved and the mere mention in the RFP under project related activity/ milestone about Railway siding and the Railway lines from nearby station to site cannot imply that the Railways is the only mode of transportation when the siding has not been made, albeit on account of land acquisition problems." The court, however, left a word of caution as, "We may, however, in the end, extend a word of caution. It should certainly not be an endeavour of commercial courts to look to implied terms of contract. In the current day and age, making of contracts is a matter of high technical expertise with legal brains from all sides involved in the process of drafting a contract. It is even preceded by opportunities of seeking clarifications and doubts so that the parties know what they are getting into. Thus, normally a contract should be read as it reads, as per its express terms. The implied terms is a concept, which is necessitated only when the Penta-test referred to aforesaid comes into play. There has to be a strict necessity for it..."

18

TIME, EXEMPTION AND *FORCE MAJURE* CLAUSES

Remember that time is money!

– Benjamin Franklin 1706–90
Advice to a Young Tradesman (1748)

TIME CLASUE

The general rule in contract is that a party will be discharged only where he has performed precisely his obligations under the contract.[1] 'Time' is a point in or period of duration at or during which something is alleged to have occurred.[2] —Where, by the contract, a promisor is to perform his promise without application by the promisee, and no time for performance is specified, the engagement must be performed within a reasonable time. The question "what is a reasonable time" is, in each particular case, a question of fact.[3] This section would apply only when time is neither expressly fixed nor determinable from the contract.[4] When a promise

---

1 Emden's Building Contract & Practice at p.384
2 Black's Law Dictionary
3 Sec. 46 of Contract Act,1872
4 Mulla on Indian Contract Act at p.1063

is to be performed on a certain day, and the promisor has undertaken to perform it without application by the promisee, the promisor may perform it at any time during the usual hours of business on such day and at the place at which the promise ought to be performed.[5] Section 55 of Contract Act deals with the provision with regards to effect of not performing when time is essential and also not essential. It provides, "55. Effect of failure to perform at fixed time, in contract in which time is essential.—When a party to a contract promises to do a certain thing at or before a specified time, or certain things at or before specified times, and fails to do any such thing at or before the specified time, the contract, or so much of it as has not been performed, becomes voidable at the option of the promisee, if the intention of the parties was that time should be of the essence of the contract.

Effect of such failure when time is not essential.—If it was not the intention of the parties that time should be of the essence of the contract, the contract does not become voidable by the failure to do such thing at or before the specified time; but the promisee is entitled to compensation from the promisor for any loss occasioned to him by such failure.

Effect of acceptance of performance at time other than that agreed upon.—If, in case of a contract voidable on account of the promisor's failure to perform his promise at the time agreed, the promisee accepts performance of such promise at any time other than that agreed, the promisee cannot claim compensation for any loss occasioned by the non-performance of the promise at the time agreed, unless, at the time of such acceptance, he gives notice to the promisor of his intention to do so."

The concept of time clause as applicable to contracts can be summarised in following principles[6]-

1. Where a contract provides for the performance of an act within a certain number of months, the period expires on the day of month

---

5   Sec. 47 of Contract Act, 1872
6   Interpretation of Contracts by Sir Kim Lewison at pp 689 to 715

bearing the same number as the date on which the period begins or if no such day, on the last day of the month.

Following this rule means, "when time is limited by reference to calendar months no account can be taken of the fact that some months are longer or shorter than others. February equals March. In my judgment if an act is authorized to be performed on any arbitrary day in any month of the year, then one month elapses on the corresponding day of the next month, provided that the day of the act itself is excluded from computation."[7]

2. The word day may mean either a calendar daay or a period of 24 consecutive hours, according to the context.

A 'working day' normally means a calendar day which is a day of work as distinguished from a holiday. Thus a working day consists of 24 hours, and not merely of that part of the day during which work is carried on.

A day is a period running from midnight to midnight, and not a period of 24 consecutive hours, unless so intended. The Supreme Court in National Insurance Co. Ltd v Jijubai Nathuji Dabhi[8] held "This Court in New India Assurance co. V. RamDayal had held that in the absence of any specific time mentioned in that behalf, the contract would be operative from the mid-night of the day by operation of provisions of the General Clauses Act. But in view of the special contract mentioned in the insurance policy, namely, it would be operative from 4.00 p.m. on October 25, 1983 and the accident had occurred earlier thereto, the insurance coverage would not enable the claimant to seek recovery of the amount from the appellant-Company."

---

7   Dodds v Walker [1980] 1 WLR 1061
8   (1997) 1 SCC 66

3. Where, under a contract, a period of time is expressed to run from a certain day, the day named is generally excluded in computing the period. But where a period of time is expressed to begin on a certain day, the day named is generally included in computing the period. However, the context may displace the general rule.

In Lester v. Garland[9], it was stated that there was no general rule, but it was held that in the circumstances of that case the date which started time running should be excluded from the computation of time. This rule has been consistently followed since then. In India the rule is part of statute i.e. Limitation Act, 1963 where Section 12 (1) states that in computing the period of limitation for any suit, appeal or application, the day from which such period is to be reckoned, shall be excluded. In Section 12(2) the same principle is extended to computing period of limitation for an application for leave to appeal or for revision or for review of a judgment. Similarly The General Cluses Act provides that in any Act made after the commencement of this Act, it shall be sufficient, for the purpose of excluding the first in a series of days or any other period of time, to use the word "from", and, for the purpose of including the last in a series of days or any other period of time, to use the word "to".[10] Where, by any Act made after the commencement of this Act, any act or proceeding is directed or allowed to be done or taken in any Court or office on a certain day or within a prescribed period, then, if the Court or office is closed on that day or the last day of the prescribed period, the act or proceeding shall be considered as done or taken in due time if it is done or taken on the next day afterwards on which the Court or office is.[11]

---

9   (1808) 15 Ves 248
10 Sec. 9
11 Sec. 10

In some different kind of dispute, involving dishonour of cheques, a three judges bench of the Supreme Court came to decide the question "Whether for calculating the period of one month which is prescribed under Section 142(b), the period has to be reckoned by excluding the date on which the cause of action arose?" There was variance of views in Saketh India Ltd. & Ors. v. India Securities Ltd[12] and SIL Import, USA v. Exim Aides Silk Exporters, Bangalore[13]. It was held, "we are of the opinion that *Saketh* lays down the correct proposition of law. We hold that for the purpose of calculating the period of one month, which is prescribed under Section 142(b) of the N.I. Act, the period has to be reckoned by excluding the date on which the cause of action arose. We hold that SIL Import USA does not lay down the correct law. Needless to say that any decision of this Court which takes a view contrary to the view taken in Saketh by this Court, which is confirmed by us, do not lay down the correct law on the question involved in this reference."

4. Where a person is required to perform an act within a certain period the day of the date or event from which the period runs will not be included in the period; and the act may be performed at any time up to the last moment of the last day of the period.

In Easthaugh v Macpherson[14], it was held, "As a matter of definition... I should be inclined to think that 'by the date' ought to mean 'on or before the date'. By contrast if something is to be done "on the expiry of a period", it is not done within that period.[15]

5. Time stipulations are not of the essence in a non-mercantile contract unless the contract expressly so provides; or the nature of the contract or the surrounding circumstances show that time

---

12 (1999) 3 SCC 1
13 (1999) 4 SCC 567
14 [1954] 1 All ER 214, CA
15 Ketley v Gilbert [2000] EWCA Civ 354

should be taken to be of the essence. In mercantile contracts, however, time will usually be of the essence of time stipulations.

A court of equity would often relieve against a failure to comply with a time limit (for example in the case of a mortgage which could always be redeemed after contractual date for repayment had passed) unless the time was 'of the essence of the contract'. However, this passage cannot be extended into sphere of mercantile contracts. This was made clear by the House of Lords in Bunge Corp v Tradax Export SA[16].

In **Steedman v. Drinkle**,[17] it was held that where a time limit is expressed to be a 'condition precedent' or a 'condition' it is considered that it will generally be of the essence of the contract, because a 'condition' is the equivalent expression at common law for the phrase "time of essence" which is used in equity. In **Smt. Chand Rani (Dead) By Lrs. v Smt. Kamal Rani (Dead) By Lrs.**[18] the Supreme Court held in para 25- "From an analysis of the above case law it is clear that in the case of sale of immovable property there is no presumption as to time being the essence of the contract. Even if it is not of the essence of the contract the Court may infer that it is to be performed in a reasonable time if the conditions are:

1. from the express terms of the contract;

2. from the nature of the property; and

3. from the surrounding circumstances, for example: the object of making the contract."

6. Where the subject matter of the contract is of wasting nature or liable to great fluctuations in value, time will be of the essence of the contract.

---

16 [1981] 1 WLR 711
17 [1916] 1 AC 275
18 (1993) 1 SCC 519

In case of building contracts, the contractor's obligation is to 'complete' the work as specified in the contract by the date specified therein, if he fails to do this, he becomes liable to pay damages to the employer, either liquidated damages if so specified in the contract, or damages at large representing the amount of any loss caused to the employer by the delay in the completion.[19] Here the word completion is classified into two- substantial competition and practical completion. The doctrine of substantial completion permits the contractor to be paid once he has substantially performed his part of contract, less a deduction to reflect the cost of defective or outstanding work.[20]

Judge Coulson QC in **Jani-King (GB) Ltd. v Pula Enterprises Ltd**.[21] held, "..... the whole point of a commercial contract which will last for a particular period (or until a specified event has happened) is that the contracting parties are committed to both the contract and each other for a known period. It seems to me that it would make a nonsense of such an arrangement if either party could give notice of termination at any time during the term, with minimal consequences, because, say, that party has received a more attractive proposal from someone else."

EXEMPTION CLAUSE

A contractual provision providing that a party will not be liable for damages for which that party would otherwise have ordinarily been liable.[22] Exemption clauses are encountered in many different forms. Some clauses prevent one party from being liable to the other in the event of what would otherwise be a breach of their contract; some clauses limit the amount of compensation which would otherwise be payable upon a breach of contract; and other clauses require one party to indemnify the other against the consequences of that other's default. In addition clauses

---

19   Emdon's Building Contract & Practice, Lexis Nexis at p.383
20   Ibid at p.385
21   [2008] 1 All ER(Comm) 451
22   Black's Law Dictionary

which limit the time in which one party may bring claim against the other are treated in the same way as exemption clauses.[23] Professor Coote has divided the exception clauses into two classes- Type A exemption cluses whose effect, if any, is upon the accrual of particular primary rights; and Type B exception clauses which qualify primary or secondary rights without preventing the accrual of any of particular primary rights.[24] Some of the cardinal principles relating to exemptions clause in contracts are as follows[25]:

1. In interpreting an exemption clause, it must be interpreted in the context of the contract as a whole, rather than in isolation.

2. The court's traditional hostility to exclusion clauses has diminished in modern times, and it may vary with the extent of protection which the clause in question seeks to afford.

3. Exemption clauses in contracts are construes strictly, but the degree of strictness may vary with the extent of the exemption conferred by the clause.

4. An ambiguity in an exemption clause will be resolved against the party seeking to rely on the clause.

The aforesaid position of exemption clauses at common law may not be strictly applicable to Indian context but the matter is viewed in reference to the Indian Contract Act. Here, clauses in a contract excluding liability of a party in case of specified breach is enforceable at law. In Bharati Knitting Company v DHL Worldwide Express Ltd[26], the Supreme Court considering beneficial legislation as the Consumer Protection Act is, held, "It is true that the limit of damages would depend upon the terms of the contract and facts in each case. In Anson's Laws of Contract, 24th Edn. at page 152, on exemption clause with regard

---

23 Interpretation of Contracts, Sir Kim Lewison at p.571
24 Ibid, as quoted at p.571
25 Ibid at pp 574-587
26 (1996) 4 SCC 704

to notice of a printed clause, it was stated that a person who signed, a document containing contract and terms is normally bound by them even though he has not read them, and even though he is ignorant of their precise legal effect. But if the document is not signed, being merely delivered to him, then the question arises: whether the terms of the contract were adequately brought to his notice? The terms of the contract have elaborately been considered and decided, The details thereof are not necessary for us to Pursue. It is seen that when a person signs a document which contains certain contractual terms, as rightly pointed out by Mr. R.F. Nariman, learned senior counsel, that normally parties are bound by such contracts it is for the party to establish exception in a suit. But where a policy of insurance set to exclude the liability arising out of genetic disorder, the Delhi High Court held that exclusions such as the ones relating to genetic disorders do not remain merely in the realm of contracts but overflow into the realm of public law. The reasonableness of such clauses is subject to judicial review. The broad exclusion of "genetic disorders" is thus not merely a contractual issue between the insurance company and the insured but spills into the broader canvas of Right to Health. There appears to be an urgent need to frame a proper framework to prevent against genetic discrimination as also to protect collection, preservation and confidentiality of genetic data. Insurance companies are free to structure their contracts based on reasonable and intelligible factors which should not be arbitrary and in any case cannot be "exclusionary".[27]

In Skandia Insurance Co. Ltd v Kokilaben Chandravadan & Ors[28] the Supreme Court came to deal with the question whether the insurer is entitled to claim immunity from a decree obtained by the dependents of the victim of a fatal accident on the ground that the insurance policy provided "a condition excluding driving by a named person or persons or

---

27 M/S United India Insurance v Jai Parkash Tayal
28 !987 AIR 1184

by any person who is not duly licensed or by any person who has been disqualified for holding or obtaining a driving licence during the period of disqualification," and that such exclusion was permissible in the context of Section 96(2)(b)(ii)3 of Motor Vehicles Act, 1939 for claiming immunity against the obligation to satisfy the judgments against the insured in respect of third party risks. It was held, "The defence built on the exclusion clause cannot succeed for three reasons, viz:-

1. On a true interpretation of the relevant clause which interpretation is at peace with the conscience of Section 96, the condition excluding driving by a person not duly licensed is not absolute and the promisor is absolved once it is shown that he has done everything in his power to keep, honour, and fulfil the promise and he himself is not guilty of a deliberate breach.

2. Even if it is treated as an absolute promise, there is substantial compliance therewith upon an express or implied mandate being given to the licensed driver not to allow the vehicle to be left unattended so that it happens to be driven by an unlicensed driver.

3. The exclusion clause has to be 'read down' in order that it is not at war with the 'main purpose' of the provisions enacted for the protection of victims of accidents so that the promisor is exculpated when he does every- thing in his power to keep the promise.

In this judgment reliance was placed on Suisse Atlantique Societe d'Armement Maritime v. N V rotter-damsched Kolen Centrale[29] where the case involved the charter of a ship for two years' consecutive voyages between US and Europe. The ship was to be loaded at a specified rate. The owners were to be paid according to the number of voyages made during the two-year period. If the time taken for loading and unloading was longer than required, the charterers were to pay $1000 per day by way of demurrage. The charterers were

---

29   [1967] 1 AC 361

taking many extra days in loading and unloading but were allowed to continue to have the use of the ship for the remainder of the two years. Eight round trips were made. However, the owners alleged that the charterers delay in loading and unloading had made a further six trips impossible and sued for damages. The owners claimed that they were not bound by that clause because the charterers by their extraordinary delays had committed a fundamental breach of the contract. The House of Lords held that the contract did not in fact prescribe a minimum number of voyages. Therefore, there was no breach by the charterers merely by undertaking only eight voyages instead of the 14-17 voyages that the owners claimed were possible. It was further held "There is no rule of law which prevents parties to a contract agreeing to limit their respective liabilities. It is a question of the construction of the particular clause as to whether it applies to a fundamental breach or not. The court doubted the value of continuing the doctrine of fundamental breach or breach of a fundamental term. Exemption clauses may be held inapplicable to certain breaches of contract as a matter of construction of the contract. The court will be reluctant to ascribe to an exemption condition a meaning which effectively absolves one party from all duties and liabilities. It is not necessary for parties to a contract, when stipulating a condition, to spell out the consequences of breach."[30]

An interpretation of 'exemption' clause takes to the realm of distinction between 'fundamental breach' and 'breach of fundamental term'. In *Suisse Atlantique* it was also held, "There is no magic in the words 'fundamental breach'; this expression is no more than a convenient expression of saying that a particular breach or breaches of contract by one party is or are such as to go to the root of the contract which entitles the other party to treat such breach or breaches as a repudiation of the whole contract". To decide whether or not there has been a 'findamental breach' as distinct

---

30 www.thelawlane.com

from breach of a 'fundamental term', Viscount Dilhorne said that 'one has to have regard to the character of the breach and determine whether in consequence of it the performance of contract becomes something totally different from that which the contract contemplates.[31]

FORCE MAJURE CLAUSE

It is a French word which means, 'a superior force'. An event or effect that can be neither anticipated nor controlled. The term includes both acts of nature (e.g. floods and hurricanes) and acts of people (e.g. riots, strikes and wars). Force majeure clause is a contractual provision allocating the risk if performance becomes impossible or impracticable, esp. as a result of an even or effect that the parties could not have anticipated or controlled.[32] This term is used with reference to all circumstances independent of the will of man, and which it is not in his power to control, and such force majeure is sufficient to justify the non-execution of a contract. Thus war, inundations, and epidemics, are cases of force majeure.[33] *Lebeaupin* was cited with approval by the Supreme Court in M/S. Dhanrajamal Gobindram v M/S. Shamji Kalidas And Co[34] as, "The expression *"force majeure"* is not a mere French version of the Latin expression *"Vis major"*. It is undoubtedly a term of wider import. Difficulties have arisen in the past as to what could legitimately be included in *"force majeure"*. Judges have agreed that strikes, break- down of machinery, which, though normally not included in *"Vis Major"* are included in *"force majeure"*. An analysis of rulings on the subject into which it is not necessary in this case to go, shows that where reference is made to *"force majeure"*, the intention is to save the performing party from the consequences of anything over which he has no control. This is the widest meaning that can be given to *"force majeure"*, and even if

---

31 Emden's Building Contracts & Practice at p.659
32 Black's Law Dictionary
33 Lebeaupin v Richard Crispin and Co; [1920] 2 KB 714. This definition was quoted from a French legal textbook
34 1961 AIR 1285

this be the meaning, it is obvious that the condition about *"force majeure"*, in the agreement was not vague. The use of the word "usual" makes all the difference, and the meaning of the condition may be made certain by evidence about a force majeure clause, which was in contemplation of parties." Some of the broader principles of *force majeure* are[35]

1. A *force majeure* clause may, depending on its terms, be viewed as equivalent to an exemption clause.

    A *force majeure* clause is an exeptions clause and must be construed strictly.[36]

2. Where a *force majeure* clause is triggered by a specified event, an event falling within the literal words of the clause may be insufficient to trigger the clause, if it is an event that could not reasonably have been contemplated by the parties at the date of the contract. In such case the contract may be held to have been frustrated.

3. A *force majeure* will usually be interpreted as applicable only where the specified triggering event is beyond the control of the party in question, and cannot be overcome. However, this principle may be excluded by the terms of the clause.

4. A *force majeure* clause will usually be interpreted as inapplicable if the triggering event has been caused by the contracting party's own negligence.

5. A *force majeure* clause will usually be interpreted to apply only where the triggering event is the cause of the failure to perform.

6. Where a *force majeure* clause deals fully and completely with an event that would otherwise frustrate the contract, the doctrine of frustration will generally be excluded.

---

35 Interpretation of Contracts- Sir Kim Lewison
36 SHV Gas Supply v Naftomar Shipping [2006] 1 Llyod'e Rep 163

7. The party failing to perform must give notice to the other party of the impediment and its effect on its ability to perform.

19

PENALTIES AND DAMAGES

Blessed is the man who expects nothing, for he shall never be disappointed' was the ninth beautitude.

– Alexander Pope 1688-1744 Letter to Fortescue

PENALTIES

It is common to see a clause in a contract which mentions a specific amount to be paid in case of specific kind of breaches arising out of the subsisting contract, with an implicit design to avoid calculation and also to deter a party from disrupting the legal relationships. In all work contracts, this clause can be seen. In case of dispute, it is for courts to cull out whether the amount so claimed falls within the ambit of penalty or liquidated damages as it is settled that the penalty clause is not enforceable at law but the liquidated damages clause is enforceable.

According to the Black Law dictionary a contractual provision that assesses against a defaulting party an excessive monitory charge unrelated to actual harm. It quotes from a book "It not infrequently happens that contracts provide for what is to happen in the event of a breach by the parties, or by one of them. Such provisions may be perfectly simple attempts to avoid future disputes and to quantity the probable amount of any loss. That is unobjectionable. But sometimes clauses of this kind are not designed to quantify the amount of probable loss but are designed to terrorize, or frighten, the party into performance. For example, a contract may provide that the promisor is to pay £5 on a certain event, but if he fails to do so, he must then pay £500. Now a clause of that kind is called a penalty clause by lawyers, and for several hundred years it has been the law that such promises cannot be enforced. The standard justification for the law here is that it is unfair and unconscionable to enforce clauses which are designed to act in terrorem".[1] In the Book Interpretation of Contracts by Sir Kim Lewison,[2] it is defined as, "A penalty clause is a clause which without commercial justification provides for payment or forfeiture of a sum of money or a transfer of property by one party to another in the event of a breach of contract, the clause being designed to secure performance of the contract rather than to compensate the payee for loss occasioned by the breach."

In Dunlop Pneumatic Tyre Co. Ltd. v. New Garage & Motor Co. Ltd[3], the appellant supplied motor tyres, covers and tubes to the respondent dealers under an agreement whereby the respondents received certain trade discounts and agreed not to tamper with the marks on the goods, not to sell or offer the goods to any private customer or to any cooperative society at less than appellant's list prices, not to supply to persons to whom the appellants would not supply and to pay the sum of 5pounds by way of liquidated damages for every tyre, cover or tube sold or offered in breach of the agreement. The respondents sold the tyre cover to a cooperative society at below the current list price and the appellants sought the damages. The respondents pleaded that the clause was penalty. The court of first instance held the same as damages which was reversed by the court of appeal which held the same as penalty. The matter reached to the House of Lords held that

---

1   P.S. Atiyah, Promises, Morals, and Law 57-58 (1981).
2   Sweet & Maxwell, South Asian Reprint 2016 at pp 769
3   [1915] AC 79 [HL]

it was a case of liquidated damage. Lord Dunedin laid out the differences between a penalty clause and a limited damages clause:

1. Though the parties to a contract who use the words "penalty" or "liquidated damages" may prima facie be supposed to mean what they say, yet the expression used is not conclusive. The Court must find out whether the payment stipulated is in truth a penalty or liquidated damages. This doctrine may be said to be found passim in nearly every case.

2. The essence of a penalty is a payment of money stipulated as in terrorem of the offending party; the essence of liquidated damages is a genuine covenanted pre-estimate of damage (*Clydebank Engineering and Shipbuilding Co. v. Don Jose Ramos Yzquierdo y Castaneda*).

3. The question whether a sum stipulated is penalty or liquidated damages is a question of construction to be decided upon the terms and inherent circumstances of each particular contract, judged of as at the time of the making of the contract, not as at the time of the breach (*Public Works Commissioner v. Hills* and *Webster v. Bosanquet*).

4. To assist this task of construction various tests have been suggested, which if applicable to the case under consideration may prove helpful, or even conclusive. Such are:

    a. It will be held to be penalty if the sum stipulated for is extravagant and unconscionable in amount in comparison with the greatest loss that could conceivably be proved to have followed from the breach. (Illustration given by Lord Halsbury in *Clydebank Case*.

    b. It will be held to be a penalty if the breach consists only in not paying a sum of money, and the sum stipulated is a sum greater than the sum which ought to have been paid (*Kemble v. Farren*). This though one of the most ancient instances is truly a corollary to the last test. Whether it had its historical origin in the doctrine of the common law that when A. promised to pay B. a sum of money on a certain day and did not do so, B. could only recover the sum with, in certain cases, interest, but could never recover further damages for non-timeous payment, or whether it was a survival of the time when equity reformed unconscionable bargains merely because they were unconscionable,—a subject which much exercised Jessel M.R. in Wallis v. Smith —is probably more interesting than material.

c. There is a presumption (but no more) that it is penalty when "a single lump sum is made payable by way of compensation, on the occurrence of one or more or all of several events, some of which may occasion serious and others but trifling damage" (Lord Watson in Lord Elphinstone v. Monkland Iron and Coal Co).

On the other hand:

d. It is no obstacle to the sum stipulated being a genuine pre-estimate of damage, that the consequences of the breach are such as to make precise pre-estimation almost an impossibility. On the contrary, that is just the situation when it is probable that pre-estimated damage was the true bargain between the parties (Clydebank Case, Lord Halsbury; Webster v. Bosanquet Lord Mersey).

However, in India, Section 74 of Indian Contract Act, 1872 is clearly an attempt to eliminate the somewhat elaborate refinements made under the English common law in distinguishing between stipulations providing for payment of liquidated damages and stipulations in the nature of penalty. Under the common law a genuine pre-estimate to damages by mutual agreement is regarded as a stipulation naming liquidated damages and binding between the parties: a stipulation in a contract in terrorem is a penalty and the Court refuses to enforce it, awarding to the aggrieved party only reasonable compensation. The Indian Legislature has sought to across the web of rules and presumptions under the English common law, but enacting a uniform principle applicable to all stipulation naming amounts to be paid in case of breach, and stipulations by way of penalty.[4] It has further been held, "Before turning to the question about the compensation which may be awarded to the plaintiff, it is necessary to consider whether S. 74 applies to stipulations for forfeiture of amounts deposited or paid under the contract. It was urged that the section deals in terms with the right to receive from the party who has broken the contract reasonable compensation and not the right to forfeit what has already been received by the party aggrieved. There is however, no warrant for the assumption made by some of the High Courts in India, that S. 74 applies only to cases where the aggrieved party is seeking to receive some amount on breach of contract and not to cases where upon breach of contract an amount received under the contract is sought to be forfeited. The expression 'the contract contains any other stipulation by way of penalty' comprehensively applies to every covenant involving a penalty whether it is for payment on breach of contract of money or delivery of property in future, or for forfeiture of right to money or other property already delivered. Duty not to enforce the penalty clause but only to award reasonable compensation is statutorily imposed upon Courts by S. 74. In all cases, therefore, where there is a stipulation in the nature of penalty for forfeiture of an amount deposited pursuant to the terms of contact which expressly provides for forfeiture, the Court has jurisdiction to award such sum only as it considers reasonable, but not exceeding the amount specified in the contract as liable to forfeiture."[5]

Kim Lewison has discussed the following canons of penalty which has been referred to and relied upon by the Indian Courts as well.

---

[4] Fateh Chand v. Balkishan Dass, AIR 1963 SC 1405, 1410
[5] Ibid

1. Whether a clause is a penalty clause is a question of construction of the contract, to be determined at the date of the contract, and not at the date of the breach.

2. A sum of money which is payable otherwise than on breach of contract cannot be a penalty, unless the same clause governs events some of which are, and some of which are not, breaches.

3. Where a sum is payable on the occurrence of a number of events, one or more of which is breach of contract by the prayer, the sum is capable of being a penalty in circumstances in which it in fact becomes payable by virtue of the breach.

4. That fact that a sum of money payable on breach of contract is described by the contract as "liquidated damages" or "penalty" is relevant to but not decisive of its proper categorisation.

5. Since liquidated damages clauses serve the useful purpose of avoiding litigation and promoting, commercial certainly, the court should not be astute to categorise as penalties clauses described as liquidated damages clauses.

6. A sum payable in breach of contract will be held to be a penalty if it is extravagant and unconscionable in amount in comparison with the greatest loss which is likely to flow from the beach.

7. Where a sum is payable on a breach of contract to pay money, it will be a penalty if the sum payable on breach is greater than the sum which ought to have been paid under the contract. This does not, however, prohibit a requirement to pay interest at a reasonable rate.

8. A clause will not generally be construed as a penalty clause where it provides for the whole of a debt payable in instalments to become due on failure to pay one or more instalments on time.

9. There is a presumption that a stipulated sum is a penalty where it is made payable on the occurrence of one or more of several breaches, some of which may cause serious damage and others insignificant damage.

10. A clause providing for the forfeiture of a deposit will not be treated as a penalty provided that the deposit is a reasonable amount.

In **BSNL v. Reliance Communication Ltd**[6]., the Supreme Court held in para (53) "Liquidated damages serve the useful purpose of avoiding litigation and promoting commercial certainly and, therefore, the court should not be astute to categories as penalties the clauses described as liquidated damages. This principle is relevant to regulatory regimes. While categorising damages as "penal" or "liquidated damages", one must keep in mind the concept of pricing of these contracts and the level playing field provided to the operators because it is on costing and pricing that the loss to the promisee (BSNL) is measured and, therefore, all calls during the relevant period have to be seen. Since Clause 6.4.6. of interconnection agreement represents pre-estimate of reasonable compensation, Section 74 of the Contract Act is not violated. [7] It has further been held, "The fact that a sum of money is payable on breach of contract is described by the contract as "penalty" or "liquidated damages" is relevant but not decisive as to categorisation.[8] In certain cases it has been explained that forfeiture of a reasonable amount paid as earnest money does not amount to imposing a penalty. But if forfeiture is of the nature of penalty, Section 74 applies. Where under the terms of the contract the party in breach has undertaken to pay a sum of money or to forfeit a sum of money which he has already paid to the party complaining of a breach of contract, the undertaking of the nature of a penalty. (Paras 70 and 71).[9]

---

[6] (2011) 1 SCC 394
[7] (2011)1 SCC 394.
[8] Ibid
[9] V.K. Ashokan v. CCE, (2009) 14 SCC 85

DAMAGES

Notwithstanding, sanctity of contract, all contracts need not be performed. Sections-62 to 67 of Indian Contract Act cover all such contracts and contractual situations which would allow the party to obviate performance of such contracts. These six provisions are not a new species of contract or contractual situation but are merely re-enforcing provisions of earlier ones. The promisee may dispense with the performance or remit the same. Both the parties may enter into contract *de novo* or agree that let contract be never performed. Therefore, this chapter IV, in other words, essentially deal with discharge of contract by three means- Satisfaction (no action can be brought); Breach (action can be brought for damages or compensation) and Frustration (action cannot sustain) and all other matters ancillary and incidental thereto.

The main remedy against breach of contract is damages. The other remedy available in case of breach of contract is specific performance, but that remedy is not a rule rather discretionary based on principles of equity, which are granted only if it is shown that the compensation in monetary terms is grossly inadequate and in sufficient. In matter of commercial disputes, specific reliefs like- restitution and injunction are not readily granted.

Damages for breach of contract is also distinguishable from that of tort or equitable obligations like trust. The difference between the damages for tort and that for breach of contract lies in the fact that while the first requires sufferance of loss to be quantified and proved, the latter does not require any actual loss to have been suffered by the plaintiff.

According to orthodox law, damages for breach of contract are intended to put plaintiffs in the same position, so far as money is able, that they would have been in had their contracts been performed.[10] This basic measure of contract damages is as set out by **Baron Park in Robinson v.**

---

10   Contract Theory by Stephen A Smith, Oxford University Press at p 409

Harman, "Where a party sustains loss by reason of a breach of contract, he is, so far as money can do it to be placed in the same situation, with respect to damages, as if the contract has been performed".[11] This dictum has been invariably cited and approved in United Kingdom, and elsewhere. The key feature of the damages is that it is compensatory. As Lord Nicholls observed, "Leaving aside the anomalous exception of punitive damages, damages are compensatory. That is axiomatic.[12] The aim of the award is not to deter or punish, nor to strip the defendant of any gain (which would be restitutionary award), but rather to measure the loss to the claimant, that loss being the difference between the situation the claimant is in and that it would have been in.[13] This approach is often summarized by saying that the apparent aim of damages is to compensate plaintiffs' "expectation" interest (on the basis of that plaintiffs get the benefit they expected to get from performance) A more useful summary description might be to say that the apparent aim is to compensate the promisee's 'promissory' or performance interests.[14] If fundamental breach is established the next question is what effect, if any, that has on the applicability of other terms of the contract. This question has often arisen with regard to clauses excluding liability, in whole or in part, of the party in breach. I do not think that there is generally much difficulty where the innocent party has elected to treat the breach as a repudiation, bring the contract to an end and sue for damages. Then the whole contract has ceased to exist, including the exclusion clause, and I do not see how that Clause can then be used to exclude an action for loss which will be suffered by the innocent party after it has ceased to exist, such as loss of the profit which would have accrued if the contract had run its full term.[15]

---

11 [1848] 1 Ex Rep 850
12 The Law of Contract Damages by Adam Cramer, Hart Publishing, 2nd ed at p.13
13 Ibid
14 Contract Theory by Stephen A Smith, Oxford University Press at p 409
15 Maharashtra State Electricity Distribution Company Ltd. v. Datar Switchgear Limited and Ors. MANU/SC/0017/2018

Efficiency based explanation

Stephen A Smith has analysed the damages rule by comparing efficiency theories and rights-based theories. From the perspective of an efficiency theory, the fundamental purpose of an award of damages is to establish incentives for future potential contracting parties to act efficiently. This is set to be achieved by setting damages such that contracting parties have incentives to perform when, but only when, it is efficient to do so. More specifically, the normal damages rule (expectation damages) is said to encourage efficient performance because it internalizes the costs of breach to promisors. By setting damages at the value of promised performance, promisors have incentive to perform when, but only when, that value is greater than the cost of performance.[16] From an efficiency perspective, a basic function of contract law is to facilitate contract decision. According to efficiency theories, the primary way courts facilitate this decision is by protecting persons who enter contracts from losses that they might suffer if the other party reneges on the agreement. From another perspective, this protection is achieved by awarding reliance damages, not expectation damages. Reliance damages are equal to the costs incurred and profits foregone (from entering a different, but, comparable, contract) in reliance on a contract.[17] Expectation damages by contrast, require that the promisor pay a sum greater than the value of the losses caused by her promise. So far as contract decision is concerned, therefore, a rule of expectation damages will have the effect of dissuading some parties from entering beneficial contracts.[18]

Rights-based explanation

It explains damages on the basis of corrective justice. They explain compensatory damages on the basis that such orders require defendants

---

16 Ibid
17 Ibid
18 Ibid

to fulfil their duties, in corrective justice, to repair the harm caused by their wrongful actions. This principle is consistent with the principle that victims of breach have a right to compensatory damages.[19]

The specific measure of damages that corrective justice requires in contract case depends on what kind of an obligation a contractual obligation is. In particular, it depends on whether a contractual obligation is an obligation to do the very thing the defendant promised to do or whether, instead, it is an obligation to ensure that the plaintiff is not made worse off as a result of relying on the contract. In first view, which regards the wrong of breach as failing to do what was promised, is correct, compensation should, in principle, be equivalent to the value of the promise. But if the second view, which regards the wrong as failing to ensure that the plaintiff is not left worse off as a result of her reliance, is correct, then compensation should, in principle, be equivalent to the amount of reliance incurred.[20]

Adam Cramer has discussed the topic of contract damages from twin concept of 'The Breach Position' and 'The Non-Breach Position'. The breach position is a matter of working out what happened after the breach, although the principles of legal causation and mitigation alter that somewhat. The non-breach position is a matter of working out what would have happened had the breach not occurred, although this is something modified by the concepts of loss of chance or the defendant's minimum obligation rule.[21]

The essence of the contract damages enquiry is to find the net difference between the breach and non-breach positions. It is only by doing this that one can work out what loss was caused by the breach, i.e. what the claimant does not have but would have had but for the breach, and what the claimant has but would not have had but for the breach. A post-breach detriment is nothing to do with the defendant if it would have happened

---

19 Ibid
20 Ibid
21 The Law of Contract Damages by Adam Cramer, Hart Publishing, 2nd ed at p.13

anyway.[22] It is generally classified in two groups-Liquidated Damages and Unliquidated Damages. 'Liquidated Damages' means a sum which the parties have assessed by the contract as damages to be paid notwithstanding whatever may be the actual damage. The parties to a contract, as part of the agreement between them, fix an amount which is to be paid by way of damages in the event of breach. The term 'Unliquidated Damages', means a sum of money not established in advance by the contracting parties as a compensation for a breach of contract, but determined by a court after such breach occurs. Such damages are unascertained in advance.

Chapter VI of Indian Contract Act deals with the consequences of breach of contract. It contains only three sections-73, 74 and 75 and the whole law of liquidated damages, un-liquidated damages and no-damages have been provided therein. The damages for contracts and that for obligations resembling to contract are distinguished in section 73. Section 73 clearly confers a right on the party who suffers to receive compensation from a party who causes such breach. The assessment of loss or damage shall be one which naturally arose in usual course of things from such breach or which the parties knew when they made the contract to be likely to result from such breach of it. It remains prime concern for the parties to a contract of appreciating various underlying principles governing assessment of damages.

Courts have not shied away from invoking fundamental theories of contracts while coming to a conclusion. The encyclopaedic nature of the subject is reflected in altogether 18 illustrations [(a) to (r)] appended to this sections, all based on experiences of common law regime in England prior to codification of a Contract Act. Broadly, the principle underlying the assessment of damages is to put the aggrieved party monetarily in the same position as far as possible in which it would have been if the contract had been performed.[23] It would be found out the different method recognised

---

22 Ibid at p.16
23 Gaziabad Development Authority v. Union of India AIR 2000 SC 2003

by the Courts for assessment in suits as well as other proceedings like arbitration. Acceptance of foreign judgments may be viewed with reluctance in trial courts in general, but the Supreme Court of India has always been receiving the same as piece of great persuasive value, so as, all High Courts. The advent of international arbitration law in past century has gained deep momentum in the domain of international law with due recognition of municipal law as enshrined in UNICITRAL Code.

The dichotomy of 'reliance' v. 'expectation' loss has been considered by the Supreme Court[24] as, "That leaves the question with regard to reliance loss and the expectation loss. Whether the two could be maintainable simultaneously or were mutually exclusive? In Pullock & Mulla, 14th Edition, Volume II, page 1174, the primary object for protection of expectation interest, has been described as to put the innocent party in the position which he would have occupied had the contract been performed. The general aim of the law being to protect the innocent party's defeated financial expectation and compensate him for his loss of bargain, subject to the rules of causation and remoteness. The purpose of protection of reliance interest is to put the plaintiff in the position in which he would have been if the contract had never been made. The loss may include expenses incurred in preparation by the innocent party's own performance, expenses incurred after the breach or even pre-contract expenditure but subject to remoteness. The following passage from the same is considered appropriate for extraction:

"No Recovery for Both, the Expectation Loss and the Reliance loss." Although the rules as to damages seek to protect both the expectation and the reliance interests, the innocent party cannot ordinarily recover both expectation loss, viz., loss of profit, and reliance loss, viz., expenses incurred in reliance on the promise; that would involve double counting. He has to choose between the two measures. However, he cannot claim reliance losses to put himself in a better position that if the contract had been fully

---

[24] *Kanchan Udyog Ltd. v. United Spirits Ltd.* **(2017) 8 S.C.C. 237.**

performed: else, the award of damages for reliance losses would confer a windfall on the plaintiff, and would increase the damages in proportion to the claimant's inefficiency in performance, rather than in proportion to the gravity of the breach, and probably of normal principles of causation. In such cases, therefore, the plaintiff can recover the loss on account of the wasted expenditure or outlay only to the extent of the expected gain; and the onus of proving lies on the party committing the breach to show that the reliance costs (or any part of them) would not have been recouped, and would still have been wasted, had the contract been performed."

Section 74 does not pose as bigger challenge as section 73, because it deals with two classes of cases- where contract fixes an amount to be paid in case of breach and secondly, contract provides any other stipulation by way of penalty. Section 75 provides that the party rightfully rescinding the contract is entitled to compensation for any damage he has sustained through non-fulfilment of contract. Onus is on the plaintiff to lead evidence and prove the quantum of damage sustained by it. In respect of sec. 74, the Supreme Court in **Fateh Chand V. Balkishan Das** held "The section is clearly an attempt to eliminate the somewhat elaborate refinements made under the English common law in distinguishing between stipulations providing for payment of liquidated damages and stipulations in the nature of penalty. Under the common law a genuine pre-estimate of damages by mutual agreement is regarded as a stipulation naming liquidated damages and binding between the parties: a stipulation in a contract in terrorem is a penalty and the Court refuses to enforce it, awarding to the aggrieved party only reasonable compensation. The Indian Legislature has sought to cut across the web of rules and resumptions under the English common law, by enacting a uniform principle applicable to all stipulations naming amounts to be paid in case of breach, and stipulations by way of penalty.[25] Section 74 occurs in Chapter 6 of the Indian Contract Act, 1872 which reads "Of the consequences of breach of contract". It is in fact sandwiched

---

25   AIR 1963 SC 1405,

between Sections 73 and 75 which deal with compensation for loss or damage caused by breach of contract and compensation for damage which a party may sustain through non-fulfilment of a contract after such party rightfully rescinds such contract. It is important to note that like sections 73 and 75, compensation is payable for breach of contract Under Section 74 only where damage or loss is caused by such breach.[26] It is true that in every case of breach of contract the person aggrieved by the breach is not required to prove actual loss or damage suffered by him before he can claim a decree, and the Court is competent to award reasonable compensation in case of breach even if no actual damage is proved to have been suffered in consequence of the breach of contract. But the expression "whether or not actual damage or loss is proved to have been caused thereby" is intended to cover different classes of contracts which come before the Courts. In case of breach of some contracts it may be impossible for the Court to assess compensation arising from breach, while in other cases compensation can be calculated in accordance with established rules. Where the Court is unable to assess the compensation, the sum named by the parties if it be regarded as a genuine pre-estimate may be taken into consideration as the measure of reasonable compensation, but not if the sum named is in the nature of a penalty. Where loss in terms of money can be determined, the party claiming compensation must prove the loss suffered by him[27]. Once it is established that the party was justified in terminating the contract on account of fundamental breach thereof, then the said innocent party is entitled to claim damages for the entire contract, i.e. for the part which is performed and also for the part of the contract which it was prevented from performing.[28]

---

26   Kailash Nath Associates V. Delhi Development Authority 2015 Scc Online SC 19
27   Maula Bux V. Union of India ; AIR1970SC 1955
28   Maharashtra State Electricity Distribution Company Ltd. v. Datar Switchgear Limited and Ors. 2018 Scc Online SC 20

However, the plaintiff is expected to mitigate the damages. It is well settled that the two principles relating to compensation for loss or damage caused by breach of contract as laid down in sec.73 of the Indian Contract Act, 1872, read with the Explanation thereof, are (i) that, as far as possible, he who has proved a breach of a bargain to supply what he contracted to get is to be placed, as far as money can do it, in as good a situation as if the contract had been performed, but (ii) that there is a duty on him of taking all reasonable steps to mitigate the loss consequent on the breach and debars him from claiming any part of the damage which is due to his neglect to take such steps[29].

In **Southcott Estates Inc. v. Toronto Catholic District School Board**[30], Supreme Court of Canada considered the question of mitigation and awarded just nominal damages. The appellant S was a single-purpose company incorporated solely for the purpose of a specific land purchase, with no assets other than money advanced to it by its parent company for the deposit relating to such purchase. It entered into an agreement of purchase and sale for a specific property with the respondent. When the respondent failed to satisfy a condition and refused to extend the closing date, S sought specific performance of the contract. It argued that it was not required to mitigate its losses. The trial judge refused to award specific performance but awarded damages to S in the amount of $1,935,500. The Court of Appeal concluded that the respondent had breached its contractual obligations but that S had failed to take available steps to mitigate its losses. It reduced the damage award to a nominal sum. It was held, "As a separate legal entity, S was required to mitigate by making diligent efforts to find a substitute property. Those who choose the benefits of incorporation must bear the corresponding burdens. One such responsibility is to take steps to mitigate losses".

---

29   *M/s. Murlidhar Chiranjilal v. M/s. Harishchandra Dwarkadas & Anr* 1962 AIR 366
30   2012 SCC 51

There are three rules of mitigation applicable to breach of contract cases-

i. The plaintiff is not entitled to recover the loss resulting from the defendant's default if the plaintiff could have avoided the loss by taking reasonable steps.

ii. If it is found that the plaintiff avoids or mitigates the loss, he shall not recover for such avoided loss even if he takes steps that are more than what was reasonably required of him.

iii. If the plaintiff suffers loss or incurs expense by taking reasonable steps to avoid or mitigate the loss resulting from the default of the defendant, he may recover the further loss or expense from the defendant.

Yet another aspect of damages is the forfeiture/recovery/set off clauses in contract entitling one of parties to recover damages claimed from the other party by appropriating any sum which may become due to said other party under pending bills in terms of contract it was held that is clearly within the power of the court under section 41(b) because the claim for damages forms the subject matter of arbitration proceedings and the court can always say that until such claim is adjudicated upon, the appellant shall be restrained from recovering it by appropriating other amounts due to respondent.[31] The law on this point was summarised by the Supreme Court as "A claim for damages for breach of contract is, therefore, not a claim for a sum presently due and payable and the purchaser is not entitled in exercise of the right conferred upon it under Clause 18, to recover the amount of such claim by appropriating other sums due to contractor."[32] This judgment was overruled, partly, by a three Judges Bench in **H.M. Kamaluddin Ansari & Co. v. UOI & Ors**.[33] and it was held, "We are clearly of the view that an injunction order restraining respondents from

---

31 Union of India v. Raman Iron Foundary (1974) 2 SCC 231
32 Ibid
33 (1983) 4 SCC 417

withholding the amount due under other pending bills to the contractor virtually amounts to a direction to pay the amount to the contractor-appellant. Such an order was clearly beyond the purview of cl. (b) of sec. 41 of the Arbitration Act. The Union of India has no objection to the grant of an injunction restraining it from recovering or appropriating the amount Lying with it in respect of other claims of the contractor towards its claim for damages. But certainly cl. 18 of the standard contract confers ample power upon the Union of India to withhold the amount and no injunction order could be passed restraining the Union of India from withholding the amount." A similar matter again reached to the Supreme Court in **Gangotri Enterprises Ltd. v. Union of India**[34] where putting reliance on the *Raman Iron Foundary*, it was held, "A claim for damages for breach of contract is, therefore, not a claim for a sum presently due and payable and the purchaser is not entitled, in exercise of the right conferred upon it under clause 18, to recover the amount of such claim by appropriating other sums due to the contractor. On this view, it is not necessary for us to consider the other contention raised on behalf of the respondent, namely, that on a proper construction of clause 18, the purchaser is entitled to exercise the right conferred under that clause only where the claim for payment of a sum of money is either admitted by the contractor, or in case of dispute, adjudicated upon by a court or other adjudicatory authority. We must, therefore, hold that the appellant had no right or authority under clause 18 to appropriate the amounts of other pending bills of the respondent in or towards satisfaction of its claim for damages against the respondent and the learned Judge was justified in issuing an interim injunction restraining the appellant from doing so." However, the debate over the issue has been reignited in the recent judgment in State of Gujrat v. Amber Builders[35] where it has been held, "20. In our opinion, the judgment rendered in Gangotri Enterprises Limited (supra) is per incuriam because it relies upon Raman

---

34   (2016) 11 SCC 720
35   2020 Scc Online SC 13

Iron Foundry (supra) which has been specifically overruled by three Judge Bench in the case of H.M. Kamaluddin Ansari (supra)."

DOCTRINE OF QUANTUM MERUIT

The words "Quantum Meruit" in simple words means as much as deserved. The principle of Quantum Meruit is often applied where for some technical reason a contract is held to be invalid. Under such circumstances an implied contract is assumed, by which the person for whom the work is to be done contracts to pay reasonably for the work done, to the person who does the work.[36] Quantum Meruit can be best described as residual equity- a place to turn when there has been partial performance of a contract in a tricky new substantive area or where unfairness would result from contractual enforcement.[37] In order to understand the Quantum Meruit there are some explicative concepts which must be understood- (i) actions in law and actions in equity; (ii) Contracts implied in law and Contracts implied in facts (iii) Expectancy, reliance and restitution.[38]

In India section 70 of Contract Act is based on this doctrine, which provides that Where a person lawfully does anything for another person, or delivers anything to him, not intending to do so gratuitously, and such other person enjoys the benefit thereof, the latter is bound to make compensation to the former in respect of, or to restore, the thing so done or delivered. It has been held that this section goes far beyond English law.

In **Great Esatern Shipping Co. Ltd. v Union of India**[39] the Calcutta High Court held, "Section 70 and third paragraph of Section 73 of the Act are based on the doctrine of Restitution which says that you cannot unjustly enrich yourself by retaining anything delivered to you which does

---

36 Union of India v. Kamal Kumar Goswami AIR 1974 Cal 231; 1973 SCC Online Cal 78
37 Quantum Meruit: Residual Equity in Law, an article by Judy Beckner Sloan De Paul Law Review, can be seen on website core.ac.uk
38 Ibid
39 AIR 1971 Cal 150; 1970 SCC Online Cal 55

not belong to you and you must return it to the person from whom you have received it. It says that if you cannot return them In specie you must pay him their equivalent in money. Similarly if anything is done by one person for the other this doctrine says to the person who has accepted such works that you having enjoyed the benefits of such works must compensate the person who had done that work for you and if you do not want to pay him you will be guilty of enriching yourself unjustly by the labour of the other person and so you must pay to the person from whom you have received such work. Principle of restitution is not primarily based on loss suffered by the plaintiff but on the benefit which is enioyed by the defendant at the cost of the plaintiff which is wholly unjustified for the defendant to retain."

This section is not based on contract but embodies the equitable principles of restitution and unjust enrichment.[40]

The Madras High Court in **R Gangapathi Pillai v. P A Irudayasami Nadar**[41] placed reliance on Supreme Court in Subramanyam v. B. Thayyappa, 1961-1 Mad LJ (SN) 30 (SC) held, "'If a party to a contract has rendered service to the other not Intended to do so gratuitously, and the other person has obtained some benefit, the former is entitled to compensation for the value of the services rendered by him. Evidently, the respondent made additional constructions to the building and they were not done gratuitously. He was therefore entitled to receive compensation for the work done which was not covered by the agreement. The respondent claimed under an oral agreement compensation at prevailing market rates for work done by him; even if he had failed to prove an express agreement in that behalf, the court may still award, him compensation under S. 70 of the Contract Act. By awarding a decree for compensation under the statute and not under the oral contract pleaded, there was in the circumstances of this case no substantial departure from the claim made by the respondent."

---

40 Mulam Chand v. State of Madhya Pradesh AIR 1968 SC 1218;
41 AIR 1962 Mad 345: SCC Online 1961 Mad 64

The plaintiff claiming under section 70 must prove:

i. That he was doing something lawful when he did some act or delivered something, viz. when he was making payment,

ii. That he was not intending to do so or deliver gratuitously,

iii. That what he did was for the defendant,

iv. That the defendant did enjoy the benefit[42]

The Supreme Court in **State of West Bengal v. B K Mondal & Ors.**[43] explained the law as "It is plain that three conditions must be satisfied before this section can be invoked. The first condition is that a person should lawfully do something for another person or deliver something to him. The second condition is that in doing the said thing or delivering the said thing he must not intend to act gratuitously; and the third is that the other person for whom something is done or to whom something is delivered must enjoy the benefit thereof. When these conditions are satisfied s. 70 imposes upon the latter person, the liability to make compensation to the former in respect of or to restore, the thing so done or delivered. In appreciating the scope and effect of the provisions of this section it would be useful to illustrate how this section it would operate. If a person delivers something to another it would be open to the latter person to refuse to accept the thing or to return it; in that case s. 70 would not come in to operation. Similarly, if a person does something for another it would be open to the latter person not to accept what has been done by the former; in that case again s. 70 would not apply. In other words, the person said to be made liable under s. 70 always has the option not to accept the thing or to return it. It is only where he voluntarily accepts the thing or enjoys the work done that the liability under s. 70 arises."

---

42 Mulam Chand v. State of Madhya Pradesh AIR 1968 SC 1218;
43 AIR 1962 SC 779

It is for the person claiming the compensation to show that the conditions required in this section are complied with and the burden to prove is on him.

There can be no quarrel with the assessment of damages as at the date of the trial since the plaintiff prima facie had a legitimate claim for specific performance, but it does not follow that an award of damages should give him the financial equivalent of specific performance. Once he elected to terminate the contract his claim became the ordinary one of damages for loss of bargain, albeit assessed as at the date of hearing. He was entitled to be put in the position he would have occupied if the contract had been performed and this necessarily entailed as award of the difference between his actual financial and his financial position had the contract gone ahead.[44]

---

[44] Expectation Damages: Avoided Loss, Offsetting Gains and Subsequent Events by David McLauchlan in the Book Contract Damages: Domestic and International Perspectives Mohan Law House

20

PRIVITY OF CONTRACT AND SUB CONTRACTOR

"The young man knows the rules, but the old man knows the exceptions."

– Oliver Wendell Holmes Jr., U S Supreme Court Justice

In earlier law 'privity' referred mainly to the existence of a contractual relationship to which assumpsit[1] or indebitatus assumpsit[2] applied. In the nineteenth century however, 'privity' acquired another and more special sense. Now to speak of privity was to say that a contract had no legal effect except the two contracting parties, either because the 'offer' and its acceptance identified two, and only two specific persons, the offeror and offeree, or because (as it came to be said) the consideration must move from the promisee. In other words, 'privity' now meant that a third party could

---

1 Black's Law Dictionary defines assumpsit as An express or implied promise, not under seal, by one person undertakes to do some act or pay something to another; A common law action for breach of such a promise or breach of a contract.

2 A form of action in which the plaintiff alleges that the defendant contracted a debt and, as consideration, had undertaken (i.e. promised) to pay, the action was equivalent to the common-law action for debt (an action based on a sealed instrument), but could be used to enforce an oral debt. In England, indebitatus assumpsit was abolished in 1873

have no rights under a contract, even though the 'benefit' therein specified was expressly intended for him.[3]

The doctrine of privity is an offshoot of the bargain theory of contract, which runs parallel to the doctrine of consideration. It is one of the most uncertain terrains in the law of contract. In its classic use, the doctrine of privity precludes a third party from enforcing a contract or coming under an obligation of a contract and a party stranger to the contract shall not enforce a contract even though he is named there. To enforce a contract, such a third party will have to prove that it not only is a contractual party but that it has provided consideration. However, there are well-recognized exceptions like trust, agency, or the obligations created in a contract of insurance where a third party can claim the benefit without any consideration.

Tweddle v. Atkinson 121 ER 762 (QB) is the authority often referred to as the genesis of doctrine of privity of contract as applicable in England in which it was held that only the parties to a contract can enjoy the benefits of that contract or suffer the burdens on it. Consideration must move from the promisee. Whitman J held that it is now established that no stranger to the consideration can take advantage of contract, although made for himself. Fact of the case was that John Tweddle and Willam Guy each agreed to pay a sum of money to the plaintiff (Tweddle's son) in consideration of his marrying Guy's daughter. Guy failed to pay and the plaintiff sought to enforce his promise against Guy's executor and it was held that son could not enforce the promise despite the fact the contract was for his benefits since he had no consideration for it.[4] This was further affirmed in **Dunlop Pneumatic Tyre Co. Ltd v. Selfridge & Co. Ltd.**[5] However, in India position is different as held in **Debnarayan Dutt v. Chuni Lal Ghosh**[6], "If we were

---

[3] A History of Contract at Common Law by Samuel J. Stoljar , Australia National University
[4] Casebook on Contract Law by Jill Poole,7th Ed. Oxford University Press at p. 438
[5] [1915] AC 847 [HL]
[6] 1913 SCC Online Cal 167

governed by Twaddle v. Atkinson (1861) 1 B. &S. 393; 181 E.R. 762; 124 R.R. 610. there might possibly be a difficulty in our way, but it has to be borne in mind that Twaddle v. Atkinson (1861) 1 B. &S. 393; 181 E.R. 762; 124 R.R. 610. was a decision on a form of action peculiar to the Common Law Courts in England and that the case was influenced by the rule that no action in assumpsit could be maintained upon a promise unless consideration moved from the party to whom it was made. Here we have a definition of consideration which is wider than the requirement of the English law: [Section 2(d) of the Contract Act]. And it has been laid down by Sir Barnes Peacock in a Full Bench decision of this Court in relation to Courts in the mofussil [Rumbux Chittangeo›s Case (1867) B.L.R. Sup. Vol. 675. 7 W.B. 377] that in those Courts the rights of parties are to be determined according to the general principles of equity and justice without any distinction, as in England, between that partial justice which is administered in the Courts of Law and the more full and complete justice for which it is frequently necessary to seek the assistance of a Court of Equity. The rules and the fictions which have been in many cases adopted by the Common Law Courts» in England for the purpose of obtaining jurisdiction in cases which would otherwise have been cognizable only by the Courts of Equity, are not necessary to be followed in this country where the aim is to do complete justice in one suit. More than that we now have ample authority for saying that the administration of justice in these Courts is not to be in any way hampered by the doctrine laid down in Tweddle v. Atkinson (1910) I.L.R. 32 All. 410 L.R. 37 I.A. 152. That take to be» the result of the decision of the Privy Council in the recent case Khwaja Muhammad Khan v. Husaini Begam (1910) I.L.R. 32 All. 410 L.R. 37 I.A. 152." It is settled law that a person not a party to a contract cannot subject to certain well recognised exceptions, enforce the terms of the contract: the recognised exceptions are that beneficiaries under the terms of the contract or where the contract is a part of the family arrangement may enforce the covenant.[7]

---

7 M C Chacko v. State Bank of Travencore, (1969) 2 SCC 343

Under section 37 of Contract Act, it is only a party to the contract who must perform or after to perform. It is not clear, however, whether third party can sue for non-performance of obligation. The principle of contract provides a stranger cannot sue, which is called privity of contract. The doctrine of privity of contract is still received as a fundamental assumption of common law and ordinary a stranger to the contract can neither sue nor be sued on the basis of it.[8] Black's law dictionary defines privity of contract as, "The relationship between the parties to a contract, allowing them to sue each other but preventing a third party from doing so.". It is an elementary principle of English law-known as the doctrine of 'Privity of Contract' – the contractual rights and duties only affect the parties to a contract, and this principle is the distinguishing feature between the law of contract and the law of property. True proprietary rights are binding on the world in the lawyer's traditional purpose. Contractual, rights on the other hand, are only binding on, and enforceable by, the immediate parties to the contract. But this distinction, fundamental though it be, wears a little thin at times. On the one hand, there has been a constant tendency for contractual rights to be extended in their scope so as to affect more and were persons who cannot be regarded as parties to the transaction. On the others hand, few proprietary rights are literally binding on the world.[9] The reasons for limiting the operation of the contract to its parties only are many and these are the most profound:

i. The third party did not provide consideration for promise, even though consideration was provided for the promise.

ii. It is unjust to permit a person to sue on a contract when he cannot be sued upon it.

---

8   Pusha Ram V. Modern Construction Co. (P) Ltd. Kota AIR 1981 Raj 47.
9   An Introduction to law of Contract by P.S. Atiyah as quoted in Black's Law Dictionary p. 1238

iii. If non-contracting parties were permitted to enforce contracts made for their benefits, the rights of the contracting parties to vary or terminate such contract would be affected.

iv. It is unfair to call upon the promisor to be liable to two actions, from the promisee as well as the third party.

v. It is desirable to limit the potential liability of a contracting party from the possibility of wide range of parable third party claimants.[10]

Privity of contract is closely interlinked to privity of consideration. According to English law, consideration must move from the promissee and the promisee only, if it is furnished by any other person, the promisee becomes a stranger to the consideration, and therefore cannot enforce the promise. However, this postulate of English law is not applicable in India. Sec. 2 (d) of the Contract Act defines consideration as, "When, at the desire of the promisor, the promisee or any other person has done or abstained from doing, or promises to do or to explain from doing, something, such act or abstinence or promise is called a consideration for the promise." The word any other person's connotes that it is not necessary that consideration should be furnished by the promisee. The doctrine has two aspects. The first aspect is that no one but the parties to the contract is entitled under it. Contracting parties may confer rights or benefits upon a third party in the form of promise to pay, or to perform a service, or a promise not to sue. But the third party on whom such right or benefit is conferred by contract can neither sue under it not can rely on differences based on the contract.[11] The second aspect of the doctrine is that parties to a contract cannot impose liabilities on a third party. A person cannot be subject to the burden of a contract to which he is not party. It is the counterpart of the proposition that a third party cannot acquire rights under a contract.[12] Third parties

---

10 Contracts I Case and Materials by V. Keshava Rao p. 513
11 Ibid
12 Shiv Dayal V – UOI AIR 1963 Punj 538

for whose benefit a contract has been made may not sue on the contract lent the party making the contract may sue for specific performance for the subject of the third party even where damages obtainable will be nominal.[13] An employee of a tenant is never considered to the be in actual possession of tenanted premises only with the permission of his employer by virtue of his contract of employment with his employer. An employee, therefore, cannot claim any legal right of his own to occupy or to remain in possession of the tenanted premises while in employment of his employs or even thereafter qua landlord for want of any privity of contract between him and the landlord in respect of the tenanted premises.[14]

The Supreme Court held in **Essar Oil Limited V. Hindustan Shipyard Limited**[15] "It is true that the ONGC had made payment directly on several occasions. Upon purpose of the correspondence, we find that some understanding, but not amounting to any agreement or contract was arrived at between the ONGC and the respondent for making direct payment to the applicant, possibly because the respondent was not in a position to make prompt payments to two appellant. It also appears that on account of the delay in making payment to the appellant, the work of the ONGC was interested likely to be adversely affected. The ONGC was interested in getting it work done promptly and without any hands. In the circumstances, upon perusal of the correspondence, which had taken place between the ONGC and the respondent, it is clear that so as to facilitate the respondent, the ONGC had made payments on behalf of the respondent to the appellant directly..."

"Simply because some payments had been made by the ONGC to the appellant, it would not be established that there was a privity of contract between the ONGC and the appellant and only for that reason the ONGC cannot with a liability to pay the amount payable to the appellant by the

---

13 Mulla on Contract at p. 113
14 Nandkishor Savalaram V. Hanumanmal G. Biyani 2017 (2) SCC 622 : AIR 2017 SC 82
15 2015 (10) SCC 642

respondent."[16] In **Eureka Forbes Limited V. Allahabad Bank**[17] the appellant Company entered into an agreement with respondent no - 2 and 3 granting licence in their favour to use premises, plant and machineries and trademark. It was the case of the appellant had no knowledge of the fact that respondent no – 2 and 3 had availed cash credit and had hypothecated their raw materials, semi-furnished and finished products to Bank. However, citing reason of non-payment of licence fee the respondents no 2 and 3 requested the appellant to take over occupation of premises, goods etc. as agreed and by another letter stated that the appellant could see the stock and lathe machine lying in the factory premises and adjust the sale proceeds thereof towards the arrears of licence fee. After taking possession of the factory the appellant prepared an inventory of the stock in possession and as prepared an inventory of the stock in possession and as alleged by them, they had knowledge that these stocks had been hypothecated by the said respondent in favour of Bank. Thereafter the respondent Bank raised an issue as to how possession of stock and machinery was given to the appellant. The bank filed a suit against the appellant and respondent no – 2 and 3 for claiming the sum due. In the suit the appellant filed a written statement making a preliminary objection that there was no priority of contract between the Bank and the present appellant. This suit was transferred under provision of Recovery of Debts Due to Bank and Financial Institution Act, 1993. But the appellant did not appeal before the Debt Recovery Tribunal. *Ex-parte* judgment was passed and Recovery Certificate was issued. This decision firstly challenged before the Calcutta High Court and then Appellant Tribunal, which dismissed the appeal. Again, this decision was assailed before High Court under Article 227 of contribution. After a number of writ applications, appeal, revision the matter finally case before the Supreme Court whereby the impugned orders was challenged on the ground that, Tribunal had no jurisdiction

---

16 2015 (10) SCC 642; AIR 20158 Sc 3116
17 2010 (6) SCC 193

to entertain such application filed on behalf of the Bank as there was no privity of Contract between the appellant and the bank. The Supreme court held, "In the case in hand, there cannot be any dispute that the expression on "debt" has to be given the widest amplitude to mean any liability which is alleged as due from any person by a Bank during the course of business actively undertaken by the Bank either in cash or otherwise, whether secured or unsecured, whether payable under a decree or order of any court or otherwise and legally recoverable on the date of the application. In ascertaining the question whether any particular claim of any bank or financial institution would come within the purview of the tribunal under the Act; it is imperative that the entire averments made by the plaintiff in the plaint be looked into and then find out whether notwithstanding the specially created tribunal having been constituted, the averments are such that it is possible to hold that the jurisdiction of such a tribunal is ousted, with the aforesaid principle in mind, on examining the averments made in the plaint, we have no hesitation to come to the conclusion that the claim in assertion made by the plaintiff is essentially one for recovery of a debt due to it from the defendants and, therefore, is the Tribunal which has the exclusive jurisdiction to divide the dispute and not the ordinary Civil Court."

It a suit on the basis of a promissory note executed by the decreased and defendant – 10 decree was passed against the assets in the hand of the heirs of deceased executant or against the 10th defendant personally. The plaintiff's case was that the debt was borrowed to finance the business left by the grandfather of the deceased executant, after whose death his business had devolved on his widow. It was held that the plaintiff cannot have a personal decree against the defendants as they were not parties to the provisory note suit. There is no privity of contract between the plaintiff and defendants 1 to 9.[18]

---

18 P.R. Subramania Iyer V. Laxmi Ammal (1973) 2 SCC 54

In a case borrower (respondent no – 1) instituted writ petition in the high court praying for writ of mandamus directing Punjab Financial Corporation (PFC) to release the balance loan amount immediately in terms of the contract and also for damages with interest on the ground of breach of contract by not disbursing the loan (s). The borrower pleaded that it had made investments on its venture on the basis of the contract under which PFC had agreed to sanction and disburse the loan to enable it to set up its Project and on account of failure to disburse further amount, it has transferred huge losses for which damages were sought. It was held, "The original petitioner (the borrower) has sought damages and enforcement of back-to-back transactions with a party with whom there was no privity of contract coupled with the claim for damages are all contractual matters unenforceable by way of writ petitions."[19]

In another case the appellant, plaintiff had advertised for the circus run by the second defendant Balakrishnan. It laid a suit for recovery of a sum towards the advertisement charges impleading the respondent as first defendant, along with Balakrishnan as second defendant. Balakrishnan remained an *ex-parte* and *ex-parte* decree against him became final. The question of liability of first defendant C.T. Devraj was matter of consideration before the Supreme Court. The trial court decreed the suit against him on finding that there was privity of contact between the appellant and respondent. The High Court on appeal found that there was no privity of contact. The appellant in its argument before the Supreme Court relied on agreement (Ex A-3) which is bilateral agreement. It was held that between the respondent (C.T. Devraj) and Balakrishnan as the appellant was not a party to the agreement, so there is no privity of contracts between the appellant and Devraj. Though proposal sent for advertisement by the appellant was approved by Devraj, he did it on behalf of Balakrishnan. The

---

19 Punjab Financial Corporation and Another V. Garg Steel and Another (2010) 15 SCC 546 (2)

approval sought by the appellant was not given in writing so as to bind Devraj with the expenditure incurred for advertisement.[20]

In **K S Satyanarayana v. V R Narayana Rao**[21] the appellant entered into an agreement to purchase a two storied building belonging to N, the present respondent. The agreement was executed by S and an individual (defendant -2) who had been authorised in writing by N to enter into an agreement to sell the property at his discretion. S also made payment by cheque of Rs. 1 lakh each to N and the others individual (defendant 2). Thereafter, however, the agreement fell through and S demanded his money back. Def 2 Defendant no-2 paid Rs. 50,000/- but N refused outright to return any money. S filed a suit for recovery against defendant no-2 for the balance amount and against N, defendant no-1 for the entire Rs 1 lakh along with 14 % interest. The suit was decreed as against defendant 2 but dismissed as against defendant 1 on the ground that there was no privity of contract between S and defendant 1. On the same reasoning the High Court dismissed S's appeal. Allowing the appeal with interest and costs throughout, the Supreme Court held that after the first defendant admitted having received rupees one lakh from the plaintiff he could not retain that money on the specious plea that there was no privity of contract between him and the plaintiff. The amount of rupees one lakh had been given to him by the plaintiff as he wanted to purchase the ground floor of the property. The agreement to sell for the purpose was entered into through the 2nd defendant whom the 1st defendant had authorized to enter into any such agreement on his behalf. The plaintiff could not have paid to the 1st defendant rupees on lakh but for the agreement to sell in respect of the ground floor of the property. It is only on the basis of this agreement which is entered into by the 2nd defendant on the strength of written and signed authorization that the plaintiff paid Rs. one lakh each to the 1st and 2nd defendants. If the pleadings of the first defendant are accepted, then it

---

20 Aries Advertising Bureru V. C.T. Devraj (1995) 3 Sec 250
21 (1999) 6 SCC 104

would have to be said that the amount of Rs. one lakh had been given under some mistakes. In any case, it was not a payment gratuitously made. The doctrine of undue enrichment would squarely apply in the present case and the plaintiff would be entitled to restitution.[22] It was further observed, "It is unfortunate that the courts below were not attentive to the procedural laws and their duty to do substantive justice in the case. Had that been so the plaintiff would have been spared the tribulations of knocking at the doors of the highest court of land. The courts below fell into error in going into the question of privity of contract and lost right of the basic issues involved in the case."

It is a matter of common knowledge that an employer engages more than one contractor for competition of the project and they are generally from different trades. Therefore, an employer signs contracts with more than one contractor for the same project though for different and well defined areas. The employer has direct relationship with the main contractors only. The contractors, in turn engage sub-contractors for execution of the job assigned to them. It would thus be noticed that the employer has no direct relationship with the sub-contractors employed by the main contractors[23].

A sub-contractor is one who is awarded a portion of an existing contract by a contractor, esp. a general contractor. For example, a contractor who build houses typically retains sub-contractors to perform specialty work such as installing plumbing, laying carpet, making cabinetry, and landscaping- each subcontractor is paid a somewhat lesser sum than the contractor receives for the work.[24]

A sub-contractor who has not been nominated when the main contract is signed is not entitled as a matter of contract to the benefit of a clause in the main contract limiting liability although the existence of such a

---

22 (1999) 6 SCC 104
23 Emdon's building contracts and Practice at p. 549
24 Black's Law Dictionary

clause could negative any duty of care owed by the sub-contractor.[25] The legal effect is that there is no privity between the employer and the sub-contractor. In accordance with the general rules of contract law the employer and the sub-contractor cannot bring contractual claim against the other. A person can bring a claim pursuant to a contract to which he is a party, and only a party to a contract can have a claim brought against him.[26] The practical aspect of this can be seen in two ways:

First, an employer cannot sue a sub-contractor for breach of contract, be it for delays or deficiencies in the sub-contract work. Instead the employer's claim lies against the main contractor. However, this may not in practice provide an adequate remedy, for example the main contractor is insolvent or inadequately insured. The issue then arises as to whether the employer can sue sub-contractor directly. The traditional answer in accordance with the rule of privity is that it cannot. Second, and correspondingly neither can a sub-contractor bring a contractual claim, for example, for payment, against the employer. In the event therefore of the contractor's insolvency the sub-contractor cannot look to the employer[27].

The National Hydro-Electric Power Corporation Ltd. (hereinafter referred to as 'NHPC") had floated tender for award of work of construction of left side Afflux Bund from RD-00 M to RD-1700 M of Tanakpur Hydro-Electric Project, Tanakpur, Distt. Nainital, U.P. sometime in the 1980s, when Nainital was part of State of Uttar Pradesh (now Uttarakhand). In that tender, Hindustan Steel Works Construction Ltd. (HSCL) emerged as the successful tenderor to whom the contract was awarded by NHPC by entering into contract dated January 28, 1986.

The contract permitted sub - contracting thereof by HSCL with the consent of NHPC. Thus, HSCL sub- contracted the said works to respondent herein, i.e. Progressive Construction Ltd. (PCL) vide contract dated July 16,

---

25 Southern Water Authority v. Carey [1985]2 All ER 1077
26 Emdon's building contracts and Practice at p. 550
27 Ibid at p.551

1991. PCL had further sub-contracted the said work or part thereof to the appellant herein, i.e. M/s. Sharma & Associates Contractors (P) Ltd. (SAPL). This appeal relates to disputes between SAPL (the appellant) and PCL (the respondent).

Though, work was sub-contracted to the appellant, it is an admitted case between the parties that the sub-contracting of the work was not permissible by the respondent to the appellant. Be that as it may, a contract dated February 09, 1990 was signed between the appellant and the respondent (even prior to the award of work by HSCL to the respondent), though it was sealed on April 15, 1992, i.e., after the respondent was awarded the sub-contract from HSCL on July 16, 1991.

From the facts recorded upto now, it is clear that there is a main contract between the employer NHPC and HSCL which is dated January 28, 1996 and HSCL sub-contracted the work to PCL and contract between them is dated July 16, 1991, third contract which is between PCL (the respondent) and SAPL (the appellant) is dated February 09, 1990, sealed on April 15, 1992.

Disputes arose between the appellant and the respondent in respect of execution of the work. According to the appellant, certain payments were not made to it by the respondent though it had executed work. Those, disputes were referred to for adjudication to the arbitration as per arbitration clause in the contract between appellant and respondent by the High Court in petition filed by the appellant under Section 20 of the Arbitration Act, 1940.

The appellant contended that since it was a back to back contract, the manner in which the rates are revised upward and received by PCL from HSCL, benefit thereof has to be given to the appellant also. This contract is back to back as Clauses 1.2 and 9 thereof clearly show that terms of main contract to the extent they were 'sensible' stood explicitly incorporated in the contract that was entered into between HSCL and the respondent. However, we are not concerned with the dispute between HSCL and the respondent. As pointed out above, further sub-contract is signed between the respondent and the appellant. Therefore, the moot question is as to whether the principle of incorporation would enter into and extend to this sub-contract as well in the absence of any clause of back to back contract appearing in the contract that was signed between the appellant and the respondent.

Entire thrust in the argument of the learned counsel for the appellant before us was that there was back to back contract as according to him the aforesaid stipulations contained in a contract between HSCL and the respondent stood incorporated in the contract entered into between the appellant and the respondent as well. However, we do not find it to be so.

BIBLIOGRAPHY

1. A Treatise on the Specific Performance of Contacts by Fry, Universal Publishing Co. Ltd.
2. A Practical Approach to Legal Advice & Drafting by Susan Blake, Universal Law Publishing Co. Ltd.
3. A.N. Saha's Code of Civil Procedure.
4. Benion on Statutory Interpretation, Lexis Nexis
5. Black's Law Dictionary, South Asian Edition, Eighth Edition
6. Casebook on Contract Law, Jill Poole, Seventh Edition, Oxford University Press,
7. Commentary on The Commercial Courts Act, 2015, Fifth Edition, Asia Law House, Hyderabad
8. Commercial Courts Act, 2015 (Bare Act)
9. Contract Damages: Domestic and International Perspective, Djakhongir Saidov & Ralph Cunnington: First Indian Reprint 2020, Mohan Law House
10. Contract Theory by Stephen A Smith, Oxford University Press
11. Doctrine of Frustration in Law of Contract by Dr. G. P. Tripathi, Allahabad, Allahabad Law Agency
12. Emden's Building Contracts and Pracrice, Ninth Edition, Dr. P.C. Markanda, Lexis Nexis, Ninth Edition

13. Interpretation of Contract by M. A. Sujan, Universal Law Publishing Co. Ltd. Second Edition
14. Law relating to Tender and Government Contracts by T.R. Desai Universal Law Publishing Co.
15. Mulla's Code of Civil Procedure, Lexis Nexis
16. Pleadings & Practice by N.S. Bindra
17. Pollock & Mulla: Law of Contract & Specific Relief, Thirteenth Edition, Lexis Nexis Butterworth Wadhva, Vol I & II
18. Russel on Arbitration, Twenty Third Edition, Sweet & Maxwell, (South Asian Edition)
19. Sanjiva Row's Law relating to Contact Act and Tenders - Delhi Law House.
20. Sarkar on Code of Civil Procedure, Wadhwa Nagpur.
21. Sir John Woodroffe & Amir Ali's Code of Civil Procedure - Delhi Law House.
22. Supreme Court on Contract & Specific Relief, Eastern Book Company, Vol I & II
23. The Interpretation of Contracts by Sir Kim Lewison, Fifth Edition, Sweet & Maxwell- Thomson Reuters (South Asian Edition)
24. The Law of Contract Damages by Adam Krammer, Second Edition, Hart Publishing
25. The Law & Practice of Arbitration and Conciliation by O.P. Malhotra & Indu Malhotra, Second Edition, Lexis Nexis Butterworths
26. Wharton's Law Lexicon - 15th Edition Universal Law Publishing Co. Ltd.

www.ingramcontent.com/pod-product-compliance
Lightning Source LLC
Chambersburg PA
CBHW020856180526
45163CB00007B/2529